Sir Arthur Sullivan

Presenting in Word & Song, Score & Deed

the Life and Work of

SIR ARTHUR SULLIVAN

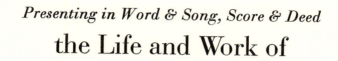

Composer for Victorian England

FROM "ONWARD, CHRISTIAN SOLDIERS"

TO GILBERT & SULLIVAN OPERA

Fully Illustrated & Annotated

COMPILED BY

REGINALD ALLEN

in collaboration with Gale R. D'Luhy

THE PIERPONT MORGAN LIBRARY
NEW YORK

DAVID R. GODINE, PUBLISHER
BOSTON

COPYRIGHT © 1975 BY THE PIERPONT MORGAN LIBRARY
29 EAST 36 STREET, NEW YORK, N.Y. 10016
PRINTED IN THE UNITED STATES OF AMERICA
LIBRARY OF CONGRESS CATALOGUE CARD NUMBER 74-32578
ISBN 0-87923-145-9

Contents

NOTE

The following abbreviations are used throughout:

Ls	Letter signed
Al	Autograph letter
Als	Autograph letter signed
MS	Manuscript
n.d.	no date
n.p.	no place

Vertical measurements are given first.

List of Illustrations

Photographs are by Charles Passela, except those of manuscripts on loan from other public libraries. All objects illustrated are in The Pierpont Morgan Library unless specified.

COVER:
Detail from cartoon by Charles Dana Gibson, 1887. (72)

THE EIGHTEEN SIXTIES

THE EIGHTEEN SEVENTIES

THE EIGHTEEN EIGHTIES

THE EIGHTEEN NINETIES

Introduction

THIS VOLUME PRESENTS the life of Sir Arthur Sullivan as seen in the archive formed first of all by his mother, and then by Sir Arthur himself. The original archive has been supplemented with dozens of autograph manuscripts and letters, printed scores, librettos, posters, drawings, prints, photographs, and memorabilia which came to The Pierpont Morgan Library before the acquisition of the papers of Sir Arthur Sullivan, and afterwards, and which today form the Gilbert & Sullivan Collection in the Library. It may well contain the most comprehensive *biographical* collection of any composer, anywhere.

W. S. Gilbert, Arthur Sullivan, and Richard D'Oyly Carte first collaborated one hundred years ago on the comic opera *Trial by Jury*. The present publication, and the exhibition held in connection with it at the Morgan Library, 13 February to 20 April 1975, is our centennial salute to this triumvirate. This is the first extensive celebration devoted to Sullivan on this side of the Atlantic, and perhaps there has not yet been one of equal scope in his own country.

Although this volume and the exhibition are biographical in nature, they do not presume to constitute a biography; nor, with respect to descriptions of published works, do they form a bibliography. It is hoped, however, that they do create (in Mr. Allen's words) a full-length portrait of Sullivan, the composer and the personage, in his time. They are part of a worldwide Gilbert & Sullivan centenary celebration, and form an American tribute to this anniversary. It is indisputable that our nationwide enthusiasm played a large part in the success of the Gilbert & Sullivan operas from their first years of production. Appropriately, the most important manuscript in the collection at the Morgan Library is the score of *The Pirates of Penzance*, the only opera by Gilbert & Sullivan which received its first performance in America. This manuscript came to the Library in 1966 as the gift of the Fellows. For this anniversary we have augmented the collection of the Morgan Library only with manuscripts in this country.

Introduction

None of this would have been possible without Reginald Allen. He is the founder, the prime mover, and the constant inspiration in building the archives at the Morgan Library, and is now the Curator of the Gilbert & Sullivan Collection.

By happy coincidence the two individuals responsible for this volume are Savoyards from earliest childhood. The two oldest amateur Gilbert & Sullivan opera companies in the country figure prominently in their lives: the Philadelphia Savoy Opera Company, founded in 1901, and the Blue Hill Troupe of New York, founded in 1924. For the past ten years Gale D'Luhy has been a singing member (mezzo-soprano) of the Blue Hill Troupe, where she met her husband, John D'Luhy (tenor). Reginald Allen's father founded the Philadelphia Savoy Company, and first met his wife-to-be at rehearsals of *The Sorcerer* in 1901; hence Mr. Allen even claims pre-birth G. & S. associations.

Mr. Allen's Gilbert & Sullivan Collection in The Pierpont Morgan Library is actually three collections in one, covering W. S. Gilbert, Gilbert & Sullivan, and Arthur Sullivan. It was started fifty years ago, while he was still an undergraduate at Harvard. In the mid-1920's he concentrated on collecting the collaborations of Gilbert & Sullivan, with only an occasional purchase of something by W. S. Gilbert alone or a letter or two from Sullivan. His *alter ego* from these earliest days was Miss Mabel Zahn of Sessler's Book Store in Philadelphia. Through her guidance there grew a network of friendly, non-competitive dealers, on both sides of the Atlantic, who were willing to co-operate with Mr. Allen in the building of his collection. Many, like the late Ralph Brown of B. F. Stevens & Brown, and the late Ifan Kyrle Fletcher, became his good friends.

The collection of W. S. Gilbert material developed quickly after these G. & S. beginnings, particularly in the mid-1930's, through Mr. Allen's contact with Townly Searle, author of the first bibliography of Gilbert, much of whose collection he later acquired. Then, after the war, through his friendship with Carroll A. Wilson, America's foremost Gilbert & Sullivan collector at that time, and later with his widow, he was able to get many rare or unique items owned by the Wilsons for the collection now at the Morgan Library.

"In collecting the works of Arthur Sullivan, since I am no musician," Mr. Allen confessed, "I needed the help of someone who might combine musicology, bibliography, and Gilbert & Sullivan enthusiasm in one person. It was a lucky day for me when Miss Zahn put me in touch with Cecil Hopkinson, then a London scholar-dealer in music books (the First Edition Bookshop), as well as bibliographer of Berlioz, Puccini, and Verdi. Mr. Hopkinson has been my valued friend and guide in the collecting of Arthur Sullivan material for almost forty years . . . nor in that time has he ignored my insatiable appetite for the works of Gilbert!"

The first full revelation of Mr. Allen's achievement as collector was twenty-five years after his graduation from college: the most comprehensive Gilbert & Sullivan exhibition which had ever been assembled, shown at the Morgan Library in 1950–1951. In 1958 the Limited Editions Club and Heritage Press published Mr. Allen's *The First Night Gilbert and Sullivan*, in which he was greatly assisted by Miss Bridget D'Oyly Carte. In 1961, when the D'Oyly Carte Opera Trust was formed, Reginald Allen was appointed a Trustee, and he remains the only non-British board member. Also in 1961, the Grolier Club of New York mounted the most complete exhibition of the works of W. S. Gilbert ever held in this country, drawn entirely from Mr. Allen's collection in the Morgan Library. Two years later the Bibliographical Society of the University of Virginia published his *W. S. Gilbert—An Anniversary Survey and Exhibition Checklist*. In 1973 he was awarded a Guggenheim Fellowship to finish his bibliography of the Gilbert & Sullivan operas. His work under this grant was interrupted to allow for the preparation of the exhibition at the Morgan Library and this volume on Sir Arthur Sullivan, which we now present nearly twenty-five years after our first Gilbert & Sullivan exhibition.

When the exhibition of 1950–1951 was held, neither Mr. Allen nor the Library had access to the Sullivan papers. The story of their pursuit and acquisition for the Morgan Library is best told by Frederick B. Adams, Jr., then Director of the Library. In his *Thirteenth Report to the Fellows of The Pierpont Morgan Library, 1963 & 1964*, he related briefly the difficulties met in acquiring the Sullivan archive, and described highlights of its extraordinary contents.

My pursuit of the Sullivan papers began in May, 1952, with a visit to Sir Newman Flower, co-author with Herbert Sullivan of the standard biography of the latter's uncle. Since Sir Newman had examined the Sullivan letters and diaries with some care in preparation for the book, he was able to describe from memory their scope and significance. Through his good offices, I was invited to tea by Mrs. Elena Bashford, Herbert Sullivan's widow, who had custody of the papers. Although Mr. Reginald Allen and I maintained these connections in ensuing years, there was no change in the situation until Mrs. Bashford's death in 1957, which brought on a deluge of complications. Title to the papers became vested in a multiplicity of heirs, and over the ensuing seven years the effort to reunite and acquire the Sullivan archive for the Library ranged over three continents. What I believe to be the final instalment reached New York in August, 1964.

With this major acquisition, our Gilbert & Sullivan collection, begun at the Library in 1949 by Mr. Allen's initial gifts, becomes beyond question the most extensive to be found anywhere. We owe thanks to many for the Sullivan papers, and firstly to the Fellows, who contributed two-thirds of their cost. Secondly, without the constant encouragement and advice of Miss Bridget D'Oyly Carte, we should have lost heart, and lost the papers too. Finally, we rejoiced in the co-operation of Mr. Homer Crotty and the Huntington Library; of Mr. J. Robert Meserve, of the Los Angeles law firm of Meserve, Mumper & Hughes . . . ; and of Miss Mabel Zahn, Philadelphia's *grande dame* of bookselling, who served as official appraiser to the interested parties. Mr. Allen acted throughout as stage manager, prompter, and property man, and deserves, as always, to be called before the footlights after the final curtain.

It is a paradox which Gilbert would have relished that the most valuable material in the Sullivan archive is Gilbert's. Here are some 175 letters from Gilbert to Sullivan, dating from 1877 to 1900, and another 22 to Herbert, commencing with condolences on his uncle's death. Here is the almost complete original manuscript of the first act of *The Pirates of Penzance*, which, to the best of our knowledge, is the only surviving manuscript of any substantial portion of a libretto of one of the comic operas . . . And here too in Gilbert's hand are all the songs and recitatives (sometimes in more than one version) for the first act of *Utopia, Limited*, and some for the second, written out for Sullivan's use in composing the music.

The most interesting part of the correspondence is that which concerns the building of the operas, which affords many insights into the methods of this remarkable partnership; the most depressing are the many contentious letters that document the quarrels between the collaborators. Gilbert enjoyed a good scrap as heartily as Sullivan disliked it, and, having practised as a barrister for four years before deserting the law for literature, he was prepared to go to court at the drop of an insult, or what he took to be one. Sullivan, on the contrary, did his best to keep from being embroiled, so that he could get on with his music and his active social life. The vigorous librettist and the lyrical composer had only their perseverance and industry in common, and the opposition of their temperaments was an essential ingredient of their successful collaboration.

Neither ever did well with a different partner . . . After their first quarrel in 1884, they rejoined to create *The Mikado*; after their second in 1888-9 (during which Gilbert wrote Sullivan that he was "incomparably the greatest English musician of the age"), they produced *The Gondoliers*, and the morning after the opening night Gilbert wrote to thank his collaborator for giving him "a chance of shining right through the twentieth century with a reflected light"; and after their third, and most acrimonious, the 1890-2 quarrel which began over charges for a carpet in the Savoy Theater, they returned with *Utopia*, in which Sullivan had so much trouble with the music for the Finale of the second act that Gilbert advised him to compose the music first, and he would write the words to fit. . . .

We have not yet had time to catalogue the several thousand letters and documents in the Sullivan archive, but they cover every phase of an extraordinarily active life, from the age of 10 until his premature death at 58. Letters from the royal family are plentiful, especially from the Duke of Edinburgh (a fellow musician). The great and near-great in the worlds of literature, music, and politics show by their letters the range of Sullivan's interests and the warmth of his companionship; among those represented are Dickens, Tennyson, Browning, Bret Harte, Kipling, "Lewis Carroll," Sir George Smart, Jenny Lind, Sir George Grove, Saint-Saëns, Massenet, Gounod, Liszt, Elgar, Nellie Melba, Emma Calvé, and Gladstone. But Sullivan also saved many letters from those who are not to be found in the biographical dictionaries, but with whom he had shared some experience or enthusiasm. The letter-press books kept by Sullivan's secretary, Walter Smythe, cover the period from January 29, 1883, to December 18, 1895; they fill many gaps in our knowledge of Sullivan's life with important, trivial, and even humorous details, as does the large file of Sullivan's letters to Smythe written when the former was away from London. The Sullivan family correspondence, mainly between the composer and his mother, covers nearly half a century in many hundreds of letters, and is invaluable as a biographical source.

The cataloguing of these thousands of items is proceeding slowly, and of course the basic archive has received additions each year. In the decade since 1964 there have been a number of important additions. Through funds from the Mary Flagler Cary Charitable Trust the Library obtained Sullivan's original manuscript score of his first success in the lyric theatre, *Cox and Box*, a comic operetta with words by F. C. Burnand. Two other outstanding groups of Sullivan material also came to the Library through the Cary Fund: the first, a splendid collection of twenty-nine autograph letters from Sullivan to Joseph Bennett, music critic (of the *Daily Telegraph*) and adaptor for Sullivan of *The Golden Legend*. These cover twenty years, from 1874 to 1893. The second is a file of more than eighty-six lots of legal documents, Sullivan's copies of contracts, agreements, assignments, etc., covering works of every description from 1880 to 1900. There is no collection in which this legal file fits so appropriately as in the Sullivan archive—a feeling fortunately shared by representatives of the heirs. And, as we go to press, through the Acquisitions Fund and Mrs. John D'Luhy, the Library has obtained an important group of thirty-nine letters from Sullivan to Wilfred Bendall, his musical assistant and secretary from 1895 to 1900.

Augmenting these family elements of the archive, the matrix of Sullivan letters within the Allen collection has grown to a total of more than five hundred, written to scores of the composer's correspondents, great and small. These give a depth and variety to Sullivan's personal papers which would not have been possible wholly within his own files. Also in the Allen collection are copies of all of Sullivan's published works, usually in first or early editions. Many are presentation copies from the composer, including a number to Mrs. Pierre Ronalds (his most intimate friend), and to her daughter, Mrs. Hay Ritchie. The Library has also recently been given by Mr. Allen a complete collection of the first editions of the librettos of the fourteen operas by Gilbert & Sullivan. The Library's file of separate sheet-music of Sullivan's ballads, songs, part-songs, and of dance arrangements from his operas is perhaps as complete as may be found anywhere. Even so there are still a few *lacunae* to challenge Mr. Allen.

Introduction

In addition to Mr. Allen, Mrs. D'Luhy and Mr. Adams, and to the Association of Fellows for its most generous support, The Pierpont Morgan Library is especially grateful to those who have joined with us and allowed their manuscripts to be part of our centennial celebration:

To John Wolfson, whose lavish representation here reveals his commitment to Arthur Sullivan, for the manuscripts of *The Sorcerer* and *The Grand Duke*, of his *Ivanhoe*, the *Incidental Music to Henry VIII*, and the *Incidental Music to The Merchant of Venice*; as well as the silver presentation cup given Gilbert for help with *The Martyr of Antioch*.

To Mr. Arthur A. Houghton, Jr., for the manuscript of *H.M.S. Pinafore*.

To the Henry W. and Albert A. Berg Collection of the New York Public Library for the manuscript of "The Absent-minded Beggar."

To the Music Division of the Library of Congress, for manuscript music themes of *Trial by Jury*.

To A Memorial Library of Music of Stanford University Libraries, for the manuscripts of *The Foresters* and of the *Idyll for 'Cello and Pianoforte*.

To the Beinecke Library, Yale University, for the three volumes of the Arthur Sullivan Diaries which record the first performances of *Ivanhoe*, 1891, *Utopia, Limited*, 1893, and *The Grand Duke*, 1896.

Charles Ryskamp
DIRECTOR

Sir Arthur Sullivan: Composer & Personage

A BIOGRAPHICAL MONTAGE from his own archive is assembled here to create a full-length portrait of the greatest English composer of the nineteenth century. For over thirty years, from the mid-1860's to his death late in 1900 at the age of fifty-eight, Arthur Sullivan was the dominant force in the musical life of Victorian England. He was, in effect, the uncrowned musician laureate of the Queen, who survived him by only two months.

"The death of Sir Arthur Sullivan, in his 59th year," wrote *The Times* in a long obituary, "may be said without hyperbole to have plunged the whole of the Empire in gloom; for many years he has ranked with the most distinguished personages, rather than with ordinary musicians. Never in the history of the art has a position such as his been held by a composer."

It was Arthur Sullivan the composer *versus* Arthur Sullivan the personage: *The Times*, when the man had been dead only twenty-four hours, pointed to this basic apposition. For Sullivan himself there had been a continuous inner struggle ever since he returned to London from Leipzig in 1861 with *The Tempest* in his portfolio, full of self-confidence and ambition—and with the curtain about to rise on a career of contradictions, a tale of two Sullivans.

Sullivan the composer was a young man in a hurry. His lavish genius evident so early in life, impelled by ambition and flattery, perhaps over-stimulated the impatience of youth. He prided himself, almost to the point of bravado, on the speed of composition which as a serious musician he should have avoided. John Goss, one of his most discerning mentors, had noticed this and, at the time of *The Prodigal Son* in December 1869, had counseled him to put out "all your strength but not the strength of a few weeks or months, whatever your immediate friends may say . . . only don't do anything so pretentious as an oratorio or even a symphony without *all your power*, which seldom comes in one fit." John Goss could not then have foreseen that his prodigal Sullivan would stray down the primrose path of comic opera. Sullivan had, in the words of his most recent biographer, Percy Young, "set out to be a great composer and spent most of his life listening to the complaints of those who considered that by not pursuing a more 'noble' end he had been guilty of some kind of moral impropriety." He was no Brahms, nor Mendelssohn, nor Handel, and admission of this to himself little by little was depressing. These were times when the success of Sullivan the personage afforded a welcome escape to the conscience of the composer.

Sullivan the personage seemed to have leaped in the early 1860's, fully armed with charisma, from the heads of the Prince of Wales and the Duke of Edinburgh. Their royal satisfaction came perhaps too early, at the expense of the development of the impatient composer. The royal family's level of critical understanding in music may have been undistinguished, but they recognized a personage in-the-bud, and adopted Sullivan the composer well ahead of his comic opera successes. These less noble creations, through their relatively brief claims on his time, their large financial return, and their constant spotlight of stage glory, served ideally to satisfy Sullivan the personage.

The obituary in *The Times* had declared that Sullivan's name stood as a synonym for music among all the English-speaking races, "with the exception of a very small and possibly unimportant class . . . principally if not entirely composed of musicians of earnest and highly cultivated taste." This was an understatement. Sullivan's unofficial laurels, his rather early knighthood, his supremacy as a colossus bestriding seven consecutive Leeds Festivals, and his theatre-born affluence had aroused the collective though mute opposition of the have-nots in the musical world. They needed only the deaths of Sullivan and Queen Victoria to become vocal and effective. Styles and tastes had changed by the time the century drew to a close. No doubt, Gilbert & Sullivan operas were beyond the assault of those seeking to depreciate Sullivan's achievement. But even those universally popular works suffered a decline at the outset of the twentieth century. And the bulk of his other compositions were swiftly consigned to the oblivion of non-performance. Even when personal animus plays no part it is not unusual for one generation to brand as commonplace the works of its predecessor. But to quote Mr. Young again, "the lesson which in modern times has taken a long time to re-learn, is that fine music sometimes is inherent in, and often arises from, the commonplace."

Well before 1975, the Victorian era had passed through adverse critical reactions into a wide renewal of appreciation. Interest in the Gilbert & Sullivan operas, similarly, had revived dramatically to greet their second century. It remains that the genius of Arthur Sullivan, serious composer, be re-explored to seek only timeless attributes of great music, unhampered by transitory opinions and comparisons. As his friend Sir George Grove wrote of Sullivan's orchestral compositions: "Form and symmetry he seems to possess by instinct; rhythm and melody clothe everything he touches; the music shows not only sympathetic genius, but sense, judgement, proportion, and complete absence of pedantry and pretension; while the orchestration is distinguished by a happy and original beauty hardly surpassed by the great masters."

As for W. S. Gilbert's appraisal of his long-time collaborator, it was expressed with characteristic bluntness: Arthur Sullivan was "incomparably the greatest English musician of the age."

Sullivan was one of those persons who never throw anything away, especially letters, and when one such collector attains world renown, along with the inescapable houseful of correspondence and memorabilia, archives are born. Sullivan inherited this collecting habit from his mother who, at least as far as anything relating to her *Wunderkind* youngest son was concerned, kept everything lovingly and with prescience. His more prosaic older brother, Fred, is represented in Maria Clementina Sullivan's treasury by very few items and those usually related to both her sons jointly.

What might be the earliest keepsake of such a mother? Clemma (as her husband, Thomas, called her) wrote in a bold hand across an envelope: "Arthur Sullivan's first shirt May 13 / 1842," and into it folded a tiny version of the hospital-shirt that ties in the back. Years later this infant who wore the shirt was to write her long letters, two or three a week. She naturally kept and replied to them conscientiously. Just as naturally Arthur kept her letters, and when she died in 1882, his memorable shirt and letters to his mother came back to him, to be kept as before. Such is the stuff that archives, and this exhibition, are made on.

This second son of Mrs. Sullivan's was no ordinary child. There was something about the dark-eyed little boy that captivated those of the musical and academic circle in which his father made a modest living. It was something more than his precocity in music and the exceptional beauty of his singing voice. A hundred years later this something would have been called charisma (and Gilbert from far away might have added, "the word is Greek"). His was a radiant appeal to both sexes, an engaging wit and talent for mixing with people great and small. It won for Arthur Sullivan recognition, warm friendship, and patronage throughout his life, from his early teens to the end of the nearly fifty years allotted him thereafter.

Letters attesting the early impact of Sullivan's magnetism include some from key figures whose influence was most appropriate to advance each step in his career. Among these were Sir George Smart, regarded as the most influential man of his day in British music, and the Reverend Thomas Helmore, Master of Children at the Chapel Royal. Both were important forces in Sullivan's becoming a Chapel Royal chorister. There followed the support of John Goss, himself a Chapel Royal figure, a highly esteemed composer of religious works and one of Sullivan's teachers at the Royal Academy of Music. It was Goss who initially recommended him for the first Mendelssohn Scholarship. When this award became the next step in Arthur's *gradus ad Parnassum*, there was again Sir George Smart, one of the Scholarship Committee, and Jenny Lind Goldschmidt, a financial backer of the scholarship and devoted *dea ex machina* in advancing the career of teen-age Sullivan.

In an early letter to his mother, Arthur described with wonder the ceremony of the first official service he rendered as a Chapel Royal chorister at a function for the "Sons of the Clergy" held at St. Paul's Cathedral. There were many other such opportunities for bringing him before the royal family, for his beautiful voice often cast him in the leading solo parts. This attention in so musically oriented a Court certainly led to his meeting Alfred, Duke of Edinburgh, himself an enthusiastic musician and of Arthur's age. They became close friends until the death of the Duke within the same year of Sullivan's own end. The archives are replete with letters from various members of the royal family, usually written and signed by a private secretary (starting "I am commanded by . . ."); but in Alfred's case more than a score are in his own hand, on an impressive array of colorful embossed letterheads from several palaces and country seats as well as from H.M.S. *Hercules*. At many of these places, including the warship, his friend Arthur was a frequent guest.

The Sullivan archives contain upwards of one hundred and fifty love letters from Rachel Scott Russell, as well as several score from her older sister Louise. Rachel was lovely, musical, intelligent, but also jealous and possessive. She and Sullivan were unofficially engaged in the mid-60's, but her mother and father (he a prominent marine engineer and board member of the Crystal Palace) opposed marriage to the young composer on the practical grounds that Sullivan was only twenty-seven and was acquiring a reputation but no money. The feeling on his side may have been somewhat less aggressive—and he was coming to value his independence. Meanwhile, the letters kept coming from Rachel (who signed herself "Passion Flower," or "Fond Dove," inspired by one of his most popular songs, "O Fair Dove! O Fond Dove!"), and from Louise, who signed herself "Little Woman" or "L.W." From the letters of these two it seems manifest that he was having an affair with each of them. At one point Henriette Scott Russell, their mother, wrote firmly to amorous Arthur that he was no longer *persona grata* in their Sydenham home unless he obeyed her ground rules. The letter-saving young man carefully kept mama's injunction and a part of his own draft reply along with the bundles of love letters from the two sisters.

Unquestionably the most important woman in Sullivan's life was an American, Mrs. Pierre Lorillard (Mary Frances) Ronalds, married but long estranged from her husband who lived in America while she lived, first in Paris, then in London. The fact that she was not divorced qualified her for acceptance in Sullivan's circle of near-royalty and minimized her as a threat to his single state. Her role served as Arthur's protectress from too serious involvement with others. From the mid-70's, and till the end, she was the dominant personal force in Sullivan's life. They wrote each other frequently, yet there is no letter from Mrs. Ronalds to Sullivan extant, letter-saver though he was.

Sullivan never married, which was certainly for the best as regards his social and musical careers. By the time he was forty he had arrived, undoubtedly with nudging from Mrs. Ronalds, at the domestic way of life, a glimpse of which spiced one of his letters to his mother written from Cairo on 26 February 1882: "My treasure of a servant that I brought with me is a failure . . . Oh the bother of servants . . . It is enough to make one marry—but the cure would be more awful than the disease. I can get rid of servants, but not of a wife—especially if she is *my* wife." Perhaps he remembered Prince Orlovsky's hedonist philosophy, "Chacun à son goût," in the pre–G. & S. classic *Die Fledermaus* (here in the Howard Dietz adaptation):

> It's nice to have a wife round the house
> As long as she's not your own.

For the purposes of this volume the life of Arthur Sullivan is divided into five periods. The first, "Child, Chorister, and Student," covers his early development to 1861. Then follow four decades of creative maturity: "The Eighteen Sixties," when he was busily trying his hand at a great variety of compositions, as well as establishing himself in the London musical and social scene; "The Eighteen Seventies," which occupied him first with church music and songs, and eventually, via *Cox and Box*, brought him into comic opera and to W. S. Gilbert;

"The Eighteen Eighties," the heyday of the G. & S. collaboration and of his two most distinguished choral works, *The Martyr of Antioch* and *The Golden Legend*; and finally, "The Eighteen Nineties," which saw his first and only grand opera, *Ivanhoe*, his most serious quarrel with Gilbert, and the fatal worsening of his always-precarious health.

As *Finale*, there is the somber subject of his funeral, told in intimate memorabilia relating to his funeral instructions, to the funeral itself, to his will, and to the dedication of the memorial to him on the Thames Embankment.

This volume's salute to the Gilbert & Sullivan Centenary, 1875–1975, focuses on the original scores of the two operas most intimately associated with the earliest popularity of Gilbert & Sullivan in America: *H.M.S. Pinafore* and *The Pirates of Penzance*. With these is the baton Sullivan used when he conducted the first performance of *The Martyr of Antioch*, and the superbly chaced silver cup which he gave to Gilbert in gratitude for helping him with the text of *The Martyr*.

These two scores lead an impressive selection of Sullivan's musical manuscripts: the complete scores of *Cox and Box*, *The Sorcerer*, *The Grand Duke*, *Ivanhoe*, *The Merry Wives of Windsor*, *Henry VIII*, the "*Exhibition Ode*," *The Foresters*, and *King Arthur*, as well as thematic sketches for *Trial by Jury* and tenor solos from *The Light of the World*. And in other fields: in instrumental music, the manuscript scores of the *Idyll for Violoncello* and *Day Dreams* (for pianoforte), and of his orchestration for the *Russian National Anthem*; in song, the manuscript scores of "The Dove Song," "Old Love Letters," "Christmas Bells at Sea," and "The Absent-minded Beggar," doubly noteworthy for its words in the hand of Rudyard Kipling.

The full spectrum of Sullivan's colorful interests and activities, musical and personal, is represented. Sheet-music of his settings for the words of some of the great poets illustrate his amazing output of songs and ballads: Shakespeare, Tennyson, Byron, Shelley, Longfellow, and many others. Letters from more than a score of contemporary musicians, authors, and opera stars reflect the character of his correspondence. Part-songs, religious music, hymns, and anthems are represented in single examples and in collections. There are other unrelated activities: his association with Henry Irving and Ellen Terry in their production of *Macbeth* at the Lyceum, his several compositions on the occasion of the wedding of the Prince of Wales, his "Grand Orchestral Concert" with Jenny Lind, and the chamber music, often *chez* Sullivan, with H.R.H. The Duke of Edinburgh playing first violin. Four large selections of letters between Gilbert and Sullivan tell the story of their three major quarrels and of the relatively calm interlude that produced *The Gondoliers*.

Here is infinite variety: from the manuscript of one of his lectures "On the Theory and Practice of Vocal Music" to his business arrangement with Edward Bok that put "The Lost Chord" in an issue of *The Ladies' Home Journal* and to the letters patent of his invention, "Sullivan Safety Shaft" ("a means for releasing draught animals from road vehicles"). And as a period piece illustrating Sullivan's *beau monde*, there is a truly fan-tastic autographed fan, originally from the family of George Henschel (he was the first director of the Boston Symphony Orchestra). Dating from 1879, this fan contains more than eighty signatures of famous authors, artists, and musicians (including Arthur Sullivan, 1880) on its sandalwood sticks, written on both sides. Three of the sticks are signed: Adelina Patti and Nellie Melba; Henry James and John S. Sargent; Mark Twain, J. R. Lowell, and W. D. Howells.

ACKNOWLEDGEMENTS

The preparation of this volume and of the exhibition has been so dependent on the devoted collaboration of one individual that, like Sir Joseph Porter, "I find it not easy to express" my gratitude. Certainly without the daily help of Gale D'Luhy throughout 1974 there would have been no work of this magnitude ready for 1975. Mrs. D'Luhy is both a trained musician and a dedicated Savoyard. She has been my Seeing Eye through countless pages of Sullivan's music that I cannot read but can only hear. And in the recent pressure of our work approaching (yes, and passing) its deadlines, her unfailing even disposition and sense of humor have been beyond thanks.

Although acknowledged among my bibliographic sources, I wish to express my particular thanks to Percy Young for the considerable help I have had from the stimulating musical opinions and collateral personal data in his biography, *Sir Arthur Sullivan* (1971). I found this work especially rewarding when used in conjunction with the Sullivan archive to which Mr. Young did not have access.

To the late Herbert Sullivan and Sir Newman Flower, authors of *Sir Arthur Sullivan, His Life, Letters and Diaries*, I am indebted for their detailed guidance through the huge wealth of source material in the Sullivan archive which, of course, was at their disposal when they collaborated on their biography in 1927. This archive is now in the Morgan Library.

To John Wolfson, himself a student of Sullivan's life and music, is due a three-fold thanks: for his generosity in lending the Library five important manuscripts from his Sullivan collection; for his success in pursuit of earliest Sullivan phonograph recording rarities; and for his musical knowledge and appraisal of Sullivan as both composer and personage, always shared with wit and enthusiasm.

To my friends of the D'Oyly Carte Opera headquarters, executives and staff, my endless gratitude and admiration. I have had only to ask and their instant help has been forthcoming, whether for photographs, elusive dates, microfilm, or checking controversial data. In particular, thank you, Miss Carte, and thank you, Albert Truelove, for all you have done for me.

To Jacques Barzun—friend, Savoyard, and scholar—whose wit and erudition in November 1950 helped launch my first G. & S. exhibition at the Library, and whose fine editorial hand, in November 1974, has been my guide in preparing this introduction.

Other individuals and institutions to whom I am indebted for help in the preparation of this volume are: The Garrick Club, Cecil Hopkinson, The Rev. Peter Joslin, Alexander Hyatt King (The British Museum), William Lichtenwanger, George Nash (Victoria & Albert Museum), Jon Newsom (Reference Department, Music Division, The Library of Congress), Michael Packard (Chappell & Co., Ltd.), The Peabody Conservatory of Music, Colin Prestige Esq., Basil Ramsey (Novello & Co., Ltd.), Terence Rees, Florian J. Shasky (Chief, Department of Special Collections, Stanford University Libraries), Dr. Jane Stedman, Dr. Lola L. Szladits (Curator, The Berg Collection, The New York Public Library), Marion Tyson-Smith, Marjorie Wynne (The Beinecke Library, Yale University).

And finally, my boundless gratitude to The Pierpont Morgan Library: to Frederick Adams, who inducted me twenty-five years ago, and to the Director, Charles Ryskamp, who has so warmly continued my association and who now brings me the fulfillment of this exhibition and volume on Sullivan; to Herbert Cahoon, Rigbie Turner, Mrs. Patricia Reyes, and my other colleagues on the Library's unique staff, always ready to help me; most particularly to Charles Passela, photographer extraordinary, whose standard of excellence has added immeasurably to this volume. And to H. H. A., *con amore*, from whom I am on loan to G. & S.

Reginald Allen
CURATOR
GILBERT & SULLIVAN COLLECTION

Child, Chorister, Student

Arthur Sullivan, ca. 1846–47, age 4–5. (1d)

ARMED with the wealth of intimate resources of the Sullivan archive, this exhibition is virtually autobiographical—the principal, in a sense, telling his own story. Naturally at first he must rely on the words of parents and of those few important architects of his career who launched it and gave it ever-increasing momentum. The crowded months and years in this stage of the boy's life, from age twelve to twenty, suggest the pages of a giant memory-book for which a Don Alhambra (*The Gondoliers*) might dictate: when everything is of the same relative unimportance, then nothing is unimportant—especially to the principal.

1a Sullivan, Sir Arthur Seymour, 1842–1900. Manuscript, signed, of an autobiographic outline [n.p., n.d.]. 4pp.

Three pages of his own manuscript autobiographic outline, written in 1873 for an article in the *Illustrated Review*, start from his birth and parentage, pass through his childhood music training, through the two-and-a-half student years in Leipzig, and lead to the threshold of his first full decade of mature creativity—the 1860's.

1b Sullivan, Maria Clementina Coghlan, 1811–1882. Photograph, head and shoulders [n.d.], taken by The Misses Bertolacci [London]. 16½ x 11 cm.

The photograph of his mother was his own treasured copy and has been reproduced by all his biographers. Maria Clementina Coghlan Sullivan, of Italian and Irish blood, was herself innately musical. Her husband, Thomas Sullivan, was a clarinetist, a musician who rose from theatre orchestra work to become Bandmaster to the Royal Military College at Sandhurst and later Professor on the staff at Kneller Hall, the Normal School for Bandmasters of the British Army. They had two sons, Frederic (b. 1839) and Arthur (b. 1842).

1c Sullivan. "Arthur Sullivan's first shirt May 13 / 1842," together with the envelope bearing that inscription in the hand of his mother, Maria Clementina Sullivan.

1d Sullivan. Photograph, three-quarter view, seated and holding a leafy branch [n.p., n.d.—ca. 1846–1847]. 10 x 6½ cm.

This earliest photograph of Arthur Sullivan, probably at age four or five, shows the large, dark eyes that appealed so to his mother [see No. 1k].

1e Sullivan. Photograph, three-quarter view, seated [n.d.—ca. 1854], taken by The Misses Bertolacci [London]. 10½ x 6½ cm.

In this photograph twelve-year-old Sullivan is wearing the working uniform of a Chapel Royal Chorister.

1f Sullivan. Als, 20 Albert Terrace [London], 21 March 1851, to his mother. 2pp.

Young Arthur's earliest extant letter, written to his mother while he was living at 20 Albert Terrace, in the house of William Gordon Plees, who ran a private school. It was Mr. Plees who first took the boy to be interviewed and auditioned by Sir George Smart, and to the Rev. Thomas Helmore who had power of appointment to the Chapel Royal. This letter, treasured by his mother, relates to these two important audition meetings.

1g Helmore, Rev. Thomas, 1811–1890. Als, 6 Cheyne Walk [London], 8 April 1854, to "Sir" [Rev. Percy Smith]. 3pp.

The Rev. Mr. Helmore wrote to Percy Smith of his reaction on meeting young Arthur. "I like Arthur Sullivan's appearance and manner—his voice is good. . . ." He went on to explain that if he was able to obviate the complication of Sullivan's being older than the usual admission age for Chapel Royal probationers, he would be glad to give him a trial. The Rev. Percy Smith was a friend of the Sullivan family who had written an apparently strong letter in behalf of the boy, which Helmore acknowledged: "Your testimonial of character, ability and sweetness of disposition is most satisfactory and weighs very much in my desire to procure his admission to the Choir of the Chapel Royal." Sullivan was appointed to the Chapel Royal within two weeks of this letter.

1h Sullivan. Als, Cheyne Walk [London], 11 May 1854, to his mother. 3pp.

As he had been appointed to the Chapel Royal the preceding month, young Sullivan was then living with the Rev. Thomas Helmore at Cheyne Walk, Chelsea. He wrote his mother describing his participation in a spectacular event for the "Sons of the Clergy" held the previous day at St. Paul's Cathedral. "We were all in our gold coats." Along with these richly dressed Chapel Royal boys were the choirs of St. Paul's, Westminster, and St. George's, Windsor. Arthur listed the procession in the order in which they ascended the aisle of the cathedral including the Archbishop of Canterbury and Prince Albert. "It was a splendid sight. About 2000 people there. There were 18 choirs." But the little boy still showed through his golden finery, reminding his mother in a vertically written postscript: "Don't forget the 13th." It was not very likely that the adoring mother would overlook his twelfth birthday.

1i Sullivan. Als, The Royal Military College, Sandhurst, 2 July 1855, to G. Grey [unidentified]. 3pp.

Arthur Sullivan's childhood was often hampered by fragile health. In this letter he wrote to G. Grey that though he had been ill at home he hoped to "be well enough to go to the Crystal Palace on Friday next." His stationery shows a fine engraving of The Royal Military College, Sandhurst, where his father was Bandmaster.

4

1j Sullivan. "O Israel," sacred song, words from Hosea XIV 1.2. London: J. Alfred Novello [n.d.]. 4pp. Plate no. 2561.

Arthur Sullivan's Opus No. 1, his first printed music, composed and published when he was thirteen. The title page states: "Composed & dedicated to Mrs. C. V. Bridgman, (Tavistock, Devon) by Arthur Sullivan, Chorister of H.M. Chapel." The publisher was J. Novello, 1855. The music occupied four pages, beautifully engraved. Chris V. Bridgman was a fellow-chorister and early friend of Arthur's.

1k Sullivan, Maria Clementina, 1811–1882. Als, Yorktown, 23 December 1855, to "my dear child" [Sullivan]. 4pp.

"My dear child," wrote his mother in a pre-Christmas letter, "I shall miss your little happy face and black eyes at my dinner table on Tuesday, but you will not be forgotten my dear." She went on to express sympathy for those parents who "have to mourn the loss of their sons fallen in this unfortunate [Crimean] war since Christmas day last." Her own small photograph of the object of her affection at age thirteen testifies to his appeal [see No. 1d].

1l Helmore, Rev. Thomas, 1811–1890. Als, 6 Cheyne Walk, 29 November 1856, to Mrs. Sullivan. 8pp.

Sullivan had won the first Mendelssohn Scholarship admitting him to the Royal Academy of Music effective September 1856. Apparently his early progress left something to be desired in the eyes of his mentors Helmore and [Sir] John Goss, English organist and composer at the Chapel Royal. This was clear in this eight-page letter to his mother from the Rev. Mr. Helmore. The Master hoped his house, where Arthur lived, would be out of quarantine and restored to normal resident student activity. Meanwhile Arthur might visit his mother next week provided he did not neglect his work. "He must in fact allow himself only so much *play* as is requisite for a healthy state of mind and body." Mr. Helmore quoted Dr. Goss as saying that Arthur "must *do more* & work harder if he hopes to satisfy the Mendelssohn Committee, & retain the [Royal Academy] Scholarship next year." The Rev. Mr. Helmore closed with the suggestion that "he ought every week to do about twelve exercises and compose a little something, a Song—or a Sanctus—or an Anthem etc. of his own. This is a practical way of testing his industry."

  With his career in jeopardy, Sullivan rose to the challenge and secured the renewal of the Mendelssohn [Royal Academy of Music] Scholarship for a second year which would carry him into 1858.

1m Helmore, Rev. Thomas, 1811–1890. Photograph, full view [n.d.], taken by Smallcombe [London]. 9½ x 6 cm.

A photograph of the Rev. Thomas Helmore from the Sullivan archive, probably belonged to Clementina Sullivan. He held the post of Priest in Ordinary to the Queen and Master of

Children at the Chapel Royal, St. James's Palace. He was the devoted friend of both Arthur's parents and particularly of the boy himself.

1n Sullivan, Thomas, 1805–1866. Photograph, among other professors at Kneller Hall in 1859, printed in the Supplement to the "Orchestral Times," September 1904. 1p.

This reproduction from a page in the Supplement to the "Orchestral Times," 19 September 1904, contains the only likeness of Thomas Sullivan in the Sullivan archive. The self-effacement of these two devoted parents is poignantly clear in the fact that the archive contains but two photographs of his mother and none of Sullivan's father.

1o Kneller Hall near Hounslow, engraved glossy card [n.d.], Harrison Engʳ., London, publisᵈ. by J. Allenson, Post Office Whitton. 9 x 12 cm.

1p Sullivan, Thomas, 1805–1866. Carte-de-visite.

This tiny bit of Sullivan archive ephemera bears the professional designation in its simplest form: "Mr. Sullivan / Professor of Music / Military School of Music, Kneller Hall." The last two lines are in microscopic lettering; the whole card is neither engraved nor printed. The humble Bandmaster-Professor had (probably himself) executed his business card with the steady hand, fine-nib pen, and practised eye of one who regularly copies band-parts on the small music cards of marching brass-players.

1q Smart, Sir George T., 1776–1867. Als, [London], 8 May 1858, to Sullivan. 1p.

By 1858 Arthur Sullivan was so outstandingly superior to other applicants that the Mendelssohn Scholarship Committee awarded him a third scholarship year with the plan to send him to Leipzig for further study. Sir George Smart, Committee member and great believer in Sullivan's potential, wrote him at about the time this great new opportunity was opening. "I wish to talk with you relative to your future prospects . . . ," wrote Sir George, and suggested four o'clock on any afternoon the following week.

1r Sullivan. Photograph, three-quarter view, signed and dated 8 September 1858, taken by Mr. Herbert Watkins [London]. 36 x 27 cm.

This portrait photograph of Sullivan was taken at the time he was about to leave for Leipzig. He signed it on the mat, dating it 8 September 1858. He was then sixteen. It is likely that this particular copy was given by him to Mrs. Helmore in whose house he had been living during his four years at the Royal Academy of Music, as it was acquired with a group of items relating to the Helmores.

6

1s Sullivan, Frederic, 1839–1877. Als, 3 Ponsonby St. [London],
14 January 1860, to "Jack" [Sullivan]. 4pp.

Often in their correspondence the two Sullivan brothers would address each other as "Jack." In this "dear Jack" letter, which older brother Fred wrote to Arthur in Leipzig, there was an abundant staccato of banter and local news. He started by telling him he had joined the Volunteers, "that is the Band of one" . . . that Walter Bache (one of Arthur's fellow-students in Leipzig) had reported that Arthur spoke disrespectfully of Fred's 'cello-playing . . . that Dr. Goss sent his kind regards . . . that Joe Barnby (who had tied with Sullivan in the original Mendelssohn Scholarship competition but lost in the play-off) was going to leave York in a year . . . and closed "I am dear Jack your affect^te brother Fred Sullivan / Lance Corporal." This was followed by a postscript, overwritten vertically: "You say you have been told by your masters that you were born to be a conductor in that case you'll have no chance in London should you aspire to such a position for the market's overstocked with omnibuses. Corp^l Sullivan."

1t Sullivan. Als, Leipzig, September 1860, to his father. 4pp.

Sullivan had again won an extension of his scholarship which kept him in Leipzig yet another year, from autumn 1859 to September 1860, by which time the scholarship funds were exhausted. But friendly advices, pressures, and generosities were visited on his father to insure the boy at least six months more. Somehow the impecunious Bandmaster was able to raise the money that accounted for his son's grateful letter of 1 September 1860.

"How shall I thank you sufficiently my dearest father, for the opportunity you have given me of continuing my studies here, I am indeed very grateful & will work very hard, in order that you may soon see that all your sacrifices (which I know you make) have not been to no purpose, & I will try to make the end of your days happy and comfortable. I had given up all idea of staying longer. . . ." He wrote that he had sent Sir George Smart "a letter from Mr. Moscheles urgently begging him to prolong my stay."

1u Sullivan. Album, Leipzig, 1860–1861, containing ten autograph
musical quotations, one pencil sketch, and two greetings, all signed, ten
dated, all to Sullivan. 14 x 22½ cm. 13pp. (the other pages are blank).

This album was started by Arthur in late 1860 when he expected to be leaving for London. Eight of its signators contributed prior to the end of the year. The remaining five carried its pages into April 1861, as Sullivan's father had found it possible to keep his son at the Conservatorium for another half-year. His friends and fellow-students, in writing messages in its pages, were expected to contribute some bit of musical autograph as well, and many did. Four of these represented one family, the Barnetts. Sullivan had written Sir George Smart when he first arrived: "The whole family of Mr. John Barnett the composer are living over here, for the sake of two daughters & a son who are in the Conservatorium." Barnett senior (John Francis Barnett, 1802–1890) was studying in Leipzig at the same time as his daughters

Clara Kathleen and Rosamond and his son Domenico. Each had a page in Arthur's album, three with musical manuscript passages. The father and both daughters, with whom young Sullivan more than likely had enjoyed some non-academic *legato* moments, wrote their musical greetings. Their brother celebrated the opportunity with a sketch (non-musical) which commented on Sullivan's initials, the middle one "S" for Seymour, which he was to drop more than a decade later. Other pages feature Walter Bache (1842–1888), pianist exponent of his teacher Liszt; Edward George Dannreuther (1844–1905), pianist and writer; Paul David (1840–1932), violinist, teacher, the son of Ferdinand who taught Sullivan; Franklin Taylor (1843–1919), pianist and teacher [later, Franklyn]; *et al*.

1v Sullivan, Thomas, 1805–1866. Als, [London], 13 January 1861, to "my dear boy" [Sullivan]. 4pp.

This long letter emphasized the combination of professional wisdom and parental love of the musician-father for his composer-son. His conclusions (in cross-writing) gave this counsel: "Do pray finish the *Tempest* before you leave. Make up your mind to be cut to pieces by the knowing ones when you produce anything in London—if you escape you will be lucky indeed. Even Handel himself has been taking it lately from Chorley—Prodigious!! . . . Mother has just favoured me with a kiss for writing you as she calls it a nice long letter. What a *Casta Diva* your mother is my dear. I hope you will always love her. I assure you she has borne your absence with ladylike fortitude. . . ."

That young Sullivan followed his father's advice was immediately evident as can be noted [see Nos. 1w, 2g]. The *Tempest* music had a first "Prüfung" performance in Leipzig on 6 April 1861.

1w Sullivan. Als, Berlin, 11 April 1861, to his mother. 3pp.

In a quick trip from Leipzig to Berlin, Arthur wrote his mother: "The 'Tempest' was performed in the 'Prüfung' last Saturday [6 April, in Leipzig], & was most successful. I was called forward three times afterwards." He also told her that Madame Klingemann had written him a letter enclosing an introduction to Mr. P. Mendelssohn [in Berlin], "he has invited me to dine with him today. He is the brother of *the* Mendelssohn & is a very rich banker. Tannhäuser is being given tonight in the Opera House, I shall go & hear it . . . Then, au revoir, this is probably the last letter I shall write you from Germany . . . I shall see you all again in a day or two."

So ended Arthur Sullivan's student years.

1x Sullivan. Diploma, awarded to "herr Arthur Seymour Sullivan aus London, Conservatorium der Musik zu Leipzig am 10 April 1861." It is signed by the Directors and Professors. 32 x 43 cm.

The Eighteen Sixties

Arthur Sullivan, ca. 1864, age 22. (6g)

IN the 1860's variety was the spice of Sullivan's creative life. Instrumental music: only in this decade did he continue his student interests in purely instrumental fields of composition. His *Tempest* music (originally a Leipzig product); three works for the 'cello (the *Idyll*, the *Concerto in D*, and *Duo Concertante*); three works for the piano (*Thoughts*, *Day Dreams*, and *Twilight*); his *Symphony in E* (*The Irish*); his additional accompaniments to Handel's *Jeptha*; three marches; three overtures ("*In Memoriam,*" *Marmion*, and the overture to the unfinished opera, *The Sapphire Necklace*). For chorus and orchestra there were the masque, *Kenilworth*, and the oratorio, *The Prodigal Son*. For the theatre: a ballet, *L'Ile Enchantée*, and two comic operas, *Cox and Box* and *The Contrabandista*. Songs with pianoforte: he composed more than two dozen in this period. And religious music: there were some nine part-songs, two anthems, and several miscellaneous hymns. Toward the latter part of the decade it was the voice—solo and choral, in combination with pianoforte, organ, or orchestra—that was closest to him. Whether for the salon, the concert stage, the church, or the theatre—he composed for them all, as though groping, through those prolific 1860's.

2a Sullivan. Als, 3 Ponsonby St., London, 22 April 1861, to Sir George [Smart]. 3pp.

Arthur Sullivan's first order of business on his return from Leipzig was to write a letter of appreciation to Sir George Smart and the Mendelssohn Scholarship Committee of which he was President. "... [M]y heartfelt thanks for the means & opportunities you have placed at my disposal ... You have thus given me the first step in life, that which is most important to a young Artist—a first rate education. ..."

2b Sullivan. An application form for admission to the Reading Room of the British Museum, signed and dated 21 May 1862, by Arthur S. Sullivan and Campbell Clarke. 2pp.

(Sir) Campbell Clarke (1835–1902) was Librarian at the British Museum from 1852 to 1870. The collection at the Morgan Library contains two memory-book pages inscribed by Sullivan for Lady Campbell Clarke many years later (1897 and 1899), on which occasions he used the musical quote of "I have a song to sing, O" along with his signature [see No. 67g].

THE TEMPEST

2c Sullivan. *The Music to Shakespeare's Tempest*. Piano score arranged from the score by Franklyn Taylor, London: Cramer, Beale & Wood [n.d.]. 105pp. 34 x 27 cm. Plate no. 8028.

The Music to Shakespeare's Tempest was composed and dedicated to his esteemed friend Sir George Smart. This copy of the cornerstone of Sullivan's composing career is a presentation from him to Jenny Lind Goldschmidt. On the recto of a front end-paper is written in the composer's hand: "Mad^me Goldschmidt from Arthur S. Sullivan, Oct. 1862," while on its verso facing the title page, Otto Goldschmidt had signed his name. The wrappers are the original blue cloth.

2d Smart, Sir George T., 1776–1867. Als, No. 12 Bedford Square [London], 11 October 1862, to Sullivan. 1p.

Probably at the same time Sullivan sent a presentation copy of the *Tempest* to the Goldschmidts, he left a copy personally at the house of his friend and patron Sir George Smart. In this letter Sir George thanked Sullivan for dedicating the music to him and for bringing him a copy of it. He closed "with every good wish for your prosperity believe me to be your sincere Friend George T. Smart."

2e Sullivan. *The Music to Shakespeare's Tempest*. Full score, London & New York: Novello, Ewer & Co., 1891. Original printed grey boards, the first edition. 204pp. 35 x 28 cm. Plate no. 7752.

Provenance: on the front end-paper is written "J. Hampton Feb 1894" and "to G. R. Sinclair Xmas 1907." This copy bears the signature of its former owner G. R. Sinclair, organist of Hereford Cathedral and the original of the eleventh of Elgar's "Enigma" (Portraits) Variations.

2f Sullivan. Musical quotation, signed, St. James's Hall, 20 February 1865, "Where the bee sucks," from *The Music to Shakespeare's Tempest*. 1p.

No. 12, "Where the bee sucks" (pages 190–200), was probably the "pretty song" that Jenny Lind liked to sing according to Otto Goldschmidt's letter of 10 December 1862.

2g Sullivan. Al [incomplete], 3 Ponsonby St. [London], 23 November 1862, to Mrs. Lehmann. 4pp.

At this time young Sullivan formed a warm, long-lasting friendship with Mrs. Frederic Lehmann, who started as "Dear Mrs. Lehmann" and developed into "Nina," "Ni," and "Dear Heart" in his correspondence. In a long letter of which the archive has only the first four pages, it was manifest that Sullivan was gifted socially and recognized Mrs. Lehmann as an attractive asset in his ever-increasing circle of musical and literary friends. He mentioned "They did a little 'Tempest' at the C. Palace concert yesterday [22 November] and he [Joachim], Clay, & myself dined at Grove's afterwards. . . ." He wondered if the "necklace" would be given in Paris, a reference to the opera, *The Sapphire Necklace*, he was composing to a libretto by Chorley, a friend of the Lehmanns.

The archive includes another long and important letter of 23 January 1863 from Sullivan to Mrs. Lehmann giving her (with flirtatious asides) a vivid, entertaining account of Charles Hallé's performance of *The Tempest* at one of his "Gentlemen's Concerts" of his orchestra in Manchester: "I sat with the Hallés in the two front rows (I on one only, of course) A splendid Hall, & well filled—nearly 3000 I was told—

<blockquote>
Overture — Egmont — Beet:
Song — Miss Banks.
Music to the 'Tempest'. A.S.S.!
</blockquote>

Well, I felt calm & collected, & smiled blandly at the few people that I knew. The 'Storm' begins, ends, & is warmly applauded—Things go on, the 3rd-Act Prelude, also warmly applauded, at which your correspondent looks gratified, & wishes that a certain lady friend of his, could hear the way in which certain points were taken up & certain passages got through without bungle—however, the audience warms up & applauds everything—especially the 4th Act Overture, which your correspondent thought as near perfection as anything he had ever heard. The band was superb—so bright! Well it is all over—& loud applause follows. The band applaud at me. Hallé leans over & applauds at me. The audience see that something is up & continue. At last, Hallé beckons to me to come up. I wink, I nod. I interrogate with my eyebrows, & at last rush madly from my seat & up the platform. When I show myself, my breath is literally taken away by the noise. It is gratifying though I bow six times, twice to the Orchestra (who throughout have been so kind & friendly) & shake hands with Hallé—then down again, & all is over."

2h Goldschmidt, Otto, 1829–1907. Als, St. Leonard's on Sea, 10 December 1862, to Mr. Sullivan. 4pp.

Friendship with the Goldschmidts burgeoned in this first year of Sullivan's return to London. On 10 December 1862 Otto Goldschmidt wrote "Will you come Christmas *eve* to spend quietly with us & help to light the tree." He explained they were afraid to ask others because of son Walter's recent "Scarlatina," but with eight weeks passed, the house would be purified. "If you come, will you stay the night & go to *your* Service next morning, or have you to go home the same evening. We have been playing your Tempest & Mad^{me} Goldschmidt has been repeatedly singing the pretty song & the Duet [probably No. 12, 'Where the Bee Sucks,' and No. 9, 'Honour, Riches, Marriage, Blessing']. She likes the work *very much*."

2i Lind, Jenny (Madame Otto Goldschmidt), 1820–1887. Photograph, full view, seated with her son (Walter), taken by Hermann Krone, Paris and Dresden [n.d.]. 10 x 6½ cm.

"I WAS AT ROSSINI'S"

2j Sullivan. Memo, not signed, Paris, 10 December 1862. 4pp.

A big moment for twenty-year-old Sullivan was his first meeting with Rossini. It took place on 10 December 1862, and he recorded the occasion in a diarylike memo. He really worked at and made the most of this opportunity. On the first attempted visit he found Rossini out. So Arthur tried again a half-hour later. "The old gentleman was very kind & affable, asked me if I sang, as every composer for the voice ought to be able to sing—invited me to his reception the same evening." Naturally Sullivan went. The very next day, Thursday the 11th, he was back at Rossini's at 9:30 in the morning. "I found him alone composing a little pianoforte piece for his dog! He played me a new Minuet in [?]♭, very pretty & quaint." But eager Arthur must have returned the next day too, 12 December, for that is the date of Rossini's inscription on the photograph he gave him: "Offert a mon jeune Collègue Arthur S. Sullivan Paris 12 D. 1862.   G. Rossini."

2k Rossini, Gioachino, 1792–1868. Photograph, full-length view, seated, signed and dated 12 December 1862. Framed: 12 x 17 cm.

THE ROYAL WEDDING

A spectacular propulsion that placed Sullivan in the orbit of the royal family burst unaccountably and without warning in 1863. The forthcoming marriage, on 10 March of that year, of Edward, Prince of Wales, to Princess Alexandra of Denmark prompted a spate of special music to celebrate the occasion. Arthur Sullivan composed *three* of these numbers, each of them "Dedicated to H.R.H. The Prince of Wales," a privilege so carefully controlled by the royal family that the mere request for it could not be made without preparation that assured it to be welcome. So—little more than a year out of Leipzig—the twenty-one-year-old Sullivan was already on his way to being unofficial musician laureate.

3a Sullivan. "The Bride from the North," song, words by Henry F. Chorley, London: Cramer, Beale & Wood (1863), Plate no. 832.

"The Bride from the North," sheet-music with an attractive drawing of the Princess in her bridal veil on the cover, is mentioned by Percy Young (p. 273) as having no copy extant. This copy may well be unique.

3b Sullivan. "The Princess of Wales March on Danish Airs," London: Cramer, Beale & Wood (1863), performed by the Military Bands on the occasion of Her Royal Highness' arrival in London (with a presentation inscription from Sullivan).

3c Sullivan. "The Procession March," [lacking covers] [1863] (with presentation inscription from Sullivan on the dedication page).

3d Sullivan. "The Royal Wedding—Grand March," London: Cramer [n.d.] (the music is identical with the preceding). Plate no. 8361.

The other two were marches, covering the two most dramatic events: the arrival of Princess Alexandra, "The Princess of Wales March on Danish Airs," and the wedding itself, "The Procession March," also published as "The Royal Wedding—Grand March." Both copies bear presentation inscriptions from Sullivan to Mrs. Helmore, wife of the Rev. Mr. Helmore, who had first appointed Arthur to the Chapel Royal, and in whose home he lived at that time.

3e Sullivan. Als, 3 Ponsonby St. [London], 6 February 1863, to Mr. C. Salaman. 3pp.

In a letter of 6 February 1863 to Charles Salaman (one of the founders, and the Hon. Secretary, of the Musical Society of London), Sullivan first acknowledged his gratitude for being elected to the Society, and then told Salaman: "You know it [the next concert of the M.S.] comes just after the P. of Wales' marriage, &, (as you may probably not know) I am engaged to write a grand March for the occasion, which is to be performed [by] all the military bands on the wedding day." Sullivan wondered if his new March might be performed at the next Musical Society concert. "Please consider this *strictly private*, as no one yet knows about my engagement."

L'ILE ENCHANTÉE

4a Sullivan. Manuscript of "Short Chronological Memoranda," not signed nor dated, 1 Queen's Mansions [London]. Pages 1 and 2 (of twelve pages).

Sullivan wrote twelve pages of memoranda as notes for Charles Willeby in 1893 at the time Willeby was preparing the first lengthy biographical sketch on Sullivan which appeared in *Masters of English Music*, pages 1 to 102, published by James R. Osgood, McIlvaine & Co., London, 1893, as one of the *Masters of Contemporary Music* series. Later this sketch served as the basis for Sullivan's first full biography, *Sir Arthur Sullivan: Life, Letters and Reminiscences* by Arthur Lawrence, London, 1899. Pages 1 and 2 of these memoranda describe most interestingly the young composer's first experience working for the stage, in this instance a ballet, *L'Ile Enchantée* (first performed 14 May 1864 at Covent Garden).

Conductor Michael Costa at Covent Garden had engaged Sullivan as house organist to give him theatre experience. So it was natural for him to be asked to try his hand at composing for ballet. "I learned a great deal from it, for I had to adapt my music to the requirements of the inventors (Mons: Desplaces, balletmaster, and Mr. A. Harris, stage master), the scenepainter, Mr. W. Beverly, and the stage machinist, Mr. Sloman, and the *première danseuse*, Mad^{lle}. Salvioni."

4b Sullivan. *L'Ile Enchantée*, ballet. A copyist's manuscript of the orchestral parts, with the added variation for Mad^{lle}. Carmine, Covent Garden, 1864. 124pp. 31 x 24½ cm.

L'Ile Enchantée was never published. But for more than thirty-five years, until his death, Sullivan kept the copyist's score, including the page of "repititeurs" [sic] along with the name of the second danseuse, about which he gave so amusing a description on page 2 of the memoranda: "A variation (solo dance) was required at the last moment, for the second danseuse just arrived. 'What on earth am I to do?' I said to Harris, 'I haven't seen her dance yet and don't know her style.' 'I'll see' said Harris and took the young lady aside. In five minutes he returned. 'I've arranged it with her, this is exactly what she wants. (giving it me rhythmically) tiddle-iddle-um, tiddle-iddle um, rum-tirum-tirum, 16 bars of that; then rum-tum, rum-tum, heavy you know, 16 bars, & then finish up with the overture to William Tell, last movement, 16 bars & coda.' In ten minutes time I had composed it & written a répétiteur part and it was at once rehearsed."

One of the uses Sullivan was to make of his unpublished *L'Ile Enchantée* was confessed in a letter he wrote eleven years later to his great friend, the critic Joseph Bennett [see No. 41b].

The letter, dated 17 December 1874, concerns the details of Sullivan's incidental music to *The Merry Wives of Windsor*, which had been first performed at the Theatre Royal, Manchester, on 31 August 1874. "All the music is new," wrote Sullivan, "but (& this is not necessarily for publication) if you remember a Ballet called 'L'ile enchantée' which I wrote for the Italian Opera Covent Garden many years ago, you will recognize two themes. The 1st, in the Prelude & the 2nd in the scene between Anne Page & the children. . . . ."

THE SAPPHIRE NECKLACE

5a Sullivan. *Overture, The Sapphire Necklace*, arranged for military band by Charles Godfrey Junr., London: S. A. Chappell [n.d.]. 9pp. Plate no. 344.

In 1863–1864 Sullivan was involved in setting an opera of a libretto by his friend Henry F. Chorley, the critic of whom his father had written banefully only two years earlier [see No. 1v]. Chorley's age and creative heavy-handedness seem strange qualifications for youthful, witty, socially adept Sullivan. Perhaps a mutual friend (Mrs. Lehmann?) was responsible; or perhaps the career-minded Sullivan, recalling his father's references to Chorley the critic, deliberately sought to woo and win his support. At any rate, *The Sapphire Necklace* was never completed nor published. It wasted the composer's valuable time. A year later the poor quality of Chorley's libretto for Sullivan's masque, *Kenilworth*, was again a hazard to his success.

5b Sullivan. Als, Richmond Lodge, Belfast [n.d.—September 1863], to his mother. 4pp.

In a letter to his mother, from Richmond Lodge, Belfast, September 1863, Sullivan wrote her, "A note has just come, the joint production of Miss Dickens & Mrs. Lehmann, to tell me that Dickens is perfectly enchanted with the Minuet theme in my Opera (at the beginning of the Overture) which the latter plays continually to him at his request. He thinks it quite sufficient even to make the opera a success." By this time it was doubtful if Sullivan had any such great expectations.

5c Dickens, Charles, 1812–1870. Als, London, 4 November 1863, to Frederic Lehmann. 1p.

"Your bright boy is recovering without a check, I hope?" wrote the great man of Arthur. "I send my love to him, and his mother." As was so frequently the case, young Sullivan had evidently been in poor health. Dickens' closing paragraph is worthy of note, written as it was just twenty years after *The Christmas Carol*. "At this present writing I'm in some doubt whether I have anything inside my head, or no. The Christmas Nº has so addled it this week, that I don't recognize it as mine." The letterhead is: "Office of All the Year Round, a weekly journal conducted by Charles Dickens."

KENILWORTH

Early in 1864, on the recommendation of Michael Costa, Sullivan was invited to compose a work for the Birmingham Festival to be held in September of that year. The resulting effort was *Kenilworth, A Masque of the Days of Queen Elizabeth*. Henry Chorley again, as in the case of *The Sapphire Necklace*, wrote the words, again of a quality not likely to stimulate the composer—nor did they. The work was not regarded as a milestone in Sullivan's career by the musical intelligentsia, even though the composer reported an enthusiastic reception on the evening itself. But the personable young Sullivan made social capital of the occasion in any event, scoring a hit with the Harrold family at Edgbaston with whom he must have lived as houseguest all or part of the time he was in Birmingham.

6a Sullivan, and H. F. Chorley, 1808–1872. *Kenilworth, a Masque of the days of Queen Elizabeth*, Op. 4, arranged from the score by Franklyn Taylor. London: Chappell & Co. [n.d.]. Brown morocco, gilt, with decorative end-papers. Second edition, revised and corrected. [i], 1–72pp. 36 x 26½ cm.

The copy of the vocal score is the second edition, revised and corrected. Its provenance is not known, but from the elaborate nature of the binding, gilt edges, its tooled legend of the performance at the Birmingham Musical Festival, and its splendid preliminary inserted pages of photographs and signatures it must have been prepared by or for an official of the Festival, perhaps Mr. J. O. Mason, Chairman of the Orchestral Committee. There are two inserted leaves, on heavier paper, bound between the title page and the first page of music, which contain: on recto of [i], photographs of Chorley, Lemmens-Sherrington, Sullivan, Santley, Palmer, and Cummings; and on the facing verso of [ii], their signatures, boldly written—Arthur S. Sullivan, Henry F. Chorley, H [Helen] Lemmens-Sherrington, Bessie Palmer, William H. Cummings and C [Charles] Santley.

6b Sullivan. Als, 47 Claverton Terrace [London], 3 March 1864, to Mr. Costa. 3pp.

In this letter to his sponsor for the Birmingham Festival, conductor Michael Costa, Sullivan reported the good news that the Committee had accepted his work. He asked that Costa would let him show him the score "before it is printed for performance—Chappell's have agreed to buy it. . . ."

6c Sullivan. Als, Birmingham [n.d.], to his father. 3pp.

In this letter to his father, on stationery of the Union Club, Birmingham, Sullivan begged him "to run down tomorrow" for the performance of *Kenilworth*. "You see 1st you will never have another opportunity of hearing the work performed in such a magnificent style again – 2nd It is a great event in my career & one which I should like you to witness." From such evidence it is clear this letter was written 7 September 1864.

6d Sullivan. Al [incomplete], Birmingham, 11 September 1864, to his father. 4pp.

An incomplete companion letter to his father, dated four days later, 11 September, after the performance: "I know you will like to hear from me that the Cantata was undoubtedly a great success." The rehearsal had gone so well on Monday night (the 5th) that "I had no fear of its not going well on Thursday because the rehearsal inspired me with much confidence, both in myself & the Orchestra. I was dreadfully nervous when I first went up on the platform on the night of the concert . . . It went very well indeed, though not quite so well as at the rehearsal . . . the pieces which pleased most . . . were the 1st Chorus, The Shakespeare Duet, and the Brisk Dance. I was tremendously applauded at the end & recalled to the platform."

6e Sullivan. "How Sweet the Moonlight Sleeps," duet, No. 7 (Scene from the "Merchant of Venice"), from *Kenilworth*. For voice and piano, London: Chappell & Co. [n.d.]. [i], 47–55pp. Plate no. 12607.

The Duet, composed to words of Shakespeare and borrowed for inclusion in *Kenilworth*, provided an agreeable departure from words by Chorley. It was sung by Mme Lemmens-Sherrington, soprano, and William Cummings, tenor, who was substituting for the famous Mario on the occasion of its first performance in Birmingham.

6f Harrold, Caroline. Album, Edgbaston, Birmingham, 1864. 56pp. 22½ x 16 cm.

Nostalgia, in old *papier maché* and mother-of-pearl inlay, emanates from Caroline Harrold's memory book. Her very inaugural page was inscribed for her by Arthur S. Sullivan with a musical quotation, dated 13 September 1864, at which time he was living at her mother's house in Edgbaston, when his *Kenilworth* was first performed. A tiny contemporary photo head of the composer was carefully glued next to his signature.

6g Sullivan. Photograph, full-length view, taken at Birmingham [n.d.—ca. 1864]. 10½ x 6½ cm.

On the reverse side of this photograph, his mother had written: "Arthur Seymour Sullivan, Born May 13, 1842." And in Arthur's hand had been added: "Found in dear Father's desk, 1866." [See page 9.]

SYMPHONY IN E (THE IRISH)

7a Sullivan. Als, Holywood, Belfast, 30 August 1863, to his mother. 4pp.

Visiting in Ireland, Arthur wrote his mother a characteristic newsy letter while taking life easy (which he seemed to have felt needed apology): "It is true I am not working much, but I shall feel the practical results when I return to London. My life is a lazy one, as I do little else but lie on the grass (if it is fine) or lie in the drawing-room . . . but already I feel my ideas assuming a newer & *fresher* colour, & I shall be able to work like a horse on my return. Why, the other night as I was jolting home from Holestone (15 miles from here) through the wind & rain on an open jolting car the whole first movement of a Symphony came into my head with a real Irish flavour about it—besides scraps of the other movements. I shall get it ready for the Musical Society next season. . . ." This "next season" was to be three years delayed.

7b Sullivan. *Symphony in E (The Irish), for Orchestra*. Full score, London: Novello and Company, Limited, copyright, 1915. Original printed grey boards. [i], [1]–204pp. 32 x 26½ cm. Plate no. 11434.

Sullivan's only symphony, although composed in 1863, was not performed until programed by Augustus Manns at the Crystal Palace, Saturday, 10 March 1866. Its reception, reflected by *The Times*, left little for a twenty-four-year-old composer to desire. As quoted by Young (p. 41): "The symphony . . . is not only by far the most noticeable composition that has proceeded from Mr. Sullivan's pen, but the best musical work, if judged only by the largeness of its form and the number of beautiful thoughts it contains, for a long time produced by any English composer. . . ." It was performed in April of the same year by the Musical Society, as Sullivan had hoped in his letter to his mother; it received a third programing in July at a spectacular almost-all-Sullivan concert in St. James's Hall [see No. 11a], which would have been beyond his wildest hopes in 1863.

7c Sullivan. Als, Crystal Palace [London], Friday [n.d.], to Millais. 1 p.

In a one-page note to the painter John Everett Millais, written from the Crystal Palace on the day preceding the first performance (Friday, 9 March), Sullivan wistfully hoped that Millais could attend the concert: "I want so much for you to hear this new symphony. You see it can only be heard at intervals as it is unlike a picture to hang up for inspection always."

THREE WORKS FOR THE VIOLONCELLO

8 Sullivan. *An Idyll for the Violoncello*. Manuscript, signed and dated 31 July 1865. 3 leaves. 35½ x 26 cm. Unpublished.

Loaned by Stanford University Libraries, A Memorial Library of Music.

The manuscript of the *Idyll for violoncello and pianoforte* consists of three pages, the first, a title page in Sullivan's hand: "An Idyll. / for the Violoncello / composed for and dedicated to his friend / Col: P. Paget, / (Farnham) / by / Arthur S. Sullivan. / 31 July 1865." On page 2 the music, *Andante cantabile*, begins, finishing on page 3 at the bottom of which the composer had signed and dated the manuscript: "Arthur S. Sullivan / London. 31 July 1865."

Until this catalogue was in preparation, the *'Cello Idyll* was considered unpublished. Suddenly a British collector, the Rev. Peter Joslin, discovered a complete published record of this work. It is not a musical publication in the usual sense, but five pages in an elaborate compendium of works by famous writers, graphic artists, and musicians in a tall folio, *Souvenir of the Charing Cross Hospital Bazaar* held at the Royal Albert Hall 21 and 22 June 1899. Compiled and edited by Herbert Beerbohm Tree, The Nassau Press, St. Martin's Lane, W.C., and Southwark, S.E., 1899. Represented among the contributors are thirty-nine authors (including four Sullivan librettists—Burnand, Pinero, Grundy, and Hood, but not Gilbert), nine composers, and forty-four artist-illustrators. The *Idyll* appears on pages 181–185, with page 181 bearing only the title without the dedication, a facsimile signature of "Arthur Sullivan" (not "Arthur S. Sullivan" of the original), a reproduction of a photograph of the composer, and, in tiny type, the legend "Composed for an Album."

9a Sullivan. *Concerto in D Major for violoncello.* A copyist's manuscript, dated: "7/2/87," [n.p.], solo violoncello part. 14 leaves. 36 x 26 cm. Unpublished.

Sullivan's *Concerto for violoncello in D Major* bears on the title page of this copyist's score of the 'cello part only, "Composed expressly for and dedicated to Signor Alfredo Piatti." It was not published but is known to have been composed in 1866 and to have been first performed by Piatti at the Crystal Palace, 24 November 1866. Percy Young quotes *The Musical Standard*'s enthusiastic reaction: "The chief attraction of this work is found in the *Andantino*, which is a gem of loveliness, and gave the great 'cello player a fine opportunity for the display of his unequalled cantabile . . . The *Molto vivace* is marked by Mr. Sullivan's invariable elegance, and is more interesting than usual with music written with the primary object of bringing out the 'points' of a brilliant performer . . . Mr. Sullivan has now added another leaf to his fast gathering laurels. . . ."

9b Sullivan. Als, 47 Claverton Terrace [London], 8 April 1867, to J. H. Nunn. 1p.

In this "Dear Sir" letter to one J. H. Nunn, A.R.A., dated 8 April 1867, Sullivan stated: "The Concerto for the violoncello you speak of is in press but is not yet published – The slow movement is also being arranged for the organ." One wonders what happened to this work. Why was it not published in 1867? And why was the organ arrangement of the slow movement lost to posterity when reported in preparation by the earlier-quoted *Musical Standard*? And to what purpose was it worth a copyist's time to make a copy manuscript twenty years after the Piatti performance?

10 Sullivan. *Duo Concertante for violoncello & pianoforte, Op.* 2. Composed for and dedicated to his friend, Brinley Richards. London: Brewer & Co. [n.d.—ca. 1880's]. It was first published by Lamborn Cock, Addison & Co., 1868. 17pp. (pianoforte) and 4pp. (violoncello).

An example of Sullivan's chamber music is the third of these three 'cello works of his 1860's.

THE GRAND ORCHESTRAL CONCERT

"In such a night as this"—indeed! The occasion of Arthur Sullivan's Grand Orchestral Concert, Wednesday evening, 11 July 1866, at St. James's Hall, marked the zenith of Jenny Lind's assistance to the young composer. It was a dream-come-true concert conducted by Sullivan himself. The program contained two of his own songs ("Sweet day, so cool" and "Orpheus with his lute") sung by Jenny Lind; his Duet "In such a night as this," from *Kenilworth*, sung by Edith Wynne and W. H. Cummings; his "O mistress mine," sung by Charles Santley; his Overture to *The Sapphire Necklace*; his "Brisk Dance," from *Kenilworth*; and his *Symphony in E*—all conducted by the composer.

11a   Sullivan.   Programme, Book of Words, Grand Orchestral Concert, St. James's Hall, 11 July 1866. London: Lamborn Cock, Addison & Co. Original printed purple wrappers. [1]–11pp.

This copy of the Programme and Book of Words, in mint condition, probably belonged to the Goldschmidts as it was obtained with a number of their letters.

It was after this Grand Orchestral Concert that Sullivan received the rapturous letter from John Goss who, with Jenny Lind in the background, had been most instrumental in his nomination for the Mendelssohn Scholarship and had been one of his principal mentors throughout.

11b   Goss, Sir John, 1800–1880.   Als, 16 Sutherland Terrace [London], 16 July 1866, to Arthur Sullivan. 3pp.

"It was a great triumph—& that Madame Goldschmidt should have given her help crowned it to perfection! Her you can never repay except in the way that the greatest of artists, as herself desire! I mean by going on, on, on, on, until (as I hope) you may prove a worthy compeer of the Greatest of the Symphonists." These words were written to Sullivan on 16 July 1866, a few days after the Grand Orchestral Concert, by John Goss, his professor from his earliest days at the Royal Academy of Music.

OVERTURE IN C, "IN MEMORIAM"

The impact of his father's death on Sullivan's composition of the *Overture "In Memoriam"* is best recounted in his own words [see No. 4a]. "In this year [1866] I accepted an invitation to write an orchestral work for the Norwich Festival. As the time approached I worked hard but could do nothing which satisfied me, and was in despair. At last, a month before the Festival I said to my father (to whom I was passionately attached, & who was always my best friend) 'I shall give up the Norwich work, I can't get an idea of any kind' . . . My father replied 'No you mustn't give it up, you will succeed if you resolve not to be beaten. Something will probably occur which will put new vigour and fresh thoughts into you. Don't give it up.' The words were prophetic. Three days afterwards [early morning, Sunday, 23 September] he died suddenly of aneurism, and on the evening of his funeral, I sat down to work again; and eight days afterwards the Overture 'In Memoriam' was completed, and the parts copied, ready for performance at the Norwich Festival."

12a   Grove, Sir George, 1820–1900.   Als, Crystal Palace [London], 28 September 1866, to Arthur Sullivan. 2pp.

George Grove, perhaps Sullivan's closest friend at this time of his life, wrote him this letter a few days after his father died. Its message of comfort was said to have exerted an important force to reactivate the stricken composer into work on his *"In Memoriam" Overture.*

"It was a great thing for him [Thomas Sullivan] to have lived to see you triumph. If he had died last year—or even in February of *this* year, before your Symphony was done it would have been quite a different thing to him and he could not have felt such satisfaction in the thought of your success as he did."

12b Sullivan. Als, 47 Claverton Terrace [London], 18 October 1866, to [Mrs. Lehmann]. 4pp.

His close friend Mrs. Frederic Lehmann apparently did not get in touch with him after the tragedy. In his long letter to her almost four weeks afterward, he was still able to let himself go in a paroxysm of grief, tormenting himself (and probably Nina Lehmann as well) with detailed vivid recall, from the moment his brother Fred awakened him at Sydenham at 4 o'clock in the morning.

"Oh that was a dreadful night – My dear father went to bed shortly before midnight, & at twelve was dead. He slept in the dressingroom next to my mother's bedroom, & was already in bed when she came up. He called her and complained of a pain in his side. Whilst she was applying the usual remedy of fomentation, he suddenly cried 'Oh how my head swims!' and his poor eyes rolled as in death. My mother in her agony shrieked out for a maid to come down out of bed and hold him whilst she herself ran for a doctor to save time, but it was too late, she was only away a few minutes, and before she returned he was gone. He never spoke a word but gave a long sigh and died . . . Oh it is so hard, it is so terribly hard to think that I shall never see his dear face again. . . ."

12c Sullivan. *Overture in C (In Memoriam) for Orchestra.* Arranged for piano duet by Myles B. Foster [London], Novello & Company, Limited [n.d.—ca. 1885]. Original printed grey boards. 74pp. Plate no. 6978.

12d Sullivan. Als, Stagenhoe Park, 22 August 1884, to Mr. Foster. 1p.

Sullivan wrote his arranger on stationery of Stagenhoe Park, Nr. Welwyn, a hunting lodge of his friend the Duke of Edinburgh: "I am glad to think my Overture is in such good hands —it will not be easy to arrange for the Pianoforte. . . ."

12e Sullivan. Als, Commission Britannique [Paris], 30 September 1867, to Herr Kapellmeister [Ignaz Moscheles?]. 4pp.

In a letter in German, on the eve of his departure with George Grove for Vienna, Sullivan wrote his [unidentified] Kapellmeister friend that he expected to be in Leipzig for a week in mid-October. "For this reason I have brought along two things—one symphony which has been performed frequently in England and a big overture ('In Memoriam') which I wrote for last year's music festival in Norwich. Both works have had a great success and it would please me very much if it were possible to perform one or both things in the Gewandhaus, because, naturally this honor is longed for by every composer, and especially by one who has studied in Leipzig."

That this effort was successful can be noted from the excerpt from Sullivan's Vienna Diary [see No. 16a]. "My Overture was performed in the Gewandhaus Concert tonight Thursday Oct. 17 with great success. I was recalled—& a very fair performance. . . ."

CONCERT OVERTURE, "MARMION"

13a Sullivan. *Concert Overture, "Marmion."* Copyist's manuscript, leader and band parts [n.p., n.d.]. 78pp. 31 x 24 cm. Unpublished.

Sullivan's *Marmion Overture* was composed for the Philharmonic Society and was first performed at St. James's Hall, 3 June 1867. Later in the same year a performance of a revised score took place at the Crystal Palace, 7 December.

13b Sullivan. Als, [n.p., n.d.—ca. Saturday, 25 May 1867], to Peters. 3pp.

In this jocular letter to an unidentified friend, Sullivan showed the spontaneous humor that was so much a part of his charisma. "Shall I come to you on Tuesday afternoon at *three* with a Folio of Marmion (not Rokeby) under my arm (ion). . . ." The *"Marmion"* Overture he proposed to finish on Sunday and Monday as it was due at the copyist at five o'clock Tuesday. Apparently Peters had attended the performance of *Cox and Box* at the Adelphi Theatre, 11 May 1867.

13c Lucas, Stanley [Sec., Philharmonic Society]. Als, [London], 11 November 1867, to Arthur Sullivan. 2pp.

Lucas, as Secretary of the Philharmonic Society, wrote Sullivan that George Grove, the composer's close friend and Secretary of the Crystal Palace, had asked the directors for the loan of the parts of the concert overture, *Marmion*, composed for the Society.

13d Sullivan. Als [draft], [n.p.], 15 November 1867, to Stanley Lucas. 2pp.

This is the draft of Sullivan's reply to the Stanley Lucas letter of 11 November. He thanked Lucas that he might have the parts of the *Marmion* after reimbursing the Philharmonic for copying, and he added, "As I have made a few alterations in the score, I shall of course be most happy to have the parts belonging to the Phil. Soc: corrected at my own expense."

COX AND BOX

14a Sullivan. Manuscript of "Short Chronological Memoranda," 1 Queen's Mansions [London], [n.d.—ca. 1892]. Page 3 (of twelve pages).

These memoranda were compiled by Sullivan for his biographer, Charles Willeby, twenty-four years after his busily creative 1866–1867 period when he kept no diary. Small wonder he misdated his *Symphony in E* as first performed in 1865, instead of 1866, and that he credited 1866 so completely as the "eventful year" with respect to the success of *Cox and Box*. That it was born in 1866, privately, incompletely, and with no public or press recognition appears to be the fact. But there is no other work of Sullivan's that has been so shrouded in a confusion of faulty memories and half-truths.

The emergence of this confusion, and its abettor, is found in the controversy that arose in July 1890 in the letters columns of the *World* between Arthur J. Lewis and F. C. Burnand. The former (husband of actress Kate Terry) held that the first performance of *Cox and Box* was at his house, Moray Lodge, on 26 May 1866. The latter, librettist-adaptor of Maddison Morton's farce *Box and Cox*, claimed that his own house on Belgrave Road had the prior performance on 23 May. Sullivan and the three members of the original cast were approached by Lewis for their recollections in the hope of establishing his claim to the *jus primae noctis* at Moray Lodge on 26 May 1866.

Only one of the group concerned, John Foster (the "Bouncer"), had kept a diary and also a complete set of "Moray Minstrel" programs, neither of which sources contained any record of 1866 as the *Cox and Box* year. Foster, alone, challenged the year 1866: "I must still believe April 27, 1867, to have been the first night of 'Cox and Box.' " He had forgotten the events of May 1866 altogether and, like the other principals, he had intermingled the production details of the two occasions. George Du Maurier (the original "Box") had not kept a diary in 1866, but had started one in March 1867. From this he contributed doubly important evidence. (Andrew Lamb quoted this bit in *The G. & S. Journal*, January 1968.) On 28 March 1867, Du Maurier had noted that: "Little Arthur Sullivan came and asked if I would do *Cox & Box* for charity. I said yes." First, this indicated that it was already in Du Maurier's repertoire before 27 April 1867—i.e., from an earlier performance. Secondly, it showed that Sullivan was already at work on *Cox and Box* for a public performance which at that time (28 March) must have been the benefit scheduled for 18 May at the Gallery of Illustration. Note that after the death of Charles Bennett on 2 May, the benefit for his widow was arranged for 11 May at the Adelphi Theatre, thereby becoming the first public performance.

The possibility of "an extra Moray Lodge gathering" (*G. & S. Journal*) on 26 May 1866 would fit the "try-out" character of the description of the *Cox and Box* origins in Sullivan's summarizing memorandum of 29 July 1890 to Lewis. His reference to Moray Minstrel gatherings as scheduled regularly for the final Saturday of January, February, March, and April did not include May. The lack of a printed program (a regular "M.M." feature) or of any entry in John Foster's diary, and the complete absence of any contemporary printed reference to this 1866 performance, accord with the likelihood of try-out informality. The fact that the long (fifty-seven pages of MS) duet for "Bouncer" and "Box" was not written by Sullivan till considerably later, suggests an abbreviated entertainment in May 1866 that could be, and was, augmented to fill the bill of an "M.M." gathering the following year.

14b Sullivan, and F. C. Burnand, 1836–1917. *Cox and Box*. Full score, autograph, and copyist's manuscript. Overture title page, signed and dated: "Paris, 23 Juillet 1867, Hotel Meurice." (Tipped in after the manuscript is a vocal score, Boosey & Co.; on the front wrapper is written: "Savoy 1929.") 224pp. 37 x 27½ cm.

This score, without the overture, must have been composed by Sullivan at his usual last-minute pace in time for the first public performance, 11 May 1867, at the Adelphi Theatre, London. "The ms [from Burnand] came in bit by bit, and I set it to music. I only wrote out voice parts, having no time to make a Pianoforte accompaniment," Sullivan recalled in 1890, "but at the time of the first performance at Moray Lodge I played the accompaniment myself, and no accompaniment was ever written out until long afterward, I scored it for full orchestra. Then a P.F. reduction was made."

In any event, the early authenticated public performances for charity on 11 and 18 May 1867 were certainly performed without overture, but presumably with a score prepared after the Moray Lodge performance in April. Then Sullivan left for Paris where the overture was born. A charity performance at the Theatre Royal, Manchester, on 29 July, was the first to use this additional musical manuscript.

14c Sullivan, and F. C. Burnand, 1836–1917. *Cox and Box, or The Long-lost Brothers*. Pianoforte arrangement by the composer, London & New York: Boosey & Co. [n.d.]. Original soft orange boards. [i–iv], 1–91pp. 34 x 26 cm.

The first edition of Sullivan's pianoforte arrangement of *Cox and Box* was published by Boosey in 1869, certainly no later as the title page of this copy bears the following presentation inscription to his friend the critic Joseph Bennett: "Joseph Bennett, Esq. with the kind regards of Arthur S. Sullivan May. 1869." (Checklists and biographies have consistently given 1871 as the year of publication.) It is interesting to note that two months previous to this inscription *Cox and Box* had shared the bill at German Reed's Gallery of Illustration with W. S. Gilbert's comedy *No Cards*, 29 March 1869. It was, perhaps, the first occasion that featured the names of Gilbert and Sullivan on the same program.

14d Sullivan. Als, Grove Villa [Sydenham], 26 April 1867, to his mother. 4pp.

Important dated confirmation of the first performance of the complete *Cox and Box*: Sullivan wrote "Dearest Mum" on Friday, 26 April 1867, in which he explained, "We rehearsed so late last night that I was obliged to sleep at Lewis'. . . ." He asked her, "Will you send over to Bennett [Joseph, the critic] & ask him if he wants to go to Lewis's. If so, he must make his way up to Moray Lodge about nine o'clock." Sullivan added that Lewis had given him *carte blanche* "to bring whom I like, and I like Bennett." On page 4 he drew a rough diagram showing how Jo Bennett was to get to Moray Lodge off Kensington Road.

A TRIUMVIRETTA IN CORRESPONDENCE

A Triumviretta in Correspondence (the cast—original author Maddison Morton, adaptor-librettist F. C. Burnand, and composer Sullivan): As three-cornered as the work that brought them together were the business dealings of the creators of *Cox and Box*.

14e Morton, John Maddison, 1811–1891. Als, [London], 22 February
1870, to Burnand. 3pp.

Regarding current negotiations with producer German Reed (the Gallery of Illustration), Morton wrote that he might go along with Reed's proposal even though his two colleagues were opposed.

14f Burnand, Francis Cowley, 1836–1917. Als, Garrick Club [London],
24 February 1870, to "Art" [Arthur Sullivan]. 1p.

In this letter from Burnand to Sullivan, he had evidently enclosed the above letter from Morton (22 February 1870): "I forward this to you. J. M. Morton is a Hass. Let him gang his own way. I shall do nothing without consulting you. . . ."

14g Morton, John Maddison, 1811–1891. Als, [London], 28 March 1870,
to "Sir" [Sullivan]. 1p.

Maddison Morton wrote Sullivan that he hoped to meet him at the Garrick Club at 2 o'clock Wednesday next (30 March): "can get no satisfactory idea from our friend Burnand as to future plan of campaign in the matter of 'Cox & Box.' "

14h Sullivan. Als, Beckenham, S.E., [n.d.], to "Frank" [Burnand]. 4pp.

Sullivan appeared to have been the best businessman of the three. In this undated letter (ca. 1870), he showed that he too had disagreements with Frank Burnand: "*I* don't consent to let Reed have C & B for 50 nights for £50, & have written him to say no." He closed by pointing out that Burnand had had nothing to do with *Cox and Box* since he wrote the libretto, but that he, Sullivan, had had to copy the music, teach the singers, attend the rehearsals, "& a hundred other things *besides* the composition."

THE CONTRABANDISTA

The twenty-five-year-old Sullivan in 1867 had tasted the wine of composing for the stage, and liked it. Frank Burnand, experienced punster on the staff of *Punch*, author of dozens of burlesques, recognized that partnership with Sullivan would bring him stage success of higher quality than would otherwise have been accorded his undistinguished period humor. So at this time, 1867, each saw something to gain from the other—and a second and more ambitious collaboration followed late in the year. It was a two-act comic opera, commissioned by German Reed for his newly leased St. George's Hall, where it was first performed on 18 December 1867.

15a Sullivan, and F. C. Burnand, 1836–1917. *The Contrabandista, or The Law of the Ladrones*. Pianoforte arrangement by the composer, London: Boosey & Co. [n.d.]. Original printed pink boards. [i]–[iv], [1]–87pp. 28 x 22 cm.

Boosey issued this vocal score in the same series of Comic Operettas and Musical Farces that led off with *Cox and Box*. It also appeared, perhaps, a year earlier (1870) in plain wrappers.

15b Sullivan. Als, 8 Albert Mansions [London], 13 May 1874, to Broadfield. 4pp.

A few years later, on his thirty-second birthday, 13 May 1874, he wrote a friend from a provincial engagement: "We began with the Contrabandista last night, as I found that Cox & Box killed it nearly, & the consequences was that we had a capital performance. . . ." The *Contrabandista* never achieved real popularity even though initial press was reasonably friendly—and prophetic. The *Musical Times* (as quoted by Percy Young) stated: "The excellent vein of humor so apparent in this little piece of extravagance [*Cox and Box*], as well as in the more important *Contrabandista*, justifies us in the hope that Mr. Sullivan may give us, at no distant date, a real comic opera of native manufacture." Exit Burnand, enter Gilbert. Many years later, in 1894, as a friendly gesture to his old ex-collaborator, Sullivan joined with Burnand in an enlarged version of the *Contrabandista*, *The Chieftain* [see No. 86b], even less successful than its predecessor.

THE VIENNA TRIP

An important *moment musical* in the life of twenty-five-year-old Sullivan was his trip to Vienna with George Grove—almost double Arthur's age but a very great friend and believer in the young composer. These two left London on 26 September 1867, and—with brief stops in Paris, Baden, Munich, and Salzburg—reached Vienna on 8 October. Here Carl Anton Spina, music publisher (including the works of Schubert), met them with cordiality and boundless generosity. Through him they wallowed in manuscript treasures of his and of Dr. Schneider's (where they found the *Rosamunda* music). Through him they met those few remaining who had known and dealt with the gods themselves—Beethoven and Schubert. Sullivan at so impressionable an age was not going to miss any part of these experiences which he could store up. So he kept a diary, just for this trip.

16a Sullivan. Notebook in manuscript [in pencil] with several pencil sketches, Vienna, October 1867. 15pp. written with remainder blank. 17½ x 12 cm.

This is a small notebook-diary, where he jotted down in pencil things he heard and saw, even illustrating a few with sketches. In particular he made note of the experiences recounted by Spina's ancient clerk, V. Döppler. Although quoted and requoted by biographers, the pages of this diary still have the power to thrill. Three are those describing some of Döppler's memories of Beethoven: "Beethoven wore a green Polish coat with frogs on it, and when in the shop generally leant against a wooden pillar by the counter whilst Czerny, von Seyfried [and] Stadler sat on a leather sofa. They wrote down the conversation on a slate as B was stone deaf . . . He told us that Beethoven was very absent[minded] & that, for instance, he would often order his beer, pay for it, & never drink it."

Included in the crowded pages of this little volume are also his "Notes on Franz Schubert his Grand Symphony in C from the original manuscript"; sketches of Beethoven's and Schubert's graves which he and Grove visited; a list of the complete "Musik to Rosamunda" which they discovered; and a recipe for a potent punch, "Bohle or Bole," starting take "Three bottles of Moselwein. . . ."

16b Sullivan. Als, 47 Claverton Terrace [London], 1 November 1867, to "My poor old boy" [J. W. Davison]. 2pp.

The friend to receive this interesting letter was James William Davison, a writer for *The Times*. In it Sullivan gave a condensed account of the wonderful trip he had just had with George Grove—". . . no pleasure was equal to the delight of travelling with G.G. whose looks, manners & conversation won all hearts there, even as they have won yours & mine." He listed with enthusiasm the Schubert treasures they had examined: "Two symphonies (both in C, but neither so fine as *the* C major) two overtures—(both in D.) *all* the music to Rosamunda, a String Quartett, a *lovely* Trio for Pfte, viola & cello, never performed or printed, & several little songs, perfect gems."

16c Grove, Sir George, 1820–1900. Photograph, three-quarter view, [n.d.], taken by Bingham, [Paris]. 10½ x 6½ cm.

This small cabinet photograph of George Grove was among Sullivan's papers. It was taken in Paris, perhaps on one of the many visits that these two made together, sometimes accompanied by Henry Chorley, or the Frederic Lehmanns, and at least once by Charles Dickens.

17 Sullivan. *Crépuscule* (*Twilight*), Romance pour piano. Paris: Durand & Schoenewerk [n.d.]. [i], 2–7pp. Engraved. Plate no. 2588.

In the mid-1860's when Sullivan was unofficially engaged to Rachel Scott Russell (see No. 24b and c], he dedicated a Romance for Pianoforte to her, *Twilight*, published by Chappell in 1868, and also by Kistner in Leipzig. The work here was the, apparently unrecorded, French edition of this music, published by Durand & Schoenewerk.

18   Sullivan. *Day Dreams*, Six pieces for pianoforte, No. I and II. Manuscript, signed but not dated. 1 double leaf of two facing pages of music, the reverse page is blank. 37½ x 16 cm. Published by Boosey, 1867.

This Sullivan manuscript was obtained with other autograph Sullivan material of the Frederic Lehmann's. It can be assumed that it was given by the composer to Nina (Mrs. Frederic) Lehmann with whom he shared musical experiences. The autograph is for No. I and No. II only. The former is in six staves with the composer's signature, "Arthur S. Sullivan," obviously added later. No. II is in eight staves. [There must have been at least two of these manuscripts, as this is not the autograph footnoted by Young, page 273.]

19a   Sullivan. *Additional accompaniments to Handel's 'Jeptha,' Part I*. A copyist's manuscript, [n.p., n.d.]. 142pp. 34 x 26 ½ cm. Unpublished.

In the hand of the copyist the title states: "Jeptha, an Oratorio composed in 1751 by Handel with additional accompaniments written in 1870 [sic] by Sullivan." Although unpublished, the original manuscript of this score is still in the possession of Novello. At the bottom of the last page (168) of Part II of the original is the composer's signature: "Arthur S. Sullivan begun 11 Jan^ry finished 31 [1869]."

19b   Sullivan. Als, 47 Claverton Terrace [London], 6 February 1869, to "Sir" [unidentified]. 2pp.

This "Dear Sir" letter from Sullivan dated 6 February 1869 provides the year, missing from the end of the Novello manuscript; it corrects the copyist's "1870" on the title page of the copy here. "I have been writing day & night to get 'Jeptha' ready for performance last night." This refers to the performance on 5 February 1869 by Sullivan's friend Joseph Barnby at St. James's Hall, on which occasion Sullivan's work received praise from the musical press.

20   Sullivan. *The Dove Song (Polka)*. Manuscript, signed and dated, 1869. For orchestra and voice. 4pp. 34 x 38 cm.

On the title page of this four-page fold, Sullivan wrote: "The Dove Song / (Polka) / composed expressly for the / Prince's Theatre / Manchester / (Xmas 1869) / by / Arthur S. Sullivan." According to Percy Young (p. 274), this was composed for use in a Christmas pantomime, *Froggee would a wooing go*, libretto by William Brough. Young has written (quoting from *The Manchester Guardian*), "In the 3rd scene, showing the 'Peri Lake', the peris approach: 'As they dance they sing the Dove Polka Song, wherein Mr. A. S. Sullivan has caught and retained the light, airy grace of the scene....'" Sullivan was tripping hither, tripping thither with peris many years before *Iolanthe*.

THE PRODIGAL SON

21a Sullivan. *The Prodigal Son*, an oratorio. The words selected entirely from The Holy Scriptures. Vocal score, the arrangement for pianoforte by Franklin Taylor, London: Boosey & Co., 1869. 36 x 26½ cm.

21b Williams, Philip H. Als, Forgate House, Worcester, 10 February 1869, to A. Sullivan. 2pp.

Dr. Philip H. Williams, Hon. Secretary for the Worcester Musical Festival, wrote Sullivan on 10 February 1869 that the Executive Committee had heard with great pleasure that he might be willing to write "a work" for the Festival the following September. "I beg to send a copy of a Resolution that was unanimously adopted. 'That this Committee would feel much gratification in being favoured by Mr. Sullivan with a sacred Oratorio composed by him for its first performance at the ensuing Festival.' "

21c Sullivan. Als, [n.p.], 21 August 1869, to T. Anderson. 3pp.

With the Worcester Festival only two weeks off, Sullivan wrote Mr. T. Anderson, apparently a critic, "Messrs Boosey & Co. have probably sent you a set of proofs of the 'Prodigal Son'. Pray consider them as '*private* and *privileged*' communication. They are sent in order that you may with more facility and greater knowledge review or criticise the work when it appears. I am sure I can rely upon your not 'quoting' any of the musical portion in print or showing it about freely."

21d Reeves, [John] Sims, 1818–1900. Photograph, three-quarter view, Brighton, [n.d.], taken by W. & A. H. Fry. 16½ x 10½ cm.

This cabinet portrait photograph of Sims Reeves was given to Sullivan by the famous tenor who, among many other associations with the composer, sang in the first performance of *The Prodigal Son*. The presentation inscription reads: "To Arthur, from his Prodigal Son." Indeed, the tenor part was said to have been written with Reeves in mind.

21e Goldschmidt, Jenny Lind, 1820–1887. Als, Oak Lea [London], [n.d.], Friday, to Mr. Sullivan. 4pp.

The Prodigal had been scheduled for a Crystal Palace performance, Sullivan conducting, on 18 December 1869, but Sims Reeves found himself double-booked. After much travail it was rescheduled for Saturday, 11 December. Then Reeves became ill and an unfortunate substitution had to be made. It was this performance that Jenny Lind Goldschmidt could not attend, as she wrote Sullivan in this letter on Friday, 10 December. (The Sullivan and Flower biography incorrectly attributed this letter and Reeves' absence to the opening performance of the Worcester Festival.) "I should have indeed been happy to have found out the good points in your work as I shall always—if only for old lang syne's sake—take interest in your welfare. Your old friend Jenny L. Goldschmidt."

21f Goss, Sir John, 1800–1880. Als, 15 Clarewood Terrace [London], 22 December 1869, to Sullivan. 4pp.

Unlike Jenny Lind (see preceding letter), John Goss attended the Crystal Palace performance of *The Prodigal* on Saturday, 11 December. In his long letter to Sullivan, he managed to write several most flattering comments, but closed on a note of critical advice: "You are an admirable conductor. The band seemed to me most capital in your hands, the Chorus seemed to do very well . . . All you have done is most masterly—Your orchestration superb, & your effects many of them original & first rate . . . Some day you will I hope try another oratorio, putting out all your strength, but not the strength of a few weeks or months, whatever your immediate friends may say . . . only don't do anything so pretentious as an oratorio or even a Symphony without *all your power*, which seldom comes in one fit." The old master knew the composer's predisposition to do too much too fast.

SULLIVAN AND HIS LEIPZIG MASTERS

In one of his first letters from Leipzig, young Sullivan wrote Sir George Smart, giving an account of his exacting schedule and of the imposing musical figures who were his teachers:

22a Sullivan. Als, Leipzig, 17 January 1859, to Sir George Smart. 5pp.

"I have one lesson a week from Prof. Moscheles & two from Mr. Plaidy on the Pianoforte. In counterpoint, weekly, 1 from Dr. Hauptmann & one from Mr. Richter. One composition from Herrn. Kapellmeister Rietz. On the violin 1 a week from Concertmeister Dreyschock (brother to the celebrated pianoforte player) & 2 from Mr. Röntgen. . . ." His rapport with his teachers was as warm as it had been in London.

On his departure from Leipzig, Plaidy, David, and Hauptmann contributed little autographic musical items *au souvenir*:

22b David, Ferdinand, 1810–1873. Musical quotation, Leipzig, 10 May 1861, to Sullivan. 1p.

22c Hauptmann, Moritz, 1792–1868. Musical quotation, Leipzig, 26 May 1861, to Sullivan. 1p.

22d Plaidy, Louis, 1810–1874. Musical quotation, Leipzig, July 1861, to Sullivan. 1p.

22e Moscheles, Ignaz, 1794–1870. Als [German], Belgrade, July 1864, to "Lieber Sullivan." 1p.

Of those key figures listed in his letter to George Smart, Ignaz Moscheles and his wife became enduring friends. "I cannot tell you how kind Mr. & Mrs. Moscheles are to me. From the first day I came here they have treated me more as a son than as a stranger." The continuing correspondence began in English and later shifted to German when Arthur had graduated from "Mr. Sullivan" to "Lieber Sullivan."

LETTERS FROM MUSICIANS AND AUTHORS

23a Manns, Sir Augustus, 1825–1907. Als, Crystal Palace, London, 27 February 1862, to "My dear sir" [Sullivan]. 1p.

Back in London, influential conductor Augustus Manns was to program the first performance of Sullivan's *Tempest* at the Crystal Palace on 5 April 1862. This short letter relates to that event: "My Saturday orchestra at present does consist of 10 firsts, 8 seconds, 6 violas, 5 'cellos, 5 basses...." He suggested that Sullivan make the arrangements with Miss Banks *et al.* for the first Saturday in April.

23b Goss, Sir John, 1800–1880. Als, London, 11 August 1863, to Sullivan. 4pp.

In his kindly advisory style: "... it is best for young men to be *discreet*, & this is a piece of advice I am constantly offering ... and now venture to mention to you." He then cited Mendelssohn, whom he had known personally—"He had a spirit of his own. He was quiet, & I have seen him in a passion. He knew his own talent ... but he was ... no monopolist of the talk & fun of the room."

23c Browning, Robert, 1812–1889. Als, 19 Warwick Crescent, London, 7 July 1864, to Mr. Sullivan. 2pp.

As early as 1864, great literary figures knew the young composer for what he was achieving in the setting of poetry. Introducing Sullivan to the Irish poet William Allingham, Browning wrote: "He knows and admires your music—if you know his poetry, the business of 'introduction' will not need be a long one."

23d Bennett, William Sterndale, 1816–1875. Als, London, 3 November 1864, to Sullivan. 1p.

In British music B.S. (before Sullivan) the name of William Sterndale Bennett ranked highest among nineteenth-century composers. He was an important friend and teacher to Arthur in his early years of training. And it was thoughtful of the young man to remember him in the way that prompted this note: "Many thanks for your kind present of 'The Tempest' Music, which I shall value extremely, Believe me, I shall always take a sincere interest in your career."

23e Hallé, Sir Charles, 1819–1895. Als, Manchester, 20 January 1868, to Sullivan. 4pp.

Conductor Charles Hallé of Manchester had already been of prime importance to Sullivan almost exactly five years earlier on the occasion of performing his music for the *Tempest*, January 1863 [No. 2g]. Hallé wrote that the Leeds Committee "have listened most favourably to my proposal that you should be appointed Conductor in general of the music...." Would Sullivan accept? Sullivan did not.

"YOUTH WILL NEEDS HAVE DALLIANCE"

24a Saxe Wyndham, Henry, 1867–1940. Als, The Guildhall School of Music, 10 December 1924, to Herbert Sullivan. 3pp.

In a letter of 1924 to Herbert Sullivan, Henry Saxe Wyndham, then at work on a biography of Arthur Sullivan, asked if he could mention Arthur's earliest love affair: "... in or about the years '66 or '67 he was engaged to a very pretty girl, Rachel Scott Russell ... the daughter of a well known Engineer ... it was altogether a very pretty little romance, that was, unhappily, ended by the young lady's mother who disapproved of the match."

It seems unlikely that either biographer or nephew was aware that the composer's pretty little romance might involve a triangle—that Uncle Arthur was having romances with two Scott Russell sisters at the same time, as samples of their love letters testify: those from Rachel, signing herself "Fond Dove" or "Passion Flower," and those from Louise, signing as "Little Woman"—each using an almost identical vocabulary of loving "oo's."

24b Passion Flower [Rachel Scott Russell], 1845–1882. Als, Zurich, 16 August 1868, to "My own darling" [Sullivan]. 4pp.

24c Fond Dove [Rachel Scott Russell], 1845–1882. Als, [n.p., n.d.], to "My Sweet One" [Sullivan]. 8pp.

Rachel to Sullivan: The lovers were about to be reunited in Zurich, August 1868, where Rachel in this letter briefed Arthur on what clothes he should bring with him. She preferred his velveteen coat: "You looked so sweet in it ... I like that better than anything else & so oo does it to please oo's bird—please do darling ... I always liked that coat—so oo gives up oo's will to oo's bird. ....Your little Passion Flower."

"My Sweet One" wrote Rachel in an eight-page letter, "Your letter made me a little sad, for it showed me that your love could not stand the test of absence, & that only physical contact could re-create it. Ah me! when I think of those days when cooing & purring was enough for us, till we tried the utmost—& that is why I fancy *marriage* spoils love. When you can drink *brandy*, water tastes sickly afterwards. . . . Your own Fond Dove.''

24d Rachel Scott Russell, 1845–1882. Two photographs, by J. Ganz, Zurich.

On the reverse of one (full-face) is: "Fest und Treu 25 Oct. 1868," and on the reverse of the semiprofile is: "Through Life – Till Death," both in the hand of Rachel.

24e Sullivan. "O Fair Dove! O Fond Dove!", song, words by Jean Ingelow, dedicated to Miss Rachel Scott Russell. Ashdown & Parry (1868). Plate no. 5349.

24f Louise Scott Russell, 1841–1878. Als, [Sydenham], [n.d.—ca. 1869], to "My dearest Arthur" [Sullivan]. 4pp.

24g Little Woman [Louise Scott Russell], 1841–1878. Als, [n.p., n.d.], to "Dearest Arthur" [Sullivan]. 3pp.

Louise to Sullivan: As go-between in the summer of 1868 during a temporary cooling of the Rachel-Sullivan affair, Louise wrote in behalf of her sister Rachel ("Chenny"): "My dearest Arthur . . . From my writing I suppose that there are not even to be any letters till October which is sad . . . Still I feel strongly that if there is the slightest doubt about the love, it had better not be . . . You must not dream that I am less fond of you than in the days gone by. . . . Your truly loving Louise Scott Russell."

And, probably later, writing as "your own devoted Little Woman," Louise counseled "Dearest Arthur" ardently against temptation. "[D]o not desecrate the sacred & beautiful expression of love. You owe it to your future wife during this time of probation . . . We come to you so pure & chaste . . . [Y]ou have your love [i.e., Rachel] & your little woman . . . [Y]ou have taken as your right the only thing I have to give. . . .''

In a letter from Louise ("Sweetest Little Woman") written to Sullivan 7 December 1868, she told him, "I burned *all* your letters yesterday." With her sister Louise as intermediary, lovebird Rachel did not need any rivals.

24h Henriette Scott Russell. Als, Westwood Lodge [Sydenham], 23 July [1867], to "My dear Mr. Sullivan." 3pp.

Mrs. Scott Russell to Sullivan: "It has come upon me with a shock," wrote the mother of Rachel and Louise on 23 July (ca. 1867), "to learn that you could not be content on merely the terms of intimate friendship in this family . . . It grieves me to tell you that under *NO* circumstances could I ever consent to a different relation. And therefore I ask you, if you *cannot* bring yourself to be satisfied with that which hitherto subsisted, to abstain from coming here till you can do so, and to cease all correspondence . . . I grieve that I reposed in you a confidence to which you were not equal. I did it in absolute good faith. . . ."

24i Sullivan. "If Doughty Deeds My Lady Please," song, written by Graham of Gartmore, composed and dedicated to Mrs. Scott Russell. Chappell & Co. (1866). Plate no. 13386.

24j Sullivan. Al, draft, [n.p., n.d.—ca. July 1867]. 2pp. An incomplete draft reply to Mrs. Scott Russell's letter of 23 July [1867].

Sullivan to Mrs. Scott Russell: An incomplete draft of his reply to Mrs. Scott Russell's ultimatum (ca. 23 July 1867) indicated that he could not, with self-respect, accept her proposal to renounce serious intentions and continue "to come among you." So "with indescribable grief & pain" he must of necessity accept the other alternative and "stay away from the house altogether. But, do not by this be deceived in to thinking for one instant that my feelings are changed or that in any sort of way I forego my determination to marry your daughter. . . ."

PART-SONGS—UNACCOMPANIED

In his early years Arthur Sullivan composed more than twenty part-songs for unaccompanied voices. About half of them were published by Novello in the 1860's. Six were published separately as well as in *Six Four-Part Songs* (1868), Book XIX of Novello's Part-Song Book:

25a No. 150 (No. 1—1868), "The Rainy Day," words by Longfellow (1867).

25b No. 151 (No. 2), "O hush thee, my babie," words by Sir Walter Scott (1867).

25c No. 152 (No. 3), "Evening," words from Goethe, trans. by Lord Houghton (1868).

25d No. 153 (No. 4), "Joy to the victors," words by Sir Walter Scott (1868).

25e No. 154 (No. 5), "Parting Gleams," poetry by Aubrey De Vere (1868).

25f No. 155 (No. 6), "Echoes," words by Thomas Moore (1868).

In addition, the following two, "Seaside Thoughts" (written in 1857) and "Fair Daffodils," were both published after the composer's death, the former in 1904, the later in 1903.

25g *Orpheus*, No. 368, "Seaside Thoughts," words by Bernard Barton (1904).

25h *Orpheus*, No. 728, "Fair Daffodils," words by Robert Herrick (1903).

25i Sullivan, and Henry F. Chorley, 1808–1872. "The Last Night of the Year," a four-part song. London: Novello & Co. [1864]. [1]—7pp. Plate no. 3202.

"The Last Night of the Year," published by Novello in the *Musical Times*, 1863, was also printed in standard sheet-music form. The copy bears a presentation inscription: "Sir George T. Smart, with the affect. regards of Arthur S. Sullivan. Xmas 1864."

SONGS—PIANOFORTE ACCOMPANIMENT

These selections from Sullivan's large number of songs and ballads emphasize the aristocracy of poets whose words inspired him, especially in the 1860's: Byron, Scott, Shakespeare, Shelley, and Tennyson. Association with the last named of these, the Poet Laureate, spanned the full four decades of the composer's creative life. The following examples are drawn from more than two-dozen titles in this period.

Words by Shakespeare—1862–1864:

"Where the bee sucks," *The Tempest* [see No. 2e and f], in complete vocal score: Cramer, Beale & Wood, plate no. 8028; separate: Novello, Ewer & Co.

26a "Rosalind," *As You Like It*, dedicated to William H. Cummings, Edward Ashdown, plate no. E.A. 18895.

26b "Orpheus with his lute," *Henry VIII*, dedicated to Louisa Crampton, Metzler, plate no. 1461.

26c "Sigh no more, Ladies," *Much Ado About Nothing*, dedicated to Sims Reeves, Metzler, plate no. 1517.

26d "The Willow Song," *Othello*, dedicated to Madame Sainton-Dolby, Metzler, plate no. 1655.

26e "O Mistress Mine," *Twelfth Night*, dedicated to Charles Santley, Metzler, plate no. 1436.

Words by Tennyson:

26f "What does little birdie say?", Ashdown (1867), plate no. A&P 5079.

Words by Byron:

26g "I wish to tune my quiv'ring lyre," Boosey (1868).

Words by Walter Scott:

26h "A weary lot is thine, fair maid," Chappell (1866).

Words by Shelley:

26i "Arabian Love Song," Chappell (1866).

Words by Henry Chorley:

"The Bride from the North," Cramer, Beale & Wood (1863), plate no. 832 [see 3a].

Words by Robert Graham:

"If doughty deeds my lady please," Chappell (1866), plate no. 13386 [see 24i].

Words by Jean Ingelow:

"O fair dove, O fond dove," Ashdown (1868), plate no. A&P 5349 [see 24e].

HYMNS AND ANTHEMS

"O Israel," London: J. Alfred Novello (1855), plate no. 2561 [see 1j].

Novello's Octavo Anthems:

27a No. 3, "O, love the Lord," full anthem for four voices, dedicated to John Goss (1864).

27b No. 74, "We have heard with our ears, O God," anthem for five voices (1865).

MISCELLANEOUS

27c *Choral Album*, No. 826, "Te Deum Laudamus," four voices and organ,
London: Bayley & Ferguson (1866).

27d "I sing the birth was born tonight," four voices unaccompanied, words
by Ben Jonson, Boosey (1868).

27e "Sing O Heavens," anthem for Christmas or any festival occasion,
Boosey & Co. (1868). Presentation copy to E. J. Hopkins (1818–1901):
"with the kind regards of Arthur Sullivan 1873."

27f No. 93, "I will lay me down in peace," copyist's manuscript, dated
"4/9/68," Novello (1910).

Arthur Seymour Sullivan.

Born in London. 13 May 1842
His Father was of Irish family and
his Mother of Italian parentage.

His Father was Professor (at Kneller Hall)
the normal school for Bandmasters of
the British Army, and from his parents
he derived his first musical instruction
His passion for music developed itself
at a very early age, and he began
trying to write down original compositions
when he was six. In the meantime
his general education was not neglected
and he was sent to a good school.
Having a beautiful voice, he soon
persuaded his parents to let him enter
the Choir of the Chapel Royal. St James
Palace; where he remained over three
years until he was between 15 & 16

Page 1 of early Sullivan autobiographic outline, 1873. (1a)

Arthur Sullivan's baby shirt, 1842. (1c)

Sullivan, Chapel Royal chorister (1854), at age 12. (1e)

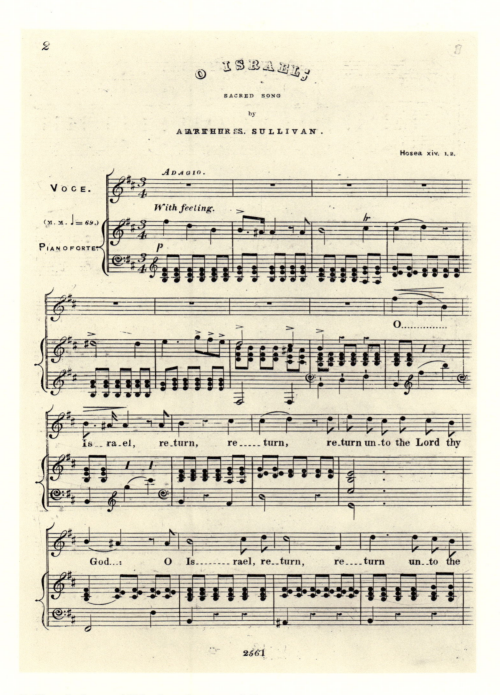

Sullivan's first published work, 1855. (1j)

6 Cheyne Walk
Chelsea 8 April
1854

My dear Sir,

I am very sorry to have neglected your letter so long.

Little Sullivan has called here this evening — & this reminds me that you are still unanswered — excuse this as the consequence of great press of other business —

I like Arthur Sullivan's appearance and manner — his voice is good — & if arrangements can be made to obviate the difficulty of his age being greater than

The Rev. Thomas Helmore to The Rev. Percy Smith, 1854. (1g)

To **a.S.S**_{ullivan}

in respect for his high talents.

Dear Sullivan! You asked me to draw something in your album — I really could not think of any thing more appropriate than the above

Leipzig 10 Sept 1860

your sincere friend Domenico Barnett

Sullivan's initials, A.S.S., lampooned in his Leipzig album, 1860. (1u)

Song commemorating marriage of the Prince of Wales, 1863. (3a)

Arthur Sullivan, 8 September 1858, age 16. (1r)

Nᵒ 12 Bedford Square,
Bloomsbury W.C,
11ᵗʰ October 1862.

My dear Sullivan

I beg you to accept my best thanks
for your kind attention by the
dedication of the Music of "The Tempest",
and also for the Copy of the same
which you left at my house
last Evening—

With every good wish for your prosperity
Believe me to be
Your sincere Friend,
George, T. Smart

To
Mʳ Arthur S. Sullivan

Sir George Smart to Sullivan, 11 October 1862. (2d)

Dickens to Frederick Lehmann, mentioning Sullivan, 1863. (5c)

Sullivan to his mother, mentioning Dickens, Belfast 1863. (5b)

rehearsal inspired me with so
much confidence, both in myself
& the Orchestra. I was dreadfully
nervous when I first went up
to the platform, on the night of
the Concert. The Hall was
crammed; the fullest evening
of the week. Very neat &
standing place was filled.
I was well received by the
Audience and the Orchestra.
and these encouraged I began.
I went very well indeed,

me that the Cantata
was undoubtedly a great
success. On Monday night
it was rehearsed (I got the
first turn, while everyone
was fresh) & went extremely
well, & people were seemingly
much pleased. I had no fear
of its not going well on
Thursday, because the

Sullivan to his father describing *Kenilworth* premiere, 1864. (6d)

49

Manuscript of *Idyll for Violoncello*, 1865. (8)

Sullivan to his mother, describing ideas for his
Symphony, Belfast 1863. (7a)

"I will lay me down in peace," song, by copyist, 9 April 1868. (27f)

Cox and Box: "No. 6 Trio. Box, Cox, Bouncer," ca. 1867. (14b)

No. 1 from *Day Dreams*, six pieces for pianoforte (1867). (18)

* Stephs said that the portrait by
Kriehuber was the most like of all

The portrait of Beethoven - pointing to the
"Missa Solennelle in D" which is in B's
Hand in the engraving he said "old!
he sketched some of that in a storm - for
he was lying under a tree writing, when
it began to rain - he was known to suffer
in his work. that he took no notice of the
rain, if it was not until his paper was
wet & his pen had gone through it that
he left off. —
He told us that Beethoven was very
absent. that, for instance, he would often
ask his fees pay for it. Never dined off —

I said "do you know Schubert?" —
"Knew him" said he - "Why I was at his
christening" and was a pupil of his
father".

Music to Rosamunde.

Overture (also used for "Zauberharf" +
"Die häusliche Krieg")

1. Entr'acte in B minor. he writes upon it
"N°1. Entr'acte nachdem I Aufzug"
allegro molto moderato: —

3ᵉ Entr'acte in - nach dem II Aufzug

Ballet music to 3rd Acte. "Zauberhafe"
Overture zum 3ten Acte.

Allegro ma non troppo
in Bmoll:

Entr'acte - nach dem 3ten Aufzug
Bb. Andantino

6. Hirtenchor. for 2 oboi n. Bb bass, 2 fagotti
and 2 clarinetti in Bb
Andante,

9. Air de Ballet. Allegretto in G.

Romanza. for sopran stimme
Fmoll.

Two pages from Sullivan's Vienna diary, 1867. (16a)

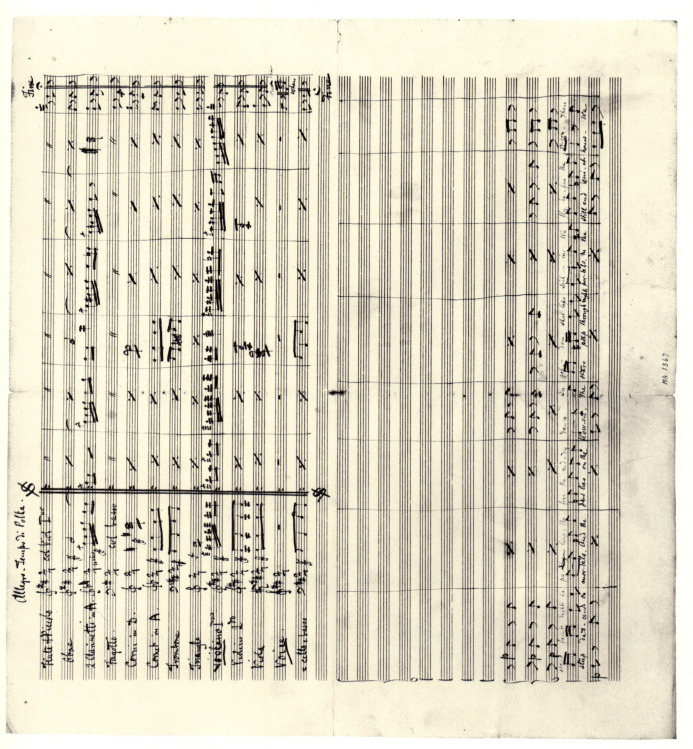

Page 1 of "The Dove Song (Polka)," 1869. (20)

found out the
good points in
your work as
I shall always.
I only felt that
long Syne's sake
take interest
in your welfare.

Your old Friend

Jenny

L. Goldschmidt

Oak Lea,
Wimbledon Park.
S.W.

Friday morning

My dear Mr Sullivan
I have just
received your
note — and write
to say how very
sorry I am not
to be able to
come to your

Jenny Lind to Sullivan about *Prodigal Son* at Crystal Palace, pages 1 and 4 (1869). (21e)

The Eighteen Seventies

Arthur Sullivan, ca. 1870, age 28. (28e)

IN the first half of this creative decade Arthur Sullivan's outpouring of settings for songs, ballads, hymns, anthems, and part-songs was so prodigious that one marvels that he had time and energy to compose major works such as *On Shore and Sea*, the *Overture di Ballo*, *Thespis*, the *Festival Te Deum*, *The Merchant of Venice*, *The Light of the World*, *The Merry Wives of Windsor*—all before 1875. Within the full ten-year period of the 1870's there were in fact more than seventy songs and more than forty-one hymns, five sacred part-songs, six anthems, and two Christmas carols. *St. Gertrude*, "Onward, Christian Soldiers," and *St. Kevin*, "Come Ye Faithful, Raise the Strain," have been sung and loved the world over for more than a century.

OVERTURE DI BALLO

The Committee for the Birmingham Musical Festival had been in touch with Sullivan as early as December 1869 in order to secure a commissioned work for the forthcoming festival of August 1870. But as late as 21 March there were still areas of disagreement to be resolved regarding the composer's expenses, and the very busy young man did not appear to be prompt with his replies. All this was in order by mid-May, according to the letters from Mr. Peyton, Secretary for the Committee, in the Sullivan files. And on 1 July, Peyton sent him the dates for the rehearsal schedule. The result of these preliminaries was Sullivan's *Overture di Ballo*.

28a Sullivan. *Overture di Ballo*. Full score, London & New York: Novello, Ewer and Co., 1889. Original printed grey boards. Title, 1–80 pp. 35 x 28 cm. Plate no. 7639.

Overture di Ballo, in the opinion of Percy Young, was "the best evidence of [Sullivan's] true genius so far, for this overture is not only a work of charm but also of wit . . . vitality and power." In it "Sullivan allowed his genius for rhythmic invention and instrumental definition full play." A contemporary critic, quoted by Lawrence, wrote: "While couched throughout in dance rhythms the overture is in strict form, and for melodic charm, graceful fancy, and delicacy of treatment it is difficult to rival it amongst modern music."

28b Peyton, R. Als, Birmingham Musical Festival, 19 May 1870, to Sullivan. 3pp.

28c Peyton, R. Als, Birmingham Musical Festival, 1 July 1870, to Sullivan. 1p.

Two letters from Mr. Peyton of the festival committee: The first, 19 May 1870, listed the wind instruments available (and a very generous selection it was, from flutes to serpents). "As to harps," he wrote Sullivan, "no performer on this instrument is engaged but we will do so with pleasure if your music requires it." (Sullivan's score did not.) The second letter, 1 July, advised him of the rehearsal schedule.

28d Sullivan. Als, Birmingham, 1 September 1870, to "Mum" [his mother]. 1p.

In a short note to "Dearest Mum" written on 1 September, the composer showed his youthful exuberance in telling his mother the evidence of his success, both the intangible of last night, and the tangible of tomorrow. "The overture was a *great success* last night, and on the strength of it they are to have my portrait in the local Illustrated paper tomorrow with a short notice. It went beautifully, and everyone who spoke to me seemed delighted."

28e Sullivan. Photograph, half view, taken by H. J. Whitlock [ca. 1870]. 10½ x 6½ cm. [See page 57.]

THE RELUCTANT LAUREATE
THE WINDOW, OR THE SONGS OF THE WRENS

The suggestion for a group of Tennyson poems, in his words "a little Liederkreis, German fashion," stemmed from George Grove, and involved Sullivan for music and Millais for illustration. Obviously the connotation of precedent, such names as Schubert and Schumann, and the réclame of association with the Laureate, appealed strongly to ambitious, twenty-five-year-old Sullivan. This sequence of letters tells the story.

29a Tennyson, Emily. Als, Farrington, 5 February 1867, to "My dear Sir" [Sullivan]. 1p.

"Mr. Tennyson bids me write and say that he will be very glad to see you on Saturday & that he hopes you will be able to prevail on Mr. Grove to accompany you."

29b Payne, J. Bertrand. Als, 44 Dover Street, Piccadilly, 7 August 1867, to Sullivan. 2pp.

It was of the utmost importance, Payne wrote, that Tennyson's new work should be out not later than February next (1868). "The Bard tells me that the revised words are quite ready." But—how long would it take Sullivan with the composition and "whether Millais could be got to 'come to time?' "

29c Millais, Sir John Everett, 1829–1896. Als, Perth, 19 August 1870, to Sullivan. 3pp.

Millais explained to Sullivan that it was too late to reassemble the drawings he had made for *The Window*. One was already being engraved (for Henry Leslie, composer-conductor), "& the other drawings are dispersed so that it is really *impossible* for me to undertake the matter again ... You must remember I did keep the drawings for months before they were parted with." And, in mentioning Tennyson's displeasure, Millais wrote "one line from him at the time would have saved the trouble."

29d Tennyson, Alfred Lord, 1809–1892. Als, Aldworth, Blackdown, Haslemere, 6 November 1870, to [Sullivan]. 1p.

". . . [S]o I must consent to the publication of the songs however much against my inclination & my judgement & that I may meet your wishes as to the time of publication I must also consent to their being published this Xmas . . . provided . . . that the fact of their having been written four years ago & of their being published by yourself [Sullivan] be mentioned in the Preface. Provided also that no one but Millais shall illustrate them." (But Millais did not.)

29e Tennyson, Alfred Lord, 1809–1892. Manuscript, written as the Preface to *The Window*, signed but not dated. This is page 2 of a letter to publisher Strahan, dated 22 November 1870. 1p. (14 lines).

29f Tennyson, Alfred Lord, 1809–1892. Als, Aldworth, Blackdown, Haslemere [n.d.], to Sullivan. 2pp.

Concerning the Preface: the Laureate's friends "failed to see in it the slightest kind of un-friendly allusion to yourself . . . & only took it as an expression of my own regret at the un-appropriateness of the time of publication [the Franco-Prussian War], & even that my words were not more worthy of your music . . . If you choose, let all your chaffing friends at the club know that you have this under my hand & seal."

29g Sullivan, and Alfred Tennyson [Poet-Laureate]. *The Window, or The Songs of the Wrens.* Vocal score, London: Strahan & Co., 1871. Original green cloth gilt-blocked, with gilt edges. [i]–[x], [1]–54pp. 32 x 25½ cm.

On the front cover the subtitle reads: "or The Loves [sic] of the Wrens." The Preface by Tennyson appears on page [v]. The volume contains twelve poems by Tennyson of which eleven are set to Sullivan's music.

29h Another copy: Dark maroon cloth boards, identically decorated to above.

Presentation inscription on half title page: "John Hollingshead Esq. with the kind regards of Arthur S. Sullivan Xmas. 1870." A year from the date of this inscription, Sullivan would be on the eve of his first collaboration with W. S. Gilbert, *Thespis*, produced by John Hollingshead.

30 [Sullivan]. Program, Buckingham Palace, Wednesday evening, 11 May 1870.

A concert program of lace-valentine beauty, listing a musical treat fit for a Queen, or at least for a Queen's immediate family. The vocal stars were Mme Trebelli-Bettini and Mlle Tietjens, among others. The composer stars from which royal program fare was drawn included: Bellini, Donizetti, Meyerbeer, Rossini, Verdi (3 numbers), Wagner, and "A. Sullivan." Mad̯ᵉ Trebelli-Bettini sang, probably from manuscript, the "New Song, 'Looking Back,' " composed expressly for and dedicated to her by Sullivan.

ARTHUR SULLIVAN—EDITOR

31 [Sullivan]. *Don Giovanni*, opera in two acts by Mozart. The Royal Edition, edited by Arthur Sullivan. Vocal score, London & New York: Boosey & Co. [n.d.]. Title, [i]–[ii], 1–256pp. Original maroon cloth boards, gilt. 26½ x 18 cm.

Starting in the late 1860's, for a few years Sullivan became editor for Boosey of the Royal Edition of vocal scores embracing the whole opera repertoire then popular. This considerable potboiler undertaking has been almost ignored by his biographers, hence its importance to his career as composer of comic operas has been overlooked. Given his intensely eager ear and memory for music, there is little wonder that he was able to write in depth such engaging parody of grand opera, drawing on his vast memory-bank from the editing of thirty-two of the most popular operas in the period. Twenty-five of these were in collaboration with Josiah Pittman, whose name follows Sullivan's on their title pages. For seven he was the sole editor, of which the copy of Mozart's *Don Giovanni* was one: "Edited by Arthur Sullivan." This copy bears the presentation inscription: "Kate Santley from her friend Arthur S. Sullivan. Nov: 1870." The recipient was wife of famed baritone Sir Charles Santley, often associated with Sullivan's festival activities. In the list of these thirty-two titles, those for which Sullivan was sole editor bear asterisks.

Auber: *Diaments de la Couronne, Fra Diavolo, Domino Noir, Masaniello.* Balfe: *Bohemian Girl.* Beethoven: **Fidelio.* Bellini: *Norma, I Puritani,* **Sonnambula.* Donizetti: *Don Pasquale, Favorita, Lucia di Lammermoor, Lucrezia Borgia.* Flotow: **Marta.* Gounod: **Faust, Mirella, Mock Doctor.* Meyerbeer: *Dinorah, Roberto il Diavolo, Gli Ugonotti.* Mozart: **Don Giovanni, Flauto Magico, Nozze di Figaro.* Rossini: **Il Barbiere, Guglielmo Tell, Semiramide.* Verdi: *Ballo in Maschera, Rigoletto,* **Trovatore, Traviata.* Wagner: *Lohengrin.* Weber: *Der Freischütz.*

MEMORANDUM—MUSIC IN THE SCHOOLS

32 Sullivan. Manuscript, signed and dated on page 5: "Arthur S. Sullivan, Garrick Club, March 1871." 5pp.

In early 1871 there had been an attack made by one Mr. Forster that threatened exclusion of music in the curricula of schools throughout England. His chief objections were based largely on the difficulty of finding competent inspectors. Sullivan, not yet turned thirty, was outraged that the youth of England were to be denied so valuable and basic an element of their cultural heritage. He wrote a paper on this subject, dated from the Garrick Club in March 1871. "I venture in the following few sentences to urge the expediency of continuing the culture of music in schools and to suggest a means by which the difficulties . . . in the way of teaching it, may be overcome." He continued, warming to his subject with youthful fervor: "Few will deny the elevating and ennobling influence of music, even if considered merely as a recreation. . . ." And then, pulling out all the stops: "Above all it is a strong uniting power. Singing is the only possible Common expression of the feeling of many. It causes a number of people with various tastes, and perhaps opposite natures to join in a common purpose. . . ." And he closed by suggesting a plan for choosing local inspectors.

LECTURES—ON THE THEORY
AND PRACTICE OF VOCAL MUSIC

33   Sullivan.   Manuscript, not signed nor dated (ca. 1870's), of two lectures "On the theory and practice of vocal music." 33pp. and 11pp.

"The object of these lectures is to give some idea of the requirements for the practice of Vocal Music with special reference to Choral singing, in a style, as plain and comprehensible as possible." Sullivan stated that the chief difference in the styles of vocal and instrumental music lay in the intervals used and in the compass of the parts, that "The voice depends on the ear for its correct guidance, and the ear is influenced in a great measure by the eye . . . We must never tax the capabilities of the singer by the use of difficult intervals, such as the ear refuses to follow . . . I confess I have great affection for them [Gregorian Chants], they are to my feeling the only kind of music which suits the sublime poetry of the Psalms . . . The monks laid the foundation of melody—they did that and more for harmony." In discussing counterpoint, Sullivan called it "the grammar of part writing." And in discussing classes of voice he mentioned women's voices—soprano, mezzo, and contralto—as about two octaves—"some with wider ranges, but I am bound to declare honestly that I had rather they did it when I am not in the room." [Yet, see No. 99b!] Near the close of his first lecture Sullivan stated: "My desire is to sharpen your critical faculties and make you form a discriminating and appreciative audience."

THE NATIONAL TRAINING SCHOOL FOR MUSIC

The concept of a National Training School for Music had stemmed initially from the Prince Consort and was brought to fruition some twenty years later by his two oldest sons, the Prince of Wales and the Duke of Edinburgh. After a Committee of Management had been formed and a building erected, the two royal friends of Arthur Sullivan pressured him into accepting the post of the School's first Principal, in January 1876. The School was opened by the Queen on 16 April 1876, Easter. Five years later, in 1881, Sullivan was succeeded by John Stainer and, only a year thereafter, the National Training School itself was succeeded by the Royal College of Music. Sullivan had always been a conscientious force in promoting musical training, and he was always a supporter of the Royal College that followed. On his death he willed to the R.C.M. his two choicest musical manuscripts: *The Golden Legend* and *The Yeomen of the Guard*.

34a Sullivan. Als, 2 Albert Street, Victoria Square, 10 January [1876], to Alan Cole. 2pp.

"Against my own inclination and judgment I have accepted the position of director of the new School." In this fashion Sullivan opened his letter to Alan Cole, son of Sir Henry Cole, a leading member of the School's Committee of Management, and one with whom the composer was to be often in disagreement. He objected to the title "Professional Director." "Of course I am professional, but the term would imply that there is another Director who is *not* professional." Why could not he be called "simply Director"?

34b Alfred, The Duke of Edinburgh, 1844–1900. Ls, National Training School for Music, Royal Albert Hall, Kensington Gore, 17 January 1876, to Sullivan. 2pp.

In a formal letter, written by a secretary but signed "Alfred", the Duke of Edinburgh acknowledged receipt of Sullivan's expressed willingness to accept the post of Principal Professor of Composition, "and to act as Principal of the School in concert with the Board of Principal Professors for a salary of £400 a year in addition to your fee as Principal Professor of Composition."

34c Alfred, The Duke of Edinburgh, 1844–1900. Als, H.M.S. *Hercules*, 24 July 1880, to Sullivan. 2pp.

H.R.H. wrote Sullivan from his Royal Navy post, commiserating with him in a matter of serious friction that had arisen between Sullivan and the Committee of the National Training School. "The report of the Examiners is very annoying but should have been treated as quite unimportant. Don't lose heart all will come right again for the public will judge on merits & without the animus displayed by the Examiners. Above all don't think of resigning just now. Excuse this short note but I am terribly busy. I will write again before long. Yours very truly Alfred."

MOMENTS MUSICAUX

35a Sullivan. Als, 47 Claverton Terrace, S.W., Wednesday (ca. November–December), 1867, to "Rev^{nd} & Dear Sir!" 3pp.

Whether or not "Rev^{nd}" is in jest, as is so much of this rollicking letter, its unspecified addressee was to have the task of keeping the cigars lighted and seeing "that any man who refuses to drink his Brandy & Soda shall be instantly ejected." They, and others who gathered at 47 Claverton Terrace Saturday night, were to hear, and some to perform, a Schubert Quartet in B flat never before heard in England. Most likely it was one of the treasures found by Sullivan and Grove a month or so earlier in Vienna. Arthur Chappell's troupe, "the Bowing Brothers of Bond St.," has not been readily identified. "Le Petit Piatti" is certainly Alfredo (1822–1901), the celebrated 'cellist; and "Serio-comic player Ries," probably Louis Ries (1830–1913), violinist. But the "boneless Blagoone" and "Striding Strauss" have not been recognized.

35b Sullivan, Maria Clementina, 1811–1882. Als, 8 Albert Mansions, S.W. [London], [n.d., ca. 1871–1877], to Mr. Shepherd. 3pp.

Sullivan's mother, as efficient concert manager for his 8 Albert Mansions household, wrote to secure the 'cellist essential for a "command" evening of chamber music. "His Royal Highness the Duke of Edinburgh will do us the honour of spending the evening with us tomorrow, and he particularly wishes to have some *very good* music, will be glad to meet you here . . . all he *requests* & *requires* is to have the benefit of your superior & very valuable assistance. *His R.H.* will take one violin—Mr. Clay [Frederic] another,—*Arthur* the Tenor [viola]—and yourself the Violincello. . . ."

35c Sullivan. Als, Eastwell Park, Ashford, Kent, 12 January 1875, to Alan Cole. 1p.

Writing from the Duke of Edinburgh's estate at Eastwell Park, Sullivan arranged with their mutual friend Alan Cole for the postponement of a concert (probably one of the Amateur Orchestral Society Concerts, encouraged by H.R.H. who enjoyed occasionally taking the first violin desk). "You are at liberty to state that it is 'postponed by H.R.H.'s desire, in order that he may be able to take part in it.' "

35d Bryan, Alfred, 1852–1899. Original drawing, brush and brown wash, white highlights, over pencil, on blue paper. [n.p., n.d.] 36½ x 26½ cm.

The Duke of Edinburgh is shown playing the violin, accompanied by Sullivan at the pianoforte.

ON SHORE AND SEA

36 Sullivan, and Tom Taylor, 1818–1880. *On Shore and Sea*, cantata. Vocal score, London: Boosey & Co., [n.d.]. Title, [1]–4, 1–51 pp. Original printed grey wrappers. 28 x 19 cm.

The Royal Albert Hall had been formally in use for only a month when the London International Exhibition opened there on 1 May 1871. It was an occasion for commissioned compositions, and Arthur Sullivan was one of those selected, along with Gounod, then living as a Franco-Prussian War refugee. This gave the two composers an opportunity for acquaintance [see Gounod's letter of 27 March 1871, No. 49b]. Sullivan's offering was a Dramatic Cantata, the words by his friend Tom Taylor.

On Shore and Sea experienced the ever-present problem of acoustical eccentricities in a new hall, and the problem in Albert Hall was compounded by its huge size. One press member could say "but little, having been unable to find the seats allotted us, or any official who could direct us to them." However, this individual "heard enough of Mr. Sullivan's Cantata . . . to learn that the Albert Hall echo has been abolished apparently at the cost of some of the audibleness of the music" (*Fun* magazine).

MERCHANT OF VENICE

37a Sullivan. *Music to the Masque in Shakespeare's "Merchant of Venice."* Score for two pianos, arranged by Joseph Rummel, London: J. B. Cramer & Co. [n.d.]. Original soft green cloth wrappers. Title, index, [1]–67, advt. pp. Plate no. 6543.

On 19 September 1871, the enterprising Manchester manager Charles Calvert produced *The Merchant of Venice* at the Prince's Theatre. A special libretto of some eighty-odd pages, with footnotes reading like a Baedeker, attested his effort to have everything historically and architecturally correct and described. As an added production value, he engaged Arthur Sullivan to write some music to accompany the action near the close of Act I, the Lorenzo Masque, the colorful revelry outside Shylock's house that serves to shroud the escape of Jessica with her lover and Shylock's ducats. Showing his partiality for music for the stage, and with his Covent Garden experience to draw on (*L'Ile Enchantée*), Sullivan wrote a seven-part *Masque* which included one vocal number, a *Serenata*, "Nel ciel seren."

The work was published by Cramer as a piano duet in 1873. This copy bears the presentation inscription from Sullivan to E. J. Broadfield, May 1874. The work is dedicated appropriately to his friend J. H. Agnew, prominent in Manchester musical affairs.

37b Sullivan. Als, The Elms, Manchester, 3 October 1871, to "J.W.D." [Davison]. 4 pp.

Always alert to his own advance press-agentry, Sullivan wrote this letter 3 October 1871 at the end of his second week in the run of *The Merchant of Venice* in Manchester, to his good friend John William Davison of *The Times*. In it he mentioned the funeral of "our poor old friend" Cipriani Potter (the Principal of the Royal Academy of Music when Sullivan was a student), explaining that he could not attend because "I have been producing some music I wrote for The 'Merchant of Venice' at the Prince's Theatre here. It will be done shortly at the Crystal Palace, so say nothing about it. But [I] leave you to form your own judgement. These are the numbers [he listed six] and form the 'Masque' at the end of the 1st Act." Signed: "A.S.S." with "Love to J. Bennett." The composer was correctly informed: the *Masque* music received its first London hearing at the Crystal Palace 28 October, Manns conducting and Madame Conneau singing the *Serenata*.

ENTER GILBERT & SULLIVAN: *THESPIS*

38a Sullivan, and W. S. Gilbert, 1836–1911. "Little Maid of Arcadee," song from *Thespis*. London: Ashdown & Parry (1872). Plate no. A&P 10,782.

Sheet-music of a song from the second Act of *Thespis, or The Gods Grown Old*, the sole Sullivan survivor of *Thespis*, "an entirely original grotesque opera" that opened on Boxing Day (26 December) 1871, at the Gaiety Theatre, Arthur Sullivan conducting. Only the entrance of the Major General's daughters in Act I of *The Pirates of Penzance* is properly identifiable *Thespis* music, but with different words. The score was never published, and has completely disappeared.

Mention of the *Thespis* score by Sullivan is rare enough to warrant interest in a pair of tantalizing letters.

38b Sullivan. Als [the top of the letter has been cut off, removing addressee, Sullivan's address, and the date], [1873], to [Joseph Rummel]. 2pp.

"Thespis is not published but if you like I will send you the Full Score of the Duet in question. Let me have a line on a Post Card." The remainder of this mutilated letter gives the clue to its recipient. "Are you still good to fulfil your promise of arranging the 'Merchant [cropped] I should like it printed immensely, & should be delighted to have your name associated with mine in the matter." The piano duet of *The Merchant of Venice* was published by Cramer in 1873, with no arranger's name on the title page. Fortunately later copies bear a corrective label "Arranged as Pianoforte Duet by J. Rummel." This evidence identifies Sullivan's addressee: "Joseph Rummell (1818–1880) was one of the most prolific arrangers of operas and operatic selections for the pianoforte who ever existed . . . His arrangements and transcriptions amount in all to fully 2000" [Grove].

38c Sullivan. Als, [Paris, 30 July 1879], to "My dear John" [Hollingshead]. 3pp.

A long, important letter from Sullivan to John Hollingshead, much quoted, although undated contains such a wealth of information that it can be dated to the day . . . and it is the last mention of the *Thespis* score as then existent. Sullivan mentioned that "on Monday last I underwent the operation of having the stone crushed, & . . . leave Paris tomorrow." He also wrote "I am detaining the parts of the 'Pinafore' so that the Directors shall not take them away from the Comique tomorrow. . . ." (The Directors tried to raid the theatre on 31 July 1879.) Enter *Thespis*: "Now will you please let me have them [the handparts of the *Merry Wives of Windsor*] and the parts of 'Thespis' also at once." Therefore the *Thespis* score existed in early August 1879.

THE *FESTIVAL TE DEUM*

The recovery of Edward, Prince of Wales, from typhoid fever prompted a celebration, and the designation of 1 May 1872 as Thanksgiving Day. The Prince had been a friend of Arthur Sullivan for almost ten years, and his brother, Alfred, Duke of Edinburgh, had evolved close musical comradery with the young composer. So, when a special Concert Festival at the Crystal Palace was organized under the leadership of the Duke for 1 May, it was natural that Sullivan would be asked to compose a major work.

39a Sullivan. *Te Deum and "Domine Salvam Fac Reginam."* Full score, London & New York: Novello, Ewer and Company [n.d.]. [i] – [iv], 1–120pp. Original printed grey boards. Plate no. 7208.

The *Festival Te Deum* was a giant affair of virtually Berlioz proportions. According to Sullivan's biographer Arthur Lawrence, there were upwards of thirty thousand people present and, as though to match such statistics, there were two thousand members of the chorus and orchestra on the stage. The vocal score was published by Novello in the same year. The full score (1887) testified to the potential volume of sound Sullivan had in mind: Chorus, 1st and 2nd violins, violas, cellos, contrabasses, organ, and also 1st and 2nd flutes, oboe, clarinet, bassoon, four horns, four trombones, and ophicleide ("the largest member of the now extinct key-bugle family"—*Grove*), and timpani. To augment this assembly, a military band was called for as well, and the score had the notice: "The small notes are only to be played in the absence of a Military Band."

39b Alfred, Duke of Edinburgh, 1844–1900. Als, [royal crest], Tuesday [n.d.], to Sullivan. 3pp.

It was on "Tuesday," probably 9 April 1872, that the Duke of Edinburgh wrote a letter to "My dear Sullivan," signed "Alfred", explaining that "The Queen cannot be present at the

Crystal Palace but she hopes that some of the Royal Family will be able to go." Whether by hope or by Command there was a very good showing: the Princess Louise, the Duke of Edinburgh, the Prince and Princess of Teck, and the Duke of Cambridge. H.R.H. went on to tell Sullivan he would see him on Friday (12 April) as to the concert arrangements, and he added: "I have obtained permission for you to dedicate your Te Deum to Her Majesty, but you had better write an application for permission to Sir Thomas Biddulph & bring it to me & I will take care you get the proper answer." He did.

39c Biddulph, Sir Thomas, 1809–1878. Als, Windsor Castle, 16 April 1872, to A. S. Sullivan. 2pp.

Sir Thomas Biddulph, Keeper of Her Majesty's Privy Purse, after hearing from the Duke, wrote "A. S. Sullivan, Esq." from Windsor Castle: "I am to say that Her Majesty rarely accords this privilege to any one, and is only induced to do so on the occasion in question, in consequence of the case, and the Performance taking place under the immediate Patronage of the Royal Family."

THE LIGHT OF THE WORLD

40a Sullivan. *The Light of the World*, an oratorio. Vocal score, London: J. B. Cramer & Co. [n.d.]. First Printing. Inscribed wrapper, dated 27 August 1873. [1]–7, 1–275pp. Original printed blue wrappers. 27½ x 21 cm. Plate no. 6735.

Public announcement in England of the betrothal of Alfred, Duke of Edinburgh, to the Grand Duchess Marie, daughter of Tsar Alexander II, was made on 12 May 1873. Composer Sullivan wasted no time. The Duke was his intimate friend. There was an important new Oratorio nearly ready for the printer which was to be launched at the Birmingham Festival in August. He swiftly sought and immediately received permission to dedicate his new work, *The Light of the World*, to his royal friend's fiancée: "to Her Imperial Highness the Grand Duchess Marie Alexandrowna of Russia." The Oratorio was performed on 27 August. The Grand Duchess' marriage to the Duke followed in January 1874. Thus, for the second printing of the score, the dedication was reworded to reflect her new title: "to Her Royal Highness, Duchess of Edinburgh." The two printings are in the Sullivan collection. The vocal score, published by Cramer, was available in time for the first performance, so the composer was able to inscribe "from Arthur Sullivan / 27 August: 1873," under the bold signature, "Shrewsbury", on the cover of the copy that belonged to the Earl of Shrewsbury, President of the Birmingham Festival.

40b Alfred, Duke of Edinburgh, 1844–1900. Als, Jugenheim, 17 July 1873, to Sullivan. 3pp.

It was in Jugenheim, 1871, as fellow guests at the Hesse-Darmstadt ducal chateau, that Alfred, Duke of Edinburgh, first had met his future wife, the Grand Duchess Marie. Two years later, back in Jugenheim after his betrothal had been announced, Alfred wrote Sullivan who obviously sent his felicitations. "I was very much touched by your very friendly letter & for all the good wishes it contained." The Duke added his wish that work Sullivan had been doing for him had not been too serious an interruption to his composing, "& that the solemn introduction to the second part has since been born to the world. Hoping that I shall be able to hear the first production of the whole work in August, I remain. . . ." (Note: H.R.H. was there!)

40c H.R.H. The Duke & Duchess of Edinburgh.   Photograph, full view, taken by F. Backofen, Darmstadt [n.d.]. 15 x 10½ cm.

40d Sullivan.   No. 24: Recitative, Tenor, and No. 31: A Ruler and the People, Tenor Solo, from *The Light of the World*. Manuscript, not signed nor dated. On the first page of No. 31 is a bookplate with the initials: "WHC". 10pp. 30 x 24 cm.

The 2nd Tenor part was sent in manuscript by Sullivan to William Hayman Cummings (1831–1915), who had been engaged as late as 18 July to replace Edward Lloyd (1845–1927). There are two numbers from this original manuscript: No. 24, Recitative for A Disciple, "Master, get thee out and depart hence," and No. 31, "We know this man whence he is." They bear Cummings' bookplate: "WHC".

40e Sullivan.   Als, 8 Albert Mansions [London], 18 July 1873, to Cummings. 2pp.

40f Sullivan.   Als, 8 Albert Mansions [London], 31 July 1873, to Cummings. 2pp.

Two letters written by Sullivan to Cummings within a two-week period in July attested the emergency need for the tenor's services. The first, dated 18 July, asked: "Will you sing the 2nd Tenor part in my Oratorio for me?" The music would be sent to him in a day or two, and assuming compliance: "may I send you Reeves' [Sims Reeves, 1818–1900, 1st Tenor] music as well to understudy, so that in case anything were to prevent his singing at the last moment, the Tenor part need not be divided but would all be in good hands?"

The second letter, dated 31 July 1873, indicated that Cummings accepted and Sullivan was very grateful. "I send the 2nd Tenor part [in manuscript], & will send the principal part for you to look through when I get it in print. Shall you be at the rehearsal on the 14th & 15th?" Cummings had been Sullivan's tenor in the first performance of his Masque, *Kenilworth*, at the Birmingham Festival in 1864.

40g Sullivan. Als, 8 Albert Mansions (blind emboss: The Mendelssohn Scholarship Foundation), 16 May 1873, to "My dear old man" [Davison]. 4pp.

Writing to his friend on *The Times*, J. W. Davison, "My dear old man," Sullivan made clear the unusually [for him] long time he had devoted to composing *The Light of the World*. "I never go out in the world as my Oratorio takes all my time and thought . . . I have stuck to my work since last Michaelmas without faltering." From Michaelmas, 29 September 1872, to the date of writing, 16 May 1873, was more than seven months. "The 1st part is done & is in rehearsal and the second is rapidly progressing. The words are all compiled from the Bible by Grove & myself. I think the book is really beautiful thanks to dear old 'G.' "

40h Sullivan. *The Light of the World*, Book of Words. A corrected printer's copy, signed: "Arthur Sullivan", [n.d.]. [1] – 15pp. 22 x 14 cm.

Sullivan's papers contained the copy of *The Light of the World* Word Book which the composer had corrected for the printer. It is a fifteen-page pamphlet of libretto size. A large version was also available "Sold for the Benefit of the General Hospital." And there was also a still larger, forty-six page "Analysis" of the Oratorio, complete with musical passages, prepared by George Grove.

THE MERRY WIVES OF WINDSOR

Sullivan's *Incidental Music to the Merry Wives of Windsor* was composed for Act V only, and served to highlight the forest scenes. As it was largely background music there were no set pieces in this score which could be conveniently excerpted for performance in band concerts, song recitals, or drawing-rooms. For this reason, and perhaps also because two of the themes had been used by Sullivan ten years earlier in his ballet *L'Ile Enchantée*, *The Merry Wives of Windsor* is one of the few scores by Sullivan which has never been published in any form.

41a Sullivan. *The Merry Wives of Windsor*, incidental music. Manuscript, full score, not signed nor dated. Contemporary half green morocco with green cloth, marbled end-papers, and marbled edges. 80pp. 34 x 27 cm.

Loaned by John Wolfson.

The illustration from the score is a rustic dance to words by Shakespeare based on one of the themes from *L'Ile Enchantée* [see No. 4b].

This music was first used at the revival produced on 19 December 1874, at the Gaiety Theatre by John Hollingshead—who had ventured to bring the first Gilbert & Sullivan collaboration, *Thespis*, on its stage three years before. "I have only had 3 weeks to do the whole thing in" wrote Sullivan in a long, informative letter to Joseph Bennett, friend and critic.

41b Sullivan. Als, 8 Albert Mansions [London], 17 December 1874, to "Jo" [Bennett]. 4pp.

Two days before the London opening at the Gaiety, Sullivan wrote Joseph Bennett a veritable program note on the *Merry Wives of Windsor* music. He listed that he had written: "(1) a Prelude (Moonlight). (2) Tripping entrance of fairies with Anne Page. (3) Song for Anne Page. (4) Scene for Anne & the children, Solo & Chorus. (5) Dance round the tree. (6) Dance & Chorus 'Fie on sinful fantasie' when they pinch Falstaff." He went on to explain the interpolation of a song to words by Swinburne [see No. 50e] at the insistence of Hollingshead. ". . . I am doubtful whether it is tender & pretty, or whether it is not commonplace." He explained to Bennett, "not necessarily for publication," the two themes he had listed from *L'Ile Enchantée*, and he also confessed, "I wouldn't write an Overture, because I did not care about competing with the very pretty one of Nicolai."

SONG—"CHRISTMAS BELLS AT SEA"

42a Sullivan, and Charles Lamb Kenney, 1821–1881. "Christmas Bells at Sea," song. Manuscript, signed and dated 21 October 187[4]. Four pages in two leaves. 30 x 22½ cm. (Published by Novello, 1875.)

This Sullivan song was a setting of words provided by his friend Charles Lamb Kenney, whose godfather was Charles Lamb. The manuscript itself consists of three pages, the last of which is dated and signed by the composer. Sullivan also drafted a title page, headed by the words "Dedicated to" which might indicate that he had someone specific in mind. But the Novello, Ewer & Co. sheet-music (1875, plate no. 5113) has no such line. The makeshift title page bears an inscription of provenance by the previous owner: "Original ms of song by Sir A. Sullivan given me by Frederic Cliffe 1925," signed "H. Saxe Wyndham." He was a musical historian and biographer: *Arthur Seymour Sullivan*, Kegan, Paul, 1926. Frederic Cliffe (1857–1931), composer, had been a pupil of Sullivan's at the National Training School.

42b Sullivan. Als, 8 Albert Mansions [London], 5 December 1874, to Kenney. 1p.

Charles Lamb Kenney, according to the D.N.B., "with the exception of Boucicault and Vivier was said to be the wittiest man of his period." Sullivan probably knew him socially, but they must also have come together at the time of editing the Boosey Royal Edition of Operas, for Kenney was the English translator of eight of them [see No. 31]. In this letter of 5 December 1874, Sullivan wrote a jocular reply to an evident inquiry as to publication and payment. ". . . Novello is keeping it until that jovial & festive season of the year, when it will electrify a vast audience at the Albert Hall. Will you write Littleton [at Novello] and demand from him a sum which shall at the same time represent an author's modesty, a publisher's generosity & poetical worth."

72

43aa Sullivan (libretto by W. S. Gilbert). *Trial by Jury*. Full score. Signed, not dated. Folio, green half morocco gilt. 164 written pages (including title), between one and sixteen filled staves to a page. 33½ x 26 cm.

The Mary Flagler Cary Music Collection, The Pierpont Morgan Library.

There is no single addition so appropriate and important to this book and to the Library's collection as Sullivan's manuscript score of Gilbert & Sullivan opus one, *Trial by Jury*. For years the score of *Trial by Jury* has not been seen publicly except in the restricted arena of the auction room. It appeared at Sotheby's in London on 13 June 1966 (as lot 178) and was bought by a Mr. "A. J. Lloyd Maxwell"; it promptly became inaccessible. Thereafter its ownership and location could not be discovered by scholars or musicians. Now suddenly, after this volume, *Sir Arthur Sullivan*, had gone to press, the manuscript of *Trial by Jury* reappeared at auction. This time it was at Sotheby Parke Bernet, New York, on 21 January 1975 (as lot 56) where it was purchased for The Mary Flagler Cary Music Collection of The Pierpont Morgan Library. This fortunate circumstance has permitted the manuscript score of the first Gilbert & Sullivan opera to join the manuscript score of Sullivan's first work for the stage, his operetta *Cox and Box*, previously purchased for The Mary Flagler Cary Music Collection.

Most scholars of the Victorian theatre date the birth of Gilbert & Sullivan opera with the first performance of *Trial by Jury*, at the Royalty Theatre, London, on 25 March 1875. Some will maintain that there is no single date of comparable importance in the history of the modern lyric theatre than this occasion which first brought together the triumvirate of W. S. Gilbert, Arthur Sullivan, and their catalyst business genius, Richard D'Oyly Carte. The next twenty-five years witnessed the spectacular, worldwide success of this collaboration: the Gilbert & Sullivan operas, initiated by *Trial by Jury*. Without this spark, who can say that any of the instantaneous hits of G. & S. that followed would ever have been written?

The names Gilbert and Sullivan had first been linked in the comic opera *Thespis*, produced by John Hollingshead in December 1871. Then for three years Sullivan had concentrated on church music, songs, and ballads, while Gilbert had been writing miscellaneous farces, comedies, and plays. They had certainly not avoided each other, but simply had moved busily in different fields. In this period Gilbert had sketched a libretto of *Trial by Jury* for impresario Carl Rosa in 1873; but this Gilbert-Rosa collaboration was dropped when Rosa's wife died in January 1874. An entire year passed, apparently with no producer interested in *Trial by Jury*. Then in the same month, December 1874, when *The Merry Wives of Windsor* with incidental music by Sullivan opened at the Gaiety Theatre, Chappell

& Company published Sullivan's "The Distant Shore," a song with words by W. S. Gilbert. The two planets were in conjunction, the stars right for the entrance of the third member of the triumvirate, Richard D'Oyly Carte.

Gilbert is said to have dropped in on D'Oyly Carte, manager of the Royalty Theatre, with his libretto sketch of *Trial by Jury* one day in mid-January 1875 at the very time the manager was looking for a piece to share the bill at the Royalty with *La Perichole*. Carte liked what he read and suggested Sullivan. Gilbert went to Sullivan's flat and read him his manuscript. Sullivan liked what he heard—and within the space of three weeks' time, in the words of the closing chorus of *Trial by Jury*, they had "settled with the job—and a good job too!"

The manuscript of this score is a most happy hundredth-birthday salute to the immortal Gilbert & Sullivan operas which it launched, 1875–1975.

TRIAL BY JURY

43a Sullivan. *Trial by Jury*. Manuscript of thematic sketches, not signed nor dated. Four leaves. 34 x 36 cm.

Loaned by The Library of Congress.

These four large unnumbered sheets of Sullivan's musical jottings contain most of the thematic material from which he constructed the score of *Trial by Jury*. There are no words of text. Some themes appear in proper sequence and key, others are scrambled at random; and two are in trial keys differing from the final score. These are the composer's working notes, comparable to pages from one of Gilbert's notebooks in which he jotted down multiple variants of a plot.

43b Sullivan. Als, 8 Albert Mansions [London], 15 June 1875, to Felix Moscheles. 2pp.

Apparently Sullivan was unable to get seats to *Trial by Jury* for the Moscheles family, his dear friends of Leipzig days. His letter to Felix Moscheles (Ignaz M.'s son) was dated 15 June 1875, three days after Royalty Theatre, at which *Trial by Jury* had been playing, had closed for the summer. "I will see what I can do about the 'Zoo,' " he wrote. This was his little comic opera that had just opened at the St. James's Theatre [see No. 44].

43c Sullivan, Frederic, 1839–1877. Photograph, in costume of the "Judge," *Trial by Jury*, taken by Lafosse, Manchester [n.d.]. 16½ x 11 cm.

This cabinet photograph of Fred Sullivan in his role of "The Learned Judge" in *Trial by Jury* has on its reverse a presentation inscription from Fred: "To W. S. Gilbert Esq / from the Learned Judge / *Fred Sullivan* / with many thanks for the valuable suggestions / made during the rehearsals / of 'Trial by Jury' / *Aug. 1875*." The photographer was Lafosse of Manchester, where *Trial by Jury* played in August while on tour after leaving the Royalty.

43d Sullivan, and W. S. Gilbert. *Trial by Jury*. Vocal score, London: Chappell & Co. [n.d.]. [i]–vi, [3]–53pp. Original tan paper wrappers. 28 x 22 cm.

The wrapper of this vocal score, first printing, omitted Gilbert's name altogether. On the title page the name W. S. Gilbert appeared, but it followed that of Arthur Sullivan. It bears an inscription by the composer, "Mrs. Hay Ritchie from Arthur Sullivan," and belonged to Fannie Ritchie, daughter of Mrs. Ronalds. She had been a cripple since childhood; was beloved by her many friends; and was "Fanette" to Sullivan, who was very fond of her.

43e Sullivan. "*Trial by Jury* Lancers." Color-lithographed sheet-music, dance music arrangement by Charles D'Albert, Chappell. Plate no. 16072.

Dedicated to Miss Nelly Bromley, who sang "The Plaintiff" in the original Royalty Theatre cast. This copy has a blind date-stamp showing: "April 10, 1876," at which time *Trial by Jury* was playing at the Opera Comique.

THE ZOO

44a Sullivan. Al [written in the third person], 9 Albert Mansions [London], 22 June 1877, to Mr. Cowper. 1p.

Undoubtedly the most recent Sullivan work for the stage to be published is *The Zoo*: first performance 1875; first published 1969. This comic opera, designated "A Musical Folly," opened at the St. James's Theatre on 5 June 1875. The words were by "Bolton Rowe," a *nom de plume* for B. C. Stephenson who in that year wrote the words to Sullivan's beautiful song "Let me dream again." Two years later, 22 June 1877, on mourning stationery for his brother, Fred, Sullivan wrote in the third-person singular: "Mr. Sullivan begs to inform Mr. Cowper that the 'Zoo' has not yet been published, nor will it until considerable alterations have been made." That there was some interest brewing in *The Zoo* was clear from the closing sentence of a letter Sullivan wrote his close friend Alan Cole on the 22nd of November the same year—only five days after the opening of *The Sorcerer*: "They [whoever that may be] want to revive the 'Zoo' at the Strand. Will you *rewrite* it with me?" Apparently this bit of collaboration never came off.

44b Sullivan, and B. C. Stephenson. *The Zoo*, a musical folly. Vocal score by Garth Morton, with a note on the libretto by Terence Rees. London: At 25, copyright 1969. Green printed wrappers. [i]–iv, [1]–108pp. 31 x 23 cm.

Mr. Terence Rees was responsible for the piano reduction of the autograph full score by Garth Morton. He made the point in his "Note on the Libretto" that there were two parallels in this work with *La Perichole* and that these were probably not lost on the London audience which had enjoyed the Offenbach work for more than two months in the spring of 1875 as the companion piece with *Trial by Jury* on the Royalty Theatre's bill. The Royalty considerately closed for the summer the week after *The Zoo* opened at the St. James's.

HENRY VIII

45 Sullivan. *Incidental Music to Shakespeare's play, Henry VIII*. Full score. Manuscript, signed and dated on the title page: "composed for the revival at the Theatre Royal, Manchester, by Arthur Sullivan, August [29] 1877." Half green morocco, gilt, with green cloth, marbled end-papers, and marbled edges. 76pp. 34 x 27 cm.
Loaned by John Wolfson.

The score consists of a "March," a "Graceful Dance," "Water Music," and "King Henry's Song," an interpolated lyric "Youth must needs have dalliance," which was published separately with a title page that must have pleased its composer: "Lyrics by Henry VIII, Music by Arthur Sullivan." The "Graceful Dance" was used only three months later as the overture to *The Sorcerer* in its original production at the Opera Comique.

The manuscript score contains the two pages of music which the composer added to the beginning of the "Graceful Dance" to make it serviceable as an overture. A brief statement of the theme, "O marvellous illusion" (from *The Sorcerer*), modulates unsatisfactorily into the opening of the "Dance" movement which begins on the following leaf. The *Henry VIII* music was not performed again as such during Sullivan's lifetime and so these two *Sorcerer* pages were never removed from the manuscript.

THE SORCERER

46a For the first performance of *The Sorcerer* on 17 November 1877, Sullivan wrote no proper overture but simply substituted a dance movement from his *Incidental Music to Henry VIII*, produced in Manchester three months before (29 August to 3 November). This was duly noted by reviewers, many of whom were inclined to regard this new comic opera as a step downward from Sullivan's artistic promise. So in 1884, when *The Sorcerer* was revived, "Revised and Partly Re-Written," with *Trial by Jury* sharing the bill, he designed a new overture consisting of a series of themes from the opera. He is said to have left the execution of this to an (as yet nameless) assistant. The pages of the manuscript, appearing toward the end of the Overture, are written in a hand other than the composer's but with corrections by Sullivan in darker ink at the bottom, strengthening the chord structure [see No. 46b].

46b Sullivan (libretto by W. S. Gilbert). *The Sorcerer*. Full score. Manuscript, not signed nor dated. One folder (containing the overture) and two volumes, half green morocco gilt. 410pp. 36 x 21½ cm.

Loaned by John Wolfson.

The final chorus of Act I, "O marvelous illusion," is one of the most heavily scored passages of the opera, and one of the most beautiful. It closely resembles the ensemble from the first act of Donizetti's *L'Elisir d'Amore*, with which both Gilbert and Sullivan were independently familar: Sullivan as co-editor of the Boosey Royal Edition of Operas, Gilbert through his first play, *Dulcamara*, a burlesque of the Donizetti original. Gilbert based his libretto of *The Sorcerer* on his own short story "The Elixir of Love," written for the Christmas number of the *Graphic*, 1876, with a bit of his *Bab Ballad* "The Rival Curates," thrown in for good measure.

46c Sullivan.   Als, 9 Albert Mansions [London], 1 November 1877, to "Mum" [his mother]. 3pp.

On Thursday night, 1 November 1877, the eve of her birthday, "yr aff. A." wrote "Dearest Mum" that "I am just putting the last few bars to my opera, & tomorrow begin the scoring, so it is a favourable occasion to write a line to wish you many happy years to come." As usual the composer was giving himself scant time, only two weeks, for the task of scoring *The Sorcerer*, during which period would come all the problems and stresses of rehearsals and final changes. "I have been *slaving* at this work," he wrote, "and hope it will be a success. Everything at present promises very well. The book is brilliant, & the music I think very pretty and good. All the Company are good & like it very much. The scoring will be a tremendous labour, but I don't mind that, as I can do it quickly, & there is no more composition to be done."

46d Sullivan.   Als, 9 Albert Mansions [London], 22 November 1877, to Alan Cole. 4pp.

Sullivan—in explaining to his friend Alan Cole why he was unable to see his father, Sir Henry, on Saturday, 17 November, regarding the National Training School—revealed the welter of work involved in the birth of *The Sorcerer*. "I had a long night rehearsal beginning at 7.30 on Friday [the final dress rehearsal, 16 November], & heaps of little things, cuts &c, to arrange on Saturday [the first night]. . . ." But the triumphant result was already apparent on the day of this letter, Thursday, 22 November. "They are doing tremendous business at the Op: Comique I am glad to say. I was on the stage last night [Wednesday, 21 November] and heard *three* encores before I left. If it is a great success it is another nail in the coffin of Opera Bouffe from the French. . . ."

46e Sullivan, and W. S. Gilbert. *The Sorcerer*. Vocal score, bearing the name "Mrs. Ronalds" boldly written at the top by the owner, Mrs. Mary Frances Ronalds, devoted friend of the composer. In the upper right corner of the title page, in Sullivan's hand, is the inscription: "Mrs. Ronalds / from her old friend / Arthur Sullivan." Metzler & Co., 1877. Original printed grey wrappers. [1]–130, advt. pp. 28 x 22 cm. Plate no. M.5001.

Colorfully lithographed sheet-music of dance arrangements followed hard on the popularity of the Sullivan score. Three were arranged by Charles D'Albert in early 1878, and may bear Metzler's blind-stamped date, often illegible.

46f "*The Sorcerer* Lancers," plate no. M.4868. Date-stamp: 11 February 1878.

46g "*The Sorcerer* Quadrille," Plate no. M.4869. Date-stamp: 1878.

46h "*The Sorcerer* Waltz," Plate no. M.5011.

H.M.S. PINAFORE

47a Sullivan. Manuscript of "Short Chronological Memoranda," not signed nor dated, 1 Queen's Mansions [London]. Page 6 (of twelve pages).

Prepared for Charles Willeby's biographical article in 1892, covering the period 1877–1878: Sullivan noted briefly the formation of the Comedy Opera Company, its first production, *The Sorcerer*, and the launching of its second, *H.M.S. Pinafore*. In a parenthesis he reminded Willeby, "(By the way, this like many of my works was written during constant physical suffering. My malady a stubborn, painful kidney condition began in 1872)." He recalled how, at the outset, *Pinafore* had failed to attract, and how, when the Directors resolved to close it, "I undertook the Promenade Concerts at Covent Garden, and performed every evening a very brilliant selection from the opera, for Orchestra and Military Band by my friend Hamilton Clarke. The Opera also 'caught on' in America, and raged like a fever through the country. For one or both of these reasons I think, a reaction set in in London, and 'HMS Pinafore' was performed for 23 months." Opening night was 25 May 1878.

47b Sullivan (libretto by W. S. Gilbert). *H.M.S. Pinafore*. Manuscript of the full score. (A page of recitative in another hand is inserted before No. 3.) Green half morocco gilt. 356 written pages. 1 volume. 34 x 25 cm.
Loaned by Arthur A. Houghton, Jr.

The original manuscript of Sullivan's miracle of success, *H.M.S. Pinafore*, was surely among the most used—and abused—volumes in his music library. Before 1900 this G. & S. war-horse had been revived twice at the Savoy (1887 and 1899) after its long initial run at the Opera Comique. And then there was the provincial exposure: in twenty-one years it had been absent from tour repertoire in only six seasons. Through countless rehearsal and performance hours by Sullivan, Alfred Cellier, and others, its pages accreted additional and altered instructions, deletions, paste-ins, renumbering, and twenty-two pages of overture which did not appear in the published vocal score until 1887 (and is not by Hamilton Clarke as alleged, nor by Sullivan). As an example: the Octet and Chorus in Act 2 was originally numbered No. 20, and was blue-crayoned to #19 (its vocal score number). After this came a passage "20½" *Moderato* ("My pain and my distress") which the vocal score includes in No. 19—and in Sullivan's hand is the instruction, "This follows immediately after the last note *sung*. The few bars for Wind, I wrote on Friday, to be cut out."

H.M.S. AS LOGGED BY W.S.G.

47c Gilbert, William Schwenck, 1836–1911. Als, 24 Boltons [London], 27 December 1877, to Sullivan. 1p.

1) The Good Ship on the ways.
This historic letter from Gilbert to Sullivan 27 December 1877 was the spark that ignited

the enduring flame of success of *H.M.S. Pinafore*. "Dear Sullivan," he wrote; "I send you herewith a sketch plot of the proposed opera. I hope & think you will like it." Gilbert had tried to see Sullivan before drawing this up in full, but found that he had gone abroad. "I should like to have talked it over with you as there is a good deal of fun in it which I haven't set down on paper. Among others a song (kind of 'Judge's Song') for the First Lord —tracing his career as office boy in cotton broker's office, clerk, traveller, junior partner & First Lord of Britain's Navy. . . ." And then, as though calming the concern he felt Sullivan might have, he explained: "Of course there will be no personality in this, the fact that the First Lord in the opera is a *radical* of the most pronounced type will do away with any suspicion that W. H. Smith is intended. . . ." (As indeed he was and as indeed it did not.)

47d Gilbert, William Schwenck, 1836–1911. Als, 24, The Boltons [London], 2 August 1879, to Sullivan. 3pp.

2) The Good Ship in troubled waters.

With D'Oyly Carte in America, and with Sullivan having just undergone a painful operation for kidney stone in Paris, the waters of the Opera Comique were anything but calm. Late in July a coup was planned by dissident Directors who, on 31 July, attempted to break up the performance and steal the properties. Gilbert wrote Sullivan about this in a long letter of 6 August 1879: "By the way on Friday night Bailey, Chappell & Drake [Directors of the Comedy Opera Company] broke into the theatre with a mob of 50 roughs, during the performance, & tried to carry off the properties. Barker [Richard Barker, acting-Manager for D'Oyly Carte] resisted their approach & was knocked down stairs & seriously hurt. There was an alarm among the audience who raised a cry of fire—appeased however by Grossmith who made them a speech from the stage. . . ." Gilbert, Sullivan, and D'Oyly Carte won ultimate victory in the courts.

ORCHESTRA SCORE PUBLISHED IN GERMANY

47e Sullivan. *Amor An Bord*, Komische Oper in zwei Acten mit Zugtundelegung des englischen Textes von W. S. Gilbert, für die deutsche Bühne bearbeitet von Ernst Dohm. Braunschweig: Henry Litolff [n.d.]. Original stiff printed grey wrappers. 1–228pp. 35 x 27 cm.

Using the title *Amor An Bord*, a full score of *Pinafore*, of course unauthorized, was printed about 1882–1884 by Henry Litolff of Brunswick, who also printed the vocal score. Its text was printed (hectograph) in German script, an adaptation by Ernst Dohm. As of 1975 this is still the only printed version of the full score. Naturally many liberties were taken with the lyrics; and rest assured there was no direct translation for: "He is an Eng-lish-man." For adaptor Dohm it was: "Ein bra-ver Kerl ist er!"

47f Sullivan, and W. S. Gilbert. *H.M.S. Pinafore or, The lass that loved a sailor*. Vocal score, second printing. [1]–105pp. Original blue-grey printed wrappers. Metzler & Co. [1878]. 28 x 22 cm. Plate no. M.5057.

On the title page of this copy Sullivan wrote: "Mrs. Hay Ritchie / from / Arthur Sullivan." Fannie Ritchie was the daughter of Mrs. Ronalds. This score starts with the opening chorus. The overture was not included in the vocal score until the subsequent printing.

Color-lithograph sheet-music of dance arrangements by Charles Godfrey, Band Master Royal Horse Guards:

47g "*H.M.S. Pinafore* Lancers," Metzler & Co. [1878]. Plate no. M.5109. Date-stamp: November 1878.

47h "*H.M.S. Pinafore* Quadrille," Metzler & Co. [1878]. Plate no. M.4931. Date-stamp: 16 July 1878.

47i "*H.M.S. Pinafore* Waltz," Metzler & Co. [1878]. Plate no. M.5081. Date-stamp: November 1878.

47j Opera Comique *H.M.S. Pinafore* poster, from the period 1878–1879. Lithographed in full color, printed by Stannard & Son, "Alfred Concanen Del. et lith." 33½ x 44 cm.

SONG—"OLD LOVE LETTERS"

48a Sullivan. "Old Love Letters," song. Manuscript, signed and dated January 1879. Six of eight pages are written, page one is a title page. 27 x 35 cm. (Published by Boosey & Co., 1879.)

This manuscript of "Old Love Letters" is dated by Sullivan both on its title page and at its close on the fifth page of music—January 1879. There is no mention of a dedication in the manuscript. All Sullivan check-lists give 1879 as Boosey's publication year for this song. The only copies seen, however, are those of a "New & Revised Edition" dedicated to Mrs. Ronalds. (The revision is on the last page of the sheet-music.) It seems unlikely that this revised form could have come out the same year as the original. Eighteen seventy-nine was a particularly busy period, what with Sullivan's serious illness, operation, recuperation, work on *The Pirates of Penzance*, and departure for America. Mid-1880, or a bit later, would seem more likely for this revision and would fit the relaxed tone of the composer's letter to his mother.

48b Sullivan. Als, 9 Albert Mansions [London], Sunday [n.d.], to "Mum" [his mother]. 3pp.

"I am having my tea & re-writing 'Old love letters'. . . ," wrote Sullivan to his mother, ". . . & have had Lloyd here today to go through it & he likes it immensely. I am copying it & sending it to Boosey." It was for Edward Lloyd (1845–1927), "the most famous English tenor of his generation" (*Grove*), that Sullivan had expressly composed this music. Lloyd sang the principal tenor role in the first *Martyr of Antioch* at Leeds on 15 October 1880. This letter may date from autumn of the same year.

48c Sullivan. Photograph, profile, signed and dated (on the mat): "Miss Shepherd from Arthur Sullivan. May: 1879." 24 x 18 cm. (with mat).

LETTERS FROM MUSICIANS AND AUTHORS

A sampling of the correspondence received by Arthur Sullivan in the seventies from well-known composers, musicians, and literary figures yields a conductor, two composers, and two widely read authors.

49a Benedict, Sir Julius, 1804–1885. Als, 2 Manchester Square [London], 4 February 1870, to Sullivan. 4pp.

Julius Benedict had been conducting and teaching in London before Sullivan was born. He had been closely connected with the Norwich Festivals, with Jenny Lind's American tour (for which he conducted), and with the Monday "Pops" concerts. This letter to Sullivan was written the year before he became Sir Julius. "The first performance of your Prodigal Son at Liverpool is fixed for Tuesday 15 March. . . ." Benedict wanted Sullivan to attend several of the rehearsals, and he submitted a list of the soloists to be engaged. "I have mentioned the 'In Memoriam Overture,'" he wrote, "which I suppose will meet with no opposition on the part of the Directors."

49b Gounod, Charles, 1818–1893. Als, [n.p., London], Lundi 27 March 1871, to Sullivan. 1p.

Charles Gounod, at the time of the Prussian occupation of Paris, became a temporary London resident. He was one of those, along with Sullivan, asked to compose a work for the opening of the London International Exhibition at Albert Hall in 1871. "Helas! mon cher ami." While Sullivan was playing his "ouverture" last Saturday, Gounod was playing a much less agreeable "fermeture": "J'étais en lit avec une Bronchite," in fact he had been sick for fifteen days. Sullivan had asked if Gounod's work for Albert Hall would be finished. "Oui." Gounod was at work on the orchestration. It was a biblical Elegie with solo and chorus. The reference was to Gounod's *Gallia* which shared the program on 1 May 1871 with Sullivan's cantata, *On Shore and Sea*.

49c Macfarren, Sir George Alexander, 1813–1887. Als, 7 Hamilton Terrace [London], 4 April 1876, to Sullivan. 1p.

Composer-Professor George Alexander Macfarren was warmly disposed toward Arthur Sullivan even though thirty years his senior. In this letter Macfarren showed his pleasure in a duty obviously pleasing to his friend. "It is the pleasantest privilege of the office I hold at Cambridge that I have to tell you, the Council of the University yesterday agreed to sanction a grace offering you the honorary Degree of Doctor of Music. . . ."

49d Trollope, Anthony, 1815–1882. Als, 39 Montagu Square [London], 17 January 1876, to Sullivan. 3pp.

Two best-selling novelists of diametrically differing fields—the towers of Barchester and the rabbit-hole of Wonderland—corresponded with the busy young composer who, in 1876, would have known as little of Phineas Finn as of the Snark. "Are you going to Paris?", wrote Trollope. "If you do will you make yourself acquainted with an American Lady one Miss Dulany . . . She sings really well, *very well indeed*. She is not beautiful but is very clever & agreable. Go & call on her like a good fellow."

49e Dodgson, C. L. ["Lewis Carroll"], 1832 – 1898. Als, Ch. Ch. [Christ Church], Oxford, 24 March 1877, to Sullivan. 3pp.

"I am the writer of a little book for children, 'Alice's Adventures in Wonderland', which has proven so unexpectedly popular. . . ." Dodgson's idea was for a possible dramatization, and he "thought (knowing your charming compositions) it would be well to get 2 or 3 of the songs in it set by you. . . ." Alas, even if 'twas brillig, there was no frabjous day for Carroll —(or for the world!). Sullivan turned him down.

SONGS—PIANOFORTE ACCOMPANIMENT

These ten examples of Sullivan's songs of the seventies need no apologies for the caliber of his poet-collaborators: Laureate Tennyson, Robert Burns, George Eliot, Longfellow, Swinburne, W. S. Gilbert (non-opera), Samuel K. Cowen, and Adelaide Proctor, whose "example" sold over a half a million copies in twenty-five years.

Words by Tennyson:

50a "St. Agnes' Eve," composed and dedicated to Mrs. Ronalds, Boosey & Co. (1879).

Words by Robert Burns:

50b "Mary Morison," Boosey & Co. (1874).

Words by George Eliot:

50c "Ay de mi, my bird," No. 2 of *The Young Mother*, *Three simple Songs*, dedicated to Lady Talbot, J. B. Cramer & Co. (1874).

Words by Henry Wadsworth Longfellow:

50d "Living Poems," composed expressly for Miss Edith Wynne, Boosey & Co. (1874).

Words by Algernon C. Swinburne:

50e "Love laid his sleepless head," dedicated to The Hon. Eliot Yorke, Boosey & Co. (1874) [interpolated in the *Merry Wives of Windsor*, No. 41b].

Words by W. S. Gilbert:

50f "Little Maid of Arcadee," *Thespis* [see No. 38a].

50g "The Love that Loves me not," dedicated to Mrs. D. B. Grant, plate no. 5133, Novello, Ewer & Co. (1875).

50h "The Distant Shore," plate no. 15873, Chappell & Co. (1875).

50i " 'Sweethearts,' " plate no. 15967, Chappell & Co. (1875).

Dance Music Arrangements by Charles D'Albert with color-lithograph covers:

50j "The Distant Shore Waltz," on Arthur Sullivan's popular song, plate no. 16466, Chappell & Co. (1875).

50k "Sweethearts Waltz," on Arthur Sullivan's popular song, plate no. 15998, Chappell & Co. (1875).

Words by Adelaide A. Proctor:

50l "The Lost Chord" [see No. 93], Boosey & Co. (1877).

Words by Samuel K. Cowan, M.A.:

50m "Old Love Letters," new & revised edition, dedicated to Mrs. Ronalds [see No. 48a and b], composed expressly for Mr. Edward Lloyd, Boosey & Co. (1879).

RELIGIOUS MUSIC

Examples of Sullivan's religious music of the period include five of the sacred part-songs, three (of his six) anthems, both his unaccompanied choruses adapted from Russian church music, and two of his Christmas carols. And in addition, the hymns, of which he composed forty-one, are all to be found in three major hymnals to which he contributed: *The Supplemental Hymn and Tune Book* (1871), *The Hymnary* (1872), and *Church Hymns with Tunes* (1874) of which he was the editor. These latter two contain thirty-eight hymns specially composed for them.

51a *The Choralist*, sacred part-songs, Boosey (1871):
> No. 164, "It came upon a midnight clear," words by E. H. Sears.
> No. 197, "Lead Kindly Light," words by John Henry Newman.
> No. 198, "Through Sorrow's Path," words by H. Kirke White.
> No. 199, "Say, watchman, what of the night?"
> No. 200, "The Way is long and dreary," words by Adelaide Procter [sic].

51b "I will worship towards Thy Holy Temple," anthem, Boosey (1871).

51c *Novello's Christmas Carols:* No. 41, "Carol for Christmas Day" (1870).

51d *Novello's Parish Choir Book:*
> No. 553, "The roseate hues of early dawn" (1872).
> No. 720, "Courage, Brother! Do not stumble" (1872).

51e *Novello's Octavo Anthems:*
> No. 34, "O God Thou Art Worthy," anthem for marriage service (1871).
> No. 100, "Mercy and Truth are met together," chorus adapted from Russian church music (1874).
> — "Turn Thee Again," chorus adapted from Russian church music (1874).
> No. 154, "I will mention," anthem for Easter (1875).

51f *The Choir:* No. 525a, "Upon the Snow-Clad Earth," carol for Christmas Tide, Metzler (1876).

51g "Onward, Christian Soldiers" (St. Gertrude) (one of "Four Popular Hymns" set to music expressly for *The Hymnary*, a Book of Church Song), Novello, Ewer and Co., printed in *The Musical Times*, 1 December 1871.

51h "Onward, Christian Soldiers," manuscript of five stanzas, signed: "S. Baring-Gould."

51i "Onward, Christian Soldiers" (St. Gertrude), in Japanese, found in *The Hymnal*, No. 1, prepared by A Union Committee, Tokyo (eighth edition, 1914).

51j *The Supplemental Hymn and Tune Book*, Novello, Ewer and Co. (1871), edited by the Rev. Robert Brown-Borthwick. Appendix to this (4ᵗʰ) edition contains Sullivan settings:
No. 68, "The Strain upraise of joy and praise."
No. 73, "Love Divine, all love excelling."
No. 74, "The Son of God goes forth to war" (from Croft).

51k *Carols New and Old*, edited by John Stainer, Novello, Ewer and Co. with George Routledge and Sons (1871), contains Sullivan's "Carol for Christmas Day," pp. 88–89, illustrated by Thomas Dalziel.

51l *The Hymnary*, *A Book of Church Song*, edited by Joseph Barnby, this copy, "Nineteenth thousand," Novello, Ewer and Co. (1872), contains twelve hymn titles composed by A. S. Sullivan for this book.

51m *Church Hymns with Tunes*, edited by Arthur Sullivan, Society for Promotion of Christian Knowledge, Clarendon Press, Oxford (1874). This copy, first printing, contains forty-five titles bearing his name as composer or arranger/harmonizer; of these, twenty-six, including two litanies, were composed for this hymnal.

51n Sullivan. Manuscript of "Litany. hy: 585. 586." The voices in unison and organ lines of one of the two litanies he composed for *Church Hymns with Tunes*, No. 585, of penitence, No. 1, "Jesu, we are far away." 6½ x 30½ cm.

Manuscript of two hymns, for *Church Hymns with Tunes*, with the presentation to Sullivan: "To his friend Arthur S. Sullivan / Two Hymn Tunes / written / for The Society's / for Promoting Christian Knowledge / New / Tune Book / by / Otto Goldschmidt / July 1873." Presentation on page 1, hymns on pages 2 and 3, page 4 is blank:

84

51o Goldschmidt, Otto, 1829–1907. Manuscript of No. 535, "To Him, who for our sins was slain," signed "O.G.", hymn, with four verses in print tipped on top. 22 x 29 cm. (two pages of a four-page fold).

51p Goldschmidt, Otto, 1829–1907. Manuscript of No. 20, "Father, by Thy Love & Power," signed "O.G. 1873," hymn, with two verses in print tipped on top. 22 x 29 cm. (two pages of a four-page fold).

Pasted to each manuscript page is what appears to be a rough type-proof of the words, intermediate to the book itself.

51q *Sunlight of Song*, Novello, Ewer and Co. with George Routledge and Sons (1875), contains two songs of Sullivan's, both illustrated by George Dalziel: "We've plowed our land" (pp. 6–8) and "The River" (pp. 40–43).

THE *RUSSIAN NATIONAL ANTHEM* AND CONCERT FOR THE TSAR—ALBERT HALL, 18 MAY 1874

52a Sullivan. *The Russian National Anthem.* Manuscript of the full score, not signed nor dated, orchestrated by Arthur Sullivan, arranged by Joseph Barnby for use on the special occasion. Brown paper wrappers with the label: "London: Novello & Co., Ltd." Nine written pages. 35 x 27½ cm.

52b Program, Albert Hall, Monday evening, 18 May 1874.

The *Russian National Anthem* was performed at the halfway point on the entrance of the Tsar. The second half started with Arthur Sullivan conducting the chorus, unaccompanied, in two arrangements from Russian church music specially made by him for this concert:

52c Two Choruses, Novello, Ewer and Co. (1874): "Turn Thee again, O Lord" and "Mercy and truth are met together."

DON GIOVANNI.

Opera,

IN TWO ACTS,

BY

MOZART.

(WITH ITALIAN AND ENGLISH WORDS).

EDITED BY ARTHUR SULLIVAN.

BOOSEY AND CO., LONDON AND NEW YORK.

The Royal Edition of Operas, edited by Sullivan for Boosey. (31)

Tennyson to Sullivan – *The Window.* (29d)

Nov. 6th 1870

"He that sweareth to his neighbour & disappointeth him not:—
So I must consent to the publication of the songs however much against my inclination & my judgement & that I may meet your wishes as to the time of publication I must also consent to their being published this X mas however much more against my inclination & my judgement ——
provided, as I stated yesterday that the fact of their having been written four years ago & of their being published by yourself be mentioned in the preface — provided also that no one but Millais shall illustrate them

Yours very truly
A Tennyson

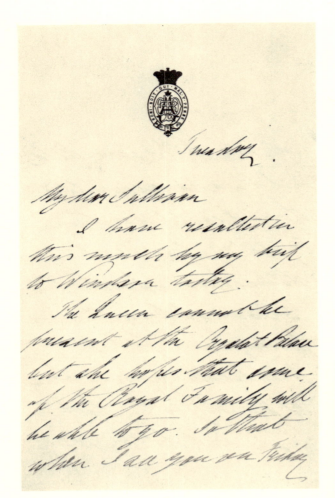

Advice from the Duke of Edinburgh (1872). (39b)

Permission from Sir Thomas Biddulph, the
Queen's Secretary. (39c)

Song, "Christmas Bells at Sea" (1874). (42a)

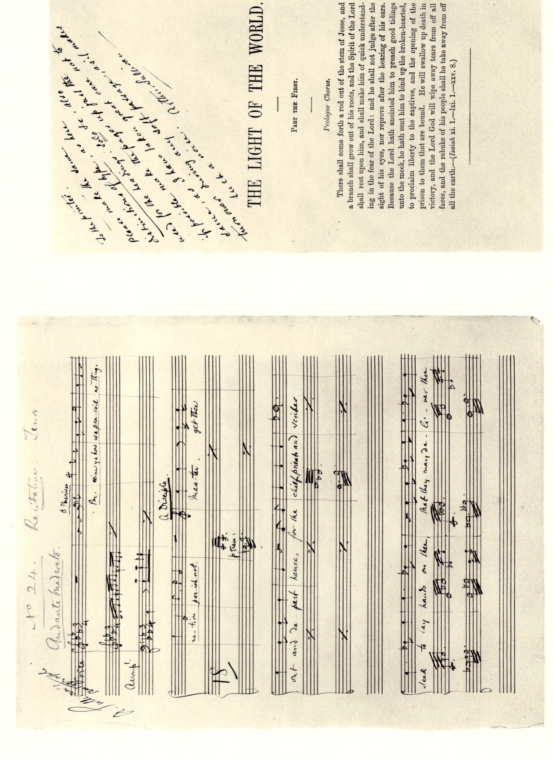

Books of Words – Sullivan's corrected proof
(1837). (40h)

No. 24, Recitative for Tenor (1873). (40d)

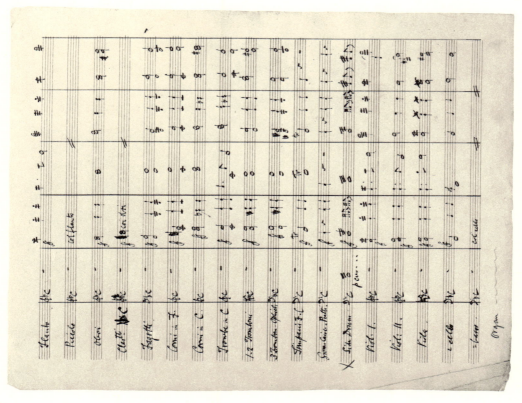

Sullivan's orchestration for the *Russian National Anthem* (1874). (52a)

The Duke of Edinburgh and Sullivan by Alfred Bryan, ca. 1870's. (35d)

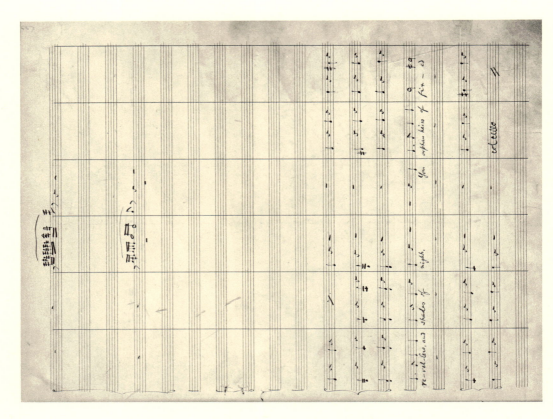

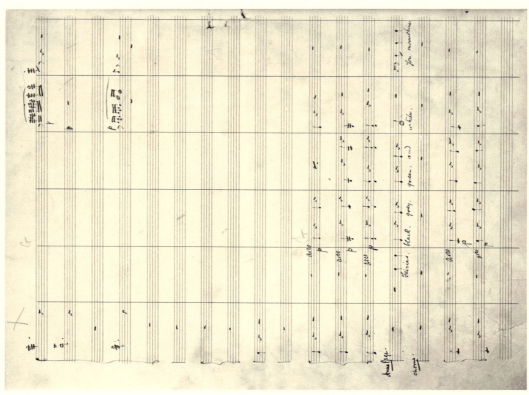

Incidental Music to *Merry Wives of Windsor* (1874). (41a)

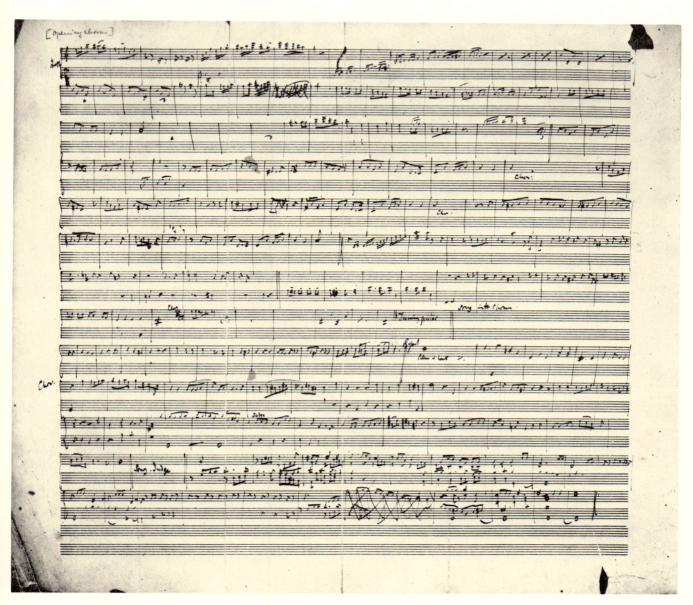

Trial by Jury, Sullivan's thematic sketches (1875). (43a)

remarkable how bright his faculties were up to the latest. I had seen him a good deal at the "Mendelssohn" Committee meetings.

How are you, old man! Thrown off some of your bothers & troubles I hope & stronger in body.

I have been producing

Some music I wrote for the "Merchant of Venice" at the Prince's Theatre here. It will be done shortly at the Crystal Palace, so I will say nothing about it. But leave you to form your own judgement. ~~so~~ These are the numbers.

Introduction
Barcarole.
Bourrée.
Grotesque dance.
Valse.
Finale.

Sullivan to J. W. Davison on *Merchant of Venice*, incidental music, 3 October 1871. (37b)

H.M.S. Pinafore, colorful early poster, ca. 1878–1879. (47j)

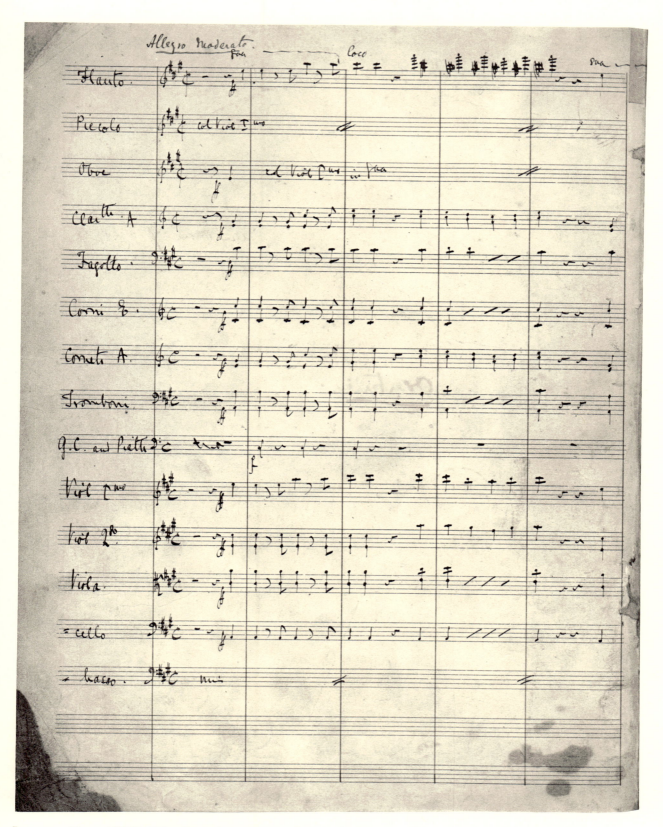

Insert to *Henry VIII*, "The Graceful Dance" (1877). (45)

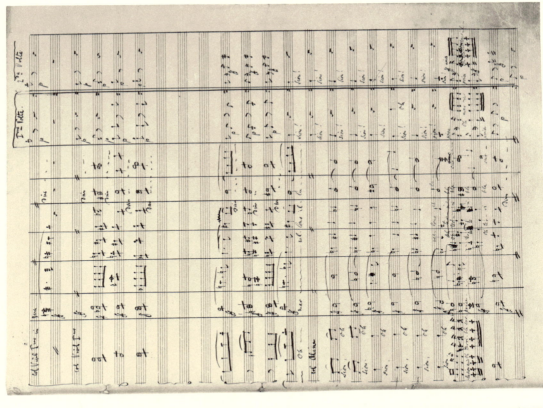

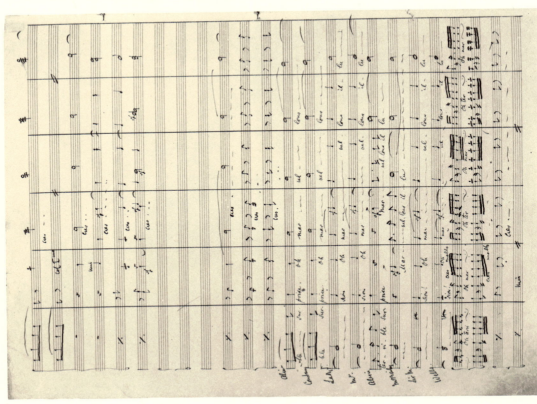

The Sorcerer, final chorus, Act I (1877). (46b)

A dance arrangement of music from *The Sorcerer*, ca. 1878. (46f)

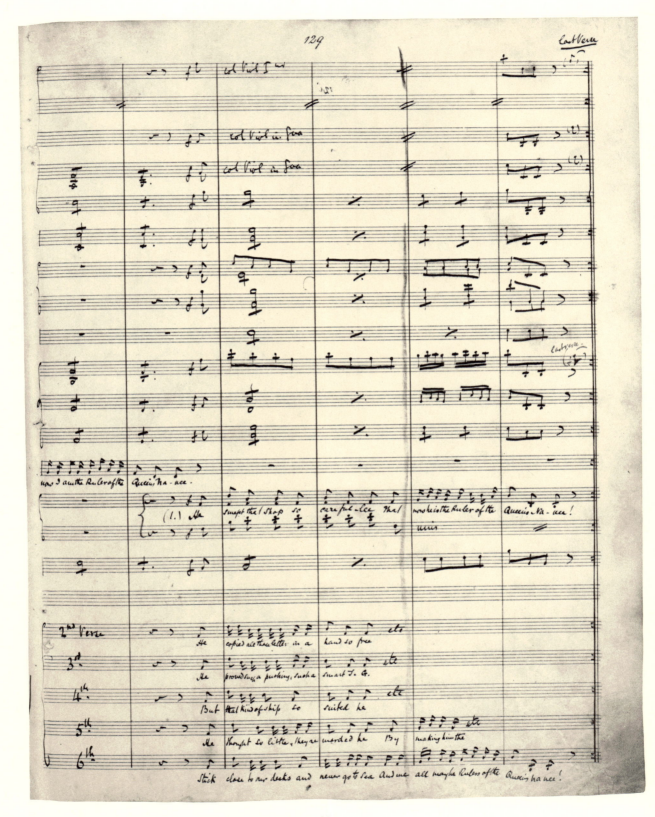

H.M.S. Pinafore, The Admiral's Song (1878). (47b)

Pinafore

24 Bolton.
27th Dec. 77.

Dear Sullivan,

I send you herewith a sketch plot of the proposed Opera. I hope & think you will like it. I called on you two days ago (not knowing that you had gone abroad) to consult you about it before drawing it up in full. I have very little doubt however but that you will be pleased with it. I should like to have talked it over with you as there is a good deal of fun in it which I haven't set down on paper. Among other things, a song (kind of "pedigree song") for the First Lord — tracing his career as office boy, clerk, traveller, junior partner & First Lord of Britain's navy. I think a splendid song can be made of this. Of course there will be no personating in this — the fact that the First Lord in the Opera is a radical of the most pronounced type will do away with any suspicion that W. H. Smith is intended. Mrs Cripps will be a capital part for Everard — I propose to have no comprimaria — & to make Hebe, the First Lord's cousin (a more important part than appears in the sketch), the contralto. Barrington will be a capital Captain, & Grossmith a first rate First Lord. The uniforms of the officers & crew will be effective — the chorus will look like sailors, & we will ask to have their uniforms made for them at Portsmouth.

I shall be very anxious to know what you think of the plot. It seems to me that there is plenty of story in it (the Sorcerer rather lacks story) with good musical situations. Josephine can have two good ballads & so can Ralph.

I hope you will have fine weather & that the change will do you a lot of good. As soon as I hear from you that the plot will do, I will set to work, sending you the first act as soon as it is finished.

Very truly yours
W S Gilbert.

Gilbert to Sullivan – The genesis of *H.M.S. Pinafore*. (47c)

up to the sticking point. They are naturally timid, but through the agency of this talisman, they are enabled to acquit themselves well. When concealed, in act 2, and the robbers approach, their courage begins to fail them (premium), but a recourse to Tarantara, has the desired effect.

I mention this that you may bear it in mind in setting the General's "Tarantara" - song - I mean that it may be treated as an important feature, & not as a mere incidental effect. I need not say that this is mere suggestion - If you don't like it, it shan't be done.

I hope your gout regained by this time.

Very truly yours
WSGilbert

---

24. THE BOLTONS,
SOUTH KENSINGTON.
6th Augt 79

My dear Sullivan

The enemy has made no further move, & I'm told that nothing can now be done till November - so I'm off today on another cruise. I shall come up on Saturday, to see Carte (who is expected on that day, & then I'm off to Trouville.

I've broken the neck of act 2 & see my way clearly to the end. I think it comes out very well.

By the way, I've made great use of the "Tarantara" business in act 2 - The police always sing "Tarantara" when they desire to work their courage

Gilbert to Sullivan – The "Tarantara" business in *The Pirates of Penzance.* (53g)

Gen.

His telling a terrible story,
But it doesn't ~~diminish~~ my story
For they would have taken my daughters
Over the billowy waters
If I hadn't, in elegant diction,
Indulged in an innocent fiction
Which is not in the same category
As a regular terrible story.

Girls, aside

His telling a terrible story
Which will tend to diminish his glory.
Though they would have taken his daughters
Over the billowy waters
It's easy in elegant diction
To call it an innocent fiction.
But it comes in the same category
As a regular terrible story.

Pirates aside:

If his telling a terrible story
He shall die by a death that is gory
One of the cruellest slaughters
That ever were known in these waters.
And we'll finish his moral affliction
By a very complete malediction
As a compliment valedictory
If his telling a terrible story!

King

Although our dark careers
Sometimes involves the crime of stealing,
We ~~are~~ rather think that we're
Not altogether void of feeling.
Although we live by strife
We're always sorry to begin it.
And what, we ask, is life
Without a touch of poetry in it?

All, Kneeling

Hail, poetry, thou heaven-born maid
Upon ~~gildest~~ ~~eeu~~
That ~~gildest~~ the Pirate's trade
Hail, flowing fount of sentiment
all hail
~~all hail~~, divine emollient!

King

You may go, for you're at liberty - our pirate rules protect you,
And honorary members of our band we do elect you!
All Hurrah!

Page 27 of Gilbert's manuscript, *The Pirates of Penzance*, Act 1 (1879). (53b)

Arthur Sullivan, May 1879, age 37. (48c)

Signature page of song, "Old Love Letters." (48a)

The Eighteen Eighties

Arthur Sullivan, 13 May 1884, age 42. (60e)

IN his creative decade of the 1880's, Sullivan concentrated on major works, particularly for the theatre: eight of the comic operas with Gilbert, *The Martyr of Antioch*, *The Golden Legend*, The *"Exhibition"* and the *"Institute"* Odes, and the *Macbeth* music. Only two anthems, one hymn, and six songs completed this ten years' work.

THE PIRATES OF PENZANCE

53a Sullivan.   Manuscript of "Short Chronological Memoranda." Page 7 (of twelve pages).

This page of Sullivan's autograph outline followed the page quoted for *The Sorcerer* and *H.M.S. Pinafore* [see No. 47a]. It started with a description of his experience in Paris as British Royal Commissioner for Music at the Exhibition. Then he described his spell of serious ill health, culminating in an operation, and weeks of rest on the Continent. On his return to London, he "wrote the 2nd Act of the 'Pirates of Penzance', left for America with Gilbert the end of October, wrote the 1st Act in New York, and produced the opera at the Fifth Avenue Theatre on New Year's Eve, with an English Company brought over by Carte . . . Returned to England in March [1880], & produced the 'Pirates' at the Opera Comique in April." In late 1879 he had received an offer from Leeds to conduct the Festival next year "and accepted it." So after launching the *Pirates* in London, "I spent much time in looking for a subject. At last settled upon Milman's poem 'The Martyr of Antioch', and began it in July. Produced at the Leeds Festival under my own direction in October."

THE GILBERT MANUSCRIPT OF ACT I

When Sullivan arrived in New York on 5 November 1879, he discovered that he had left behind his manuscript for Act I of the new opera, *Pirates of Penzance*. So he and Gilbert, in their hotel rooms between rehearsals and supervision of the first authorized American *Pinafore*, had to reconstruct the first-act libretto and musical settings from memory. This manuscript appears to be the product of their emergency work. It was found not in Gilbert's papers but in Sullivan's. That this must be *the* (or *a*) New York manuscript is suggested by such clues as the presence of the Fifth Avenue Theatre cast, in Gilbert's hand, as the *Dramatis Personae*, and the Finale in nearly identical form to that of the first American libretto. The bottom of page 27 of the manuscript is the point at which the Finale differs, lacking thirty-two lines found in the British libretto.

53b Gilbert, William Schwenck, 1836–1911. *The Pirates of Penzance*, Act I libretto. Manuscript, signed but not dated, with marginal notes in the hand of Arthur Sullivan. 31 pp. 27 x 22 cm.

Page 27 shows both collaborators at work: a tiny fragment of Sullivan's musical notation and description in the left margin—and Gilbert's four trial versions of the line "Thou gildest e'en the Pirate's trade" at the right.

53c Sullivan (libretto by W. S. Gilbert). *The Pirates of Penzance*. Manuscript of the full score, not signed nor dated. (The words on several pages in volume one have been inserted in another hand.) Green half morocco gilt. Two volumes. 492 written pages, including title. 33 x 24 cm.

The 492 written pages of this score have been bound in two volumes for convenience of conductor's use. The bulk of the work is in Sullivan's hand, both words and music. But there are a number of pages in the hand of a copyist. One such passage includes the entrance of General Stanley's daughters to the only musical element certain to have come from *Thespis*. Act I, pages 94–95, shows the closing lines of the Pirate King's Song, No. 3, "Hurrah for the Pi-rate King."

In Act 2 the music of the Pirates Chorus, "Come, friends, who plough the sea," No. 12, pages 436–437, has been sung the world over, wherever two or more Americans are gathered together, with the words "Hail, Hail the gang's all here," for more than sixty years. The origin of this piracy is so obscure as to have defied forty years of research, from Isaac Goldberg to James Fuld. Yet today, almost a century after it was written, at any performance of *The Pirates* in America the first statement of this melody in the overture will rouse murmurs and laughter of surprise recognition. It is Arthur Sullivan's contribution to American folk-music.

53d Handbill: "Royal Bijou Theatre, Paignton. For one day only, Tuesday, December 30th [1879]. An Entirely New and Original Opera. By Messrs. W. S. Gilbert and Arthur Sullivan, entitled The Pirates of Penzance, or Love and Duty, Being the first production in any country."

The gift of Miss Bridget D'Oyly Carte.

This legendary affair, held at 2 p.m. in a small theatre on the Devonshire coast, was to secure British copyright before the New York first night on 31 December. The cast was that of a *Pinafore* touring company playing in nearby Torquay.

53e The Fifth Avenue Theatre, for opening night 31 December 1879, had a small souvenir program printed on silk (both white and plum-colored copies exist) in addition to the standard tabloid-size house programs. These carried the line: "On the Opening Night the Orchestra will be conducted by Mr. Arthur Sullivan."

The gift of Miss Bridget D'Oyly Carte.

53f Opera Comique Program, printed on fringed silk.

This was used, presumably, at the opening night in London, 3 April 1880. Although the composer conducted on that occasion, there was no mention of this fact in either the silk or paper programs. Alice Barnett and Jessie Bond were missing from the cast as they were still performing in America.

53g Gilbert, W. S., 1836–1911. Als, 24, The Boltons, South Kensington [London], 6 August 1879, to Sullivan. 2pp.

After Sullivan's long summer of illness, and Gilbert's involvement in the legal activities of their Directors as well as working hard at the new opera, he wrote this friendly status report. "I've broken the neck of Act 2 & see my way clearly to the end. I think it comes out very well. By the way, I've made great use of the 'Tarantara' business in Act 2 – The police always say 'Tarantara' when they desire to work their courage up to the sticking point . . . I mention this that you may bear it in mind in setting the General's 'Tarantara', song, I mean that it may be treated as an important feature . . . I need not say that this is merely *suggestion* – If you don't like it, it shan't be done." Fortunately Sullivan must have voted no "Tarantaras" for the General.

53h "*The Pirates of Penzance* Galop," by Charles D'Albert, on Arthur Sullivan's Opera, Chappell & Co., plate no. 17096.

53i "*The Pirates of Penzance* Lancers," by Charles D'Albert, on Arthur Sullivan's Opera, Chappell & Co., plate no. 17065.

53j *The Pirates of Penzance*, one-sheet poster, Grand Theatre, Leeds, commencing Monday, 19 September [1898], Nassau Steam Press. 30 x 20 inches.

THE TRIUMVIRATE IN *VANITY FAIR* CARICATURE

54a Arthur Sullivan, on 14 March 1874, was earliest of the three to be widely recognized as a public figure, and so was drawn by Carlo Pellegrini, "Ape" (1839–1889), the originator of the *Vanity Fair* caricature series.

54b W. S. Gilbert, on 21 May 1881, following the transcendent success of his first comic operas, was drawn by Pellegrini's successor, Leslie Ward, "Spy" (1851–1922), after the opening of *Patience* at the Opera Comique.

54c Richard D'Oyly Carte, on 14 February 1891, achieved the same limelight, independent of G. & S., for a caricature by "Spy," at the time of the grand opening of his greatest venture, the Royal English Opera House at Cambridge Circus.

THE TRIUMVIRATE'S FIRST AGREEMENT

54d On Opera Comique letterhead, dated 17 May 1880, D'Oyly Carte sent this copy of a simple two-page agreement to Sullivan, with "Duplicate sent to Gilbert" written across the top. "Dear Gilbert and Sullivan," he began, "I agree to the terms and conditions of your note of assignment of yesterday, namely to pay to you two thousand nine hundred pounds (£2,900) (one half to be paid at Christmas 1880 and the remaining at Midsummer 1881) you assigning to me in consideration thereof the sole right of representation of your operas the Pirates of Penzance, the Pinafore, and the Sorcerer in Great Britain and Ireland out of London . . . R. D'Oyly Carte. To Messrs. W. S. Gilbert and Arthur Sullivan."

THE MARTYR OF ANTIOCH

How to succeed . . .

> "If you wish in the world to advance,
>   Your merits you're bound to enhance,
>   You must stir it, and stump it, and blow your own trumpet. . . ."

The words are those of W. S. Gilbert. The man who set them to music in 1887, having years before taken them to heart, was Arthur Sullivan. Two letters and a telegram tell this success story.

55a Sullivan. Letter "copy" (written by Walter Smythe, secretary to Sullivan), 9 Albert Mansions [London], 1 October 1880, to H.R.H. The Prince of Wales. 3pp.

"I am emboldened by the kindness your Royal Highness has shewn me to crave a great favour. I have completed my new sacred work 'The Martyr of Antioch' which is to be produced at the Leeds Festival the week after next, & there remains but one page to be printed: viz—the Dedication. May I be permitted to crown my work by including on it the name of Her Royal Highness The Princess of Wales? I would not venture to ask for this privilege, were it not that this is the most important work I have done for some years, and so far as I can judge, the best."

55b Knollys, Sir Francis. Telegram, Abergeldie Castle, Balmoral, [n.d.—October 1880], to Arthur Sullivan. 1p.

"I am desired by the Princess of Wales to say she has much pleasure in accepting the dedication of your new work." Sir Francis Knollys was Private Secretary to Edward for forty years, from Prince of Wales through his reign as Edward VII. Abergeldie Castle, in Edward's biographer Sir Sidney Lee's Edwardian prose, was lent by the Queen to the Prince of Wales "for his autumnal occupation."

55c Ponsonby, Sir Henry F. Als, Windsor Castle, 9 December 1880, to A. Sullivan. 1p.

". . . [I]t has given The Queen much pleasure to receive the copy of the 'Martyr of Antioch' and Her Majesty desires her best thanks to be returned to you. . . ."

55d Grove, Sir George, 1820–1900. Als, Lower Sydenham, S.E., 19 October 1880, to Sullivan. 8pp.

Only so close, knowledgable, and sensitive a friend as George Grove could have (or would have) written this letter, combining, as it did, both detailed criticism and enthusiastic praise: The codas of two of the numbers needed extending; Margarita's words at one point were not strong enough to warrant the shout of "Blasphemy"; the introduction was too light; Margarita's first scene was (too) splendid and important—"it makes her subsequent solo sound like an anticlimax!" And—"*How beautiful her first solo is!*—the expression and sentiment, and suitability of the music to the words *could not by any possibility be better*. and the music was so lovely to hear—the beautiful modulations and the cleverness of the escapes—that really I could hardly contain myself now and then."

55e Milman, William H. Als, 15, Cornwall Gardens, Queen's Gate, S.W. [London], February 1880, to Sullivan. 5pp.

In his selection of Henry Hart Milman (1791–1868), Sullivan must have called on his memory-bank as an editor of hymns. Milman, who became Dean of St. Paul's, was an intellectual of such scope that serious dramatic poems like "The Martyr of Antioch" (1822), translations of Sanskrit verse, biography, and history all flowed from him. He had died in 1868. This letter was written by his oldest son, William H. Milman, to express family appreciation that Sullivan had found in "The Martyr" a suitable subject for his Cantata: "We rejoice to think that others are as sensible to the beauty of the Poetry as we are. And we know enough of your well deserved reputation as a musician to be sure that what you do will be well done."

55f Sullivan. *The Martyr of Antioch* (Die Märtyrerin von Antiochien). Full score, London: Chappell & Co. Limited [1899], printed by C. G. Röder, Leipzig. Red half morocco gilt, marbled edges. Title, bl., dedic., bl., [1]–[2], text 3–257pp. 32 x 24 cm. Plate no. 20503.

The vocal score of the Sacred Musical Drama was published by Chappell in 1880, a piano-forte arrangement by Eugene D'Albert, son of the G. & S. dance music arranger Charles D'Albert, who had been a pupil of Sullivan's at the National Training School. A full orchestra score was printed for Chappell in 1899 by C. G. Röder in Leipzig, with both English and German texts. Margarita's first solo, No. 7, "For Thou didst die for me, oh Son of God!", was particularly praised by George Grove in the accompanying letter to Sullivan [see No. 55d].

55g Henschel, Sir George, 1850–1934. Original cartoon, "Arthur Antioch, Lord of Penzance," dated 22 October 1880, signed. 18 x 11½ cm.

This excellent profile pen-and-ink sketch, signed "G.H.", shows Sullivan with monocle and rather exaggerated sideburns. The artist was a man of prodigious accomplishment: a very successful concert singer (bass); a symphony orchestra conductor of such distinction that he became the first conductor of the Boston Symphony; a composer of many works, especially for voice; an artist who at the age of eighty-four had an exhibition of his paintings. George V knighted him in 1914 [see No. 75].

55h Sullivan, Herbert, 1868–1928. Als, 1, Queen's Mansions, 31 March 1901, to Sir Frederick Bridge. 1p.

Three months after Sullivan's death, his nephew wrote Sir Frederick Bridge—organist of Westminster Abbey, friend and pallbearer of Arthur Sullivan—to send him a few mementos: a manuscript of an anthem, a photograph, and the baton, "the one he [Sullivan] used at the 1st performance of the 'Martyr of Antioch.'"

55i Sullivan's Baton: inscribed—"The 'Martyr of Antioch' Leeds. Oct: 1880." Tapering wooden shaft, 18½ inches long, weight 1½ oz., with black silk wrist-cord.

It was a most fortunate downbeat of coincidence that conducted this baton to the Morgan Library, to be joined a few years later by the very archive of memorabilia from which Herbert Sullivan had removed it a half-century earlier.

55j Sullivan. A presentation cup to Sir W. S. Gilbert: George III, the bell-shaped body lobed and embossed at a later date with floral and foliate scrolls and two rustic figures on either side of the inscribed cartouche, with fluted and gadroon-bordered pedestal foot, the interior gilt, by Wakelin and Garrard, 1793. 8¾ inches high, 16 oz. 16 dwt.
Loaned by John Wolfson.

The inscription: "W. S. Gilbert from his friend Arthur Sullivan. Leeds Festival 1880. The Martyr of Antioch."

55k Gilbert, W. S., 1836–1911. Letter, a pencil "copy," The Boltons, South Kensington, 3 December 1880, to Sullivan. 2pp.

This pencil copy of Gilbert's letter to Sullivan thanked him for the silver chalice, the composer's gift for Gilbert's help with *The Martyr* libretto. It was copied in the hand of Nancy McIntosh, Gilbert's adopted daughter, on Grim's Dyke stationery, probably some fifteen years after Gilbert's death. Perhaps it was made at the request of Herbert Sullivan, who might have needed it for the biography of his uncle, where it is quoted in full. "It most certainly never occurred to me," wrote Gilbert, graciously, "to look for any other reward than the honour of being associated, however remotely & unworthily, in a success which, I suppose, will endure until music itself shall die."

PATIENCE

When Gilbert first conceived the plot of *Patience* he made use of his *Bab Ballad* "The Rival Curates." Then, as explained in this 1 November 1880 letter to his collaborator, he switched from clergymen to aesthetes for safer lampooning.

56a Gilbert, William Schwenck, 1836–1911. Als, 24, The Boltons [London], 1 November 1880, to Sullivan. 3pp.

"I want to see you particularly about the new piece. Although it is about two thirds finished, I don't feel comfortable about it . . . I want to revert to my old idea of rivalry between two aesthetic fanatics, instead of a couple of clergymen worshipped by a chorus of female devotees. I can get much more fun out of the subject as I propose to alter it . . . The Hussars will become aesthetic young men . . . they will all carry lilies in their hands, wear long hair & stained glass attitude . . . P.S. Let us meet to talk over the proposed change."

56b Program for *Patience*, Opera Comique, 23 April 1881 [first night]. 4pp. 25½ x 19 cm.

56c Program for *Patience*, Savoy Theatre, 10 October 1881 [opening night]. 4pp. 19½ x 12½ cm.

The pale red decorations on page 1 [No. 56b] distinguish this first-night program for *Patience* from later Opera Comique programs; also the disclosure that "On Saturday, April 23rd, there will be *no first piece.* . . ."

When the Savoy Theatre opened a half-year later, *Patience* was moved from the Opera Comique to launch the new house. On the front page of this small yellow program [No. 56c] is printed: "On Monday, October 10, 1881. Being the opening of the New Savoy Theatre at 8.30 . . . The National Anthem will be sung by the entire Company." Inside on page [3] appears the line: "On this occasion the Performance will be conducted by the Composer."

56d Sullivan, and W. S. Gilbert. *Patience; or, Bunthorne's Bride.* Vocal score, arranged from the full score by Berthold Tours, London: Chappell & Co. [1881]. Turquoise cloth boards with appropriately "aesthetic" blind and gilt-blocked decoration. 117pp. 28 x 22½ cm.

The title page states: "An Entirely New and Original Aesthetic Opera in two acts. . . ."

56e Wilde, Oscar, 1854–1900. Als, Keats House, Tite Street, Chelsea [London], [n.d.—ca. early April 1881], to Grossmith. 4pp.

It is not surprising to find that Oscar Wilde was a fan of Gilbert & Sullivan, as this letter certainly attests. "Dear Grossmith – I should like to go to the First Night of your new opera at Easter [falling on 17 April 1881, this was one week ahead of the opening]—and would be very much obliged if you would ask the box office to reserve a three guinea box for me, if there is one to be had . . . With Gilbert and Sullivan I am sure one will have something better than the dull farce of the Colonel. I am looking forward to being greatly amused." Wilde's reference to F. C. Burnand's *The Colonel*, a farce that had preceded *Patience* in satirizing aestheticism, was an indication of how *Punch* editor Burnand and *Fun* contributor Gilbert came to such bitter rivalry.

56f "*Patience* Lancers," by Charles D'Albert, on Arthur Sullivan's Opera Comique, London: Chappell & Co. [n.d.], plate no. 17183.

56g "*Patience* Polka," by Charles D'Albert, on Arthur Sullivan's Opera Comique, London: Chappell & Co. [n.d.], plate no. 17188.

56h "*Patience* Quadrille," by Charles D'Albert, on Arthur Sullivan's Opera Comique, London: Chappell & Co. [n.d.], plate no. 17181.

IOLANTHE

57a Sullivan [?]. Manuscript, not signed nor dated, of diary data for the year 1882 (1 January–9 December). Page 6 (of six pages).

Scrawled faintly at the top of page 1 of these diary entries are the words "The dark year." Indeed 1882 brought the death of his mother, the return of his painful illness, and the loss of his savings through a friend's bankruptcy. "Nov. 25 (Sat.) Received letter from E. A. Hall saying he was ruined & my money lost, just before starting for the theatre. 1st Performance of Iolanthe at the Savoy Theatre. House crammed. Awfully nervous. More so than usual on going into the orchestra. Tremendous reception. 1st Act went splendidly, the 2nd dragged & I was afraid it must be compressed. However, it finished well & Gilbert & myself were called & heartily cheered."

57b Gladstone, Sir William E., 1809–1898. Als, 10, Downing Street, 6 December 1882, to "My dear Sir" [Sullivan]. 2pp.

"I must thankfully acknowledge the great pleasure which the entertainment gave me. Nothing, I thought, could be happier than the manner in which the comic strain of the piece was blended with its harmonies of sight & sound, so good in taste and so admirable in execution from beginning to end."

TEN COLORFUL AMERICAN TRANSCRIPTIONS

In England Chappell & Co. published the standard vocal score of *Iolanthe* in 1882, arranged for pianoforte by Berthold Tours. The opera was performed in America, nearly simultaneously with its London opening, under the baton of Alfred Cellier. Although complete vocal scores were immediately available, this colorful example was published in Boston five years later, the work of Ernst Perabo (1845–1920).

57c *Iolanthe*, ten transcriptions for the piano by Ernst Perabo [from Sullivan's music], Op. 14, Boston, 1887. Geo. H. Walker & Co., Lith., Boston. 83pp. 34½ x 27 cm.

Ernst Perabo had studied in Leipzig with the same masters only a few years after Sullivan's student days. He had then moved to Boston, where (according to *Grove*) he enjoyed a distinguished career as performer and composer, especially of concert transcriptions. In a letter dated 15 October 1894, he wrote to Sullivan: "My very dear Friend ... Ten years ago last July I had the honor of playing to you my arrangements from 'Iolanthe' & was overjoyed when I heard of your kindly expressed satisfaction."

57d "*Iolanthe* Lancers," by Charles D'Albert, on Arthur Sullivan's Opera, London: Chappell & Co. [n.d.], plate no. 17647.

57e "*Iolanthe* Waltz," by Charles D'Albert, on Arthur Sullivan's Opera, London: Chappell & Co. [n.d.], plate no. 17657.

THE FIRST G. & S. CONTRACT

58 *Memorandum of Agreement*, 8 February 1883, signed by Gilbert, Sullivan and D'Oyly Carte. 3pp. 39½ x 25 cm.

This is the composer's copy of the famous triumvirate agreement which, on renewal, caused serious disagreement in 1890. In it Gilbert and Sullivan granted D'Oyly Carte for five years and thirty-one days—25 November 1882 to 25 December 1887—sole right of representation and performance of *Iolanthe* and also each and every opera theretofore written and composed and which would be thereafter written and composed jointly by Gilbert and Sullivan during said term. Carte agreed to pay each, Gilbert and Sullivan, one-third of the net profits earned by the representations after deducting all expenses and charges of producing the said operas and of all the performances of the same including: £4000 rental per annum of the Savoy, all expenses of lighting and repairs incidental to performances. . . . It was in this area of deductible expenses that Gilbert and Carte had their long, bitter battle.

KNIGHTHOOD

Arthur Sullivan's name would have led all the rest in a certain Golden Book other than Leigh Hunt's—a list of those most likely to be knighted. By 1880 it was just a question of when the honor could be conferred without seeming to stress his close friendship with the royal family. The ideal answer was to honor three distinguished men of music at the same time, the "three musical knights," as Arthur once dubbed them: George Grove (age sixty-three), G. A. Macfarren (age seventy), and Sullivan (age forty-one). They received the accolade from Queen Victoria at Windsor on 22 May 1883.

59a Gladstone, Sir William E., 1809–1898. Als, 10 Downing Street, Whitehall, 3 May 1883, to Arthur Sullivan. 2pp.

"I have the pleasure to inform you that I am permitted by Her Majesty to propose that you should receive the honor of Knighthood, in recognition of your distinguished talents as a composer and of the services which you have rendered to the promotion of the Art of Music generally in this country. I hope it may be agreeable to you to accept the proposal. Wm. Gladstone."

59b Sullivan. Letter "copy" [by Walter Smythe, secretary to Sullivan], 1 Queen's Mansions [London], 5 May 1883, to "Rt. Hon: W. E. Gladstone, M.P." 2pp.

"The honour which Her Majesty graciously desires to confer upon me, is, if possible enhanced by the kind and flattering terms in which you communicate the proposal to me. I can only say that I am grateful for, and humbly accept this mark of Her Majesty's favour. . . ."

PRINCESS IDA

60a Sullivan [?]. Manuscript, not signed nor dated, of diary data for the year 1884 (4 January – 18 November). Page 1 (of five pages).

"Difficulties / Jan. 4. Full dress rehearsal (Princess Ida) 6.30 to 2.30 a.m. I had a slight stiff neck.—acute muscular rheumatism of head & neck—dreadful pain. Morphine injected—no good. Jan. 5 Resolved to conduct first performance of new opera at night but from state I was in it seemed hopeless. At 7 p.m. had another strong hyperdermic injection to ease the pain & a strong cup of black coffee to keep me awake—managed to get up & dressed & drove to the theatre more dead than alive. Went into the orchestra at 8.10 Tremendous house—usual reception. After the performance I turned faint & could not stand—was brought home by Smythe, Cellier, Carte etc. & put to bed in dreadful pain. Ill for over a week." At the bottom of this page Sullivan wrote on 29 January: "Told Carte of my resolve not to write any more 'Savoy' pieces."

60b Two programs for *Princess Ida; or, Castle Adamant*, composed by Arthur Sullivan, written by W. S. Gilbert, Savoy Theatre, Saturday evening, 5 January 1884. Orange program, without mention of Cellier but including the composer as conducting; lavender program, with mention of Cellier. 4pp. each. 20 x 13 cm.

From Sullivan's description of his condition, there was little wonder that D'Oyly Carte did not expect him to conduct, although there were programs already printed [like the orange example] stating "The Opera will be conducted on this Occasion by the Composer." So he rushed through a second run of programs for the same date—5 January 1884—omitting this line and replacing it with "Musical Director, Mr. Frank Cellier."

60c Gilbert, William Schwenck, 1836–1911. Als, Eastbury, nr. Watford, Herts., 22 September 1883, to Sullivan. 2pp.

"Dear Sullivan, Here is Act 1. finished. I have made certain alterations in the first two or three numbers—I think you will say they are improvements," wrote Gilbert. He continued, "Don't you think the Act might end with 'Oh dainty triolet &c.' followed by the departure of the princes, Arac, Guron, & Scynthius breaking from their captors to rush after Hilarian, Cyril & Florian—to be recaptured at once, as the Act drop falls, this business to be without words, & done to symphony? It would make a good picture, I think."

60d Sullivan, and W. S. Gilbert. *Princess Ida; or, Castle Adamant*. Vocal score, arrangement for pianoforte by George Lowell Tracy (of Boston, U.S.A.), London: Chappell & Co. [n.d.]. Original printed grey wrappers. Title, [2]–134, 2 advt. pp. 28 x 22 cm. Plate no. 17,871.

The copyright notice is in Tracy's name, Stoddart & Co., Philadelphia, U.S.A. Presentation inscription on the title page: "Mrs. Hay Ritchie from Arthur Sullivan." On the front wrapper is the signature: "H. H. Ritchie."

60e Sullivan. Photograph, profile, signed and dated: "Arthur Sullivan 13 May. 1884." Taken by Levitskij [n.p.]. 16 x 10 cm. [See page 103.]

60f "*Princess Ida* Valse," by P. Bucalossi, arranged from G. L. Tracy's vocal score, 1884. London: Chappell & Co. Plate no. 17887.

60g Poster for *Princess Ida*. Clement-Smith & C⁰ʸ Lith. London
30 x 24 inches.

Featuring Princess Ida's brothers, "warriors three, sons of Gama Rex," properly armed, armoured, and bearded. The performance advertised was by one of the D'Oyly Carte Touring Companies, playing The Grand Theatre, Leeds, Monday, 19 September [1891].

QUARREL ONE—1884

61a Sullivan.   Als "copy," Légation d'Angleterre, Brussels, 28 March 1884, to Carte. 2pp.

". . . [Y]ou give me formal notice, that you may require a new Opera in six months time . . . it is impossible for me to do another piece of the character of those already written by Gilbert and myself. The reason for this decision I can give you verbally when we meet . . . P.S. I have not written to Gilbert as I much prefer talking it out with him." (Carte did not help matters by going directly to Gilbert.)

61b Gilbert.   Als, 19 Harrington Gardens [London], 30 March 1884, to Sullivan. 3pp.

"I learnt from Carte, yesterday, to my unbounded surprise, that you do not intend to write any more operas of the class with which you & I have been so long identified. I scarcely know how to deal with such an announcement, coming as it does, through a third person. You are, of course, aware that by our agreement, entered into on the 8 Feb. 1883 & extending over five years, we are bound to supply Carte . . . In all the pieces we have written together I have invariably subordinated my views to your own . . . I am, therefore, absolutely at a loss to account for the decision . . . which I hope & believe, your good feeling & strong sense of justice will induce you, on reconsideration, to recall."

61c Gilbert.   Als, Savoy Theatre / 19 Harrington Gardens, 3 May 1884, to Sullivan. 2pp.

"Your letter has caused me the gravest disappointment . . . you wish me to construct a piece which shall not deal with the supernatural or improbable . . . the time has arrived when I must state—& I do so with great reluctance—that I cannot consent to construct another plot for the next opera."

61d Sullivan. Als "copy," 1 Queen's Mansions [London], 4 May 1884, to
Gilbert. 1p.

"The tone of your letter convinces me that your decision is final and therefore further discussion is useless. I regret it very much."

61e Gilbert. Als, 19 Harrington Gardens, 8 May 1884, to Sullivan. 3pp.

"... [I]n your letter of the 6th ... in requiring me to construct another plot in which the supernatural element shall not occur, you are practically doing the very thing that you admit it would distress you to do ... [requiring] constructing plots 'on approval'? Or am I to understand that if I construct another plot in which no supernatural element occurs, you will undertake to set it? Of course I mean a consistent plot, free from anachronisms, constructed in perfect good faith & to the best of my ability."

Sullivan's letter of 6 May referred to by Gilbert in the above is missing, as is a *second* Gilbert letter of 8 May which had aroused Sullivan's "inexpressible relief."

61f Sullivan. Als, 1 Queen's Mansions [London], 8 May 1884, to
Gilbert. 3pp.

"Your letter of today is an inexpressible relief to me, as it clearly shews me that you, equally with myself are loth to discontinue the collaboration ... Your proposal to write a piece without the supernatural or improbable elements ... I gladly undertake ... without further discussing the matter...."

61g Gilbert. Als, 19 Harrington Gardens [London], 9 May 1884, to
Sullivan. 3pp.

"Thanks for your letter which quite settles the matter ... The old plot took so firm a hold on me that ... I should do well to wait (say) a month before setting to work ... Do you object to this?"

THE MIKADO

62a Sullivan [?]. Manuscript, not signed nor dated, of diary data for the year
1885 (17 January – 25 July). Page 1 (of three pages).

In a few words, Sullivan gave ample evidence of his working pressure: "Feb 21–Mar 1. All these days writing & rehearsing (Mikado) no drives, parties or recreation of any kind. Mar 3. Worked all night at Finale 1st Act, finished at 5 a.m. 63 pages of score at one sitting! [Mar.] 6. Finished scoring 2nd Act at 5.45 a.m. (Sat. morn.). [Mar.] 13. was to have dined at Lord De La Warr's to meet Prince of Wales, but had to go to full dress rehearsal, so couldn't. Very good except for Grossmith who was ill nervous. [Mar.] 14. New Opera 'The

Mikado' or The Town of Titipu' produced at Savoy Theatre with every sign of real success —a most brilliant house. tremendous reception All went very well except Grossmith whose nervousness nearly upset the piece. A treble encore for 'Three little maids' & 'The flowers that bloom in the Spring.' "

62b Sullivan (libretto by W. S. Gilbert).   *Mikado*. Full score, in English, [Leipzig: Bosworth & Co., 1893]. Original tan printed wrappers, loosely bound into red cloth covered card. No title page, 3–333, 1 bl. pp. 34 x 27½ cm.

The Germans had published the first full score of *H.M.S. Pinafore*, ca. 1882–1884 [see No. 47e]. Roughly ten years later, ca. 1893, they were also first with a full score of *The Mikado*. It was published without title page and had neither imprint nor date; but it was in fact the work of Bosworth & Co. of Leipzig, in an edition believed to have numbered only seventy-five copies.

Unlike the German *Pinafore*, "Amor an Bord," in which the text was German, this Bosworth *Mikado* had the words only in English, lithographed, not from type but in a cursive script. Since the original Sullivan manuscript of this opera was published in a facsimile edition (Gregg, 1968), it was possible for Sullivan scholar John Wolfson to compare this German score with the original. In his words, the Bosworth *Mikado* was set from Sullivan's autograph score (which must have been loaned for the purpose), note for note and mistake for mistake; it is identical. It also includes the additional scoring for the "encore" to "Flowers that bloom in the Spring" which exists in no published edition.

62c William, Prince of Prussia, 1859–1941.   Als, Potsdam, 3 June 1886, to "Sir" [Sullivan]. 3pp.

Evidence of the complete Anglo-Saxon tie stemming from the Hanover line through the family of Queen Victoria: this letter in style of penmanship as well as colloquial English could have been written by any well-educated Briton, and not necessarily by "William Prince of Prussia." The Prince, who was to become Kaiser Wilhelm II within two years, had been ill and so unable to attend the production of *The Mikado* which was viewed by his parents and sisters. "I hope that for the arrival of the Crown Prince they will have 'polished up the handle of the big front door', for he might have been a Roosian, etc., but he is a Proosian." (This "Crown Prince" became Kaiser Frederick III for one hundred days in the spring of 1888, and, on his death, from June of that year began the ill-starred reign of Sullivan's Potsdam Savoyard.)

ITALIAN PROMPT-COPY, *IL MIKADO*

62d [Gilbert, W. S.] *Il Mikado, Prosa*. Manuscript, in an unknown hand, of "Operetta in 2 Atti. Musica del Maestro Artura Sullivan. Traduzione dall'Inglese di Gustavo Macchi. Riduzione di Francesco Goirgono. Roma 26 Settembre 1899." Brown card covers. Title, 44pp., last page with pencil jottings. 32½ x 22 cm.

This colorful relic shows the wear of hard use, indicating that at the turn of the century G. & S. could attract audiences in the land of Verdi. Note the absence of Gilbert's name as the source of Sig. Macchi's translation. The title-page cover and its verso (the Dramatis Personae page) carry dated ink-stamps of permissions to perform (much like visas on a passport). Roma, Palermo, Napoli, Venetia, and Cremona are readily identifiable for performances between 1899 and 1901, the year in which Verdi died.

62e Sullivan. *Il Mikado*. Vocal score, "Opera Comica in Due Atti di W. S. Gilbert, Musica di Arturo Sullivan, Translated by Gustavo Macchi." G. Ricordi & C.: Milano-Roma-Napoli-Palermo [n.d.] Color-lithographed covers of "Three Little Maids." Title page, imprint, D.P., index [i]–[iv], 1–229pp. Overture, pp. 1–13, plate no. 102120–21. Text, pp. 14–229, plate no. 102120. 28 x 21½ cm.

MUSIK FÜR ALLE—*DER MIKADO*

62f Sullivan. *Der Mikado*, von Arthur Sullivan, verlag Ullstein & Co., Berlin u Wien, copyright 1912. Sheet music with pictorial (photograph) cover, an article "Sullivan und sein 'Mikado', von Dr. Bogumil Zepler" (pp. 1–2), and selections for voice and piano, pp. 3–20. Plate no. M.F.A.97.

In this popular "Gems from Mikado," pages 8–9 show "No. 3. Drei kleine Mädchen, eins, zwei, drei / Frisch wie die Küchlein aus dem Ei / Gab Man uns aus der Schule frei / Da sind wir all drei!"

ORIGINAL CABINET PHOTOGRAPHS

62g Rutland Barrington as "Pooh-Bah," Barraud's of Liverpool [n.d.].

62h Rosina Brandram as "Katisha," Barraud's of Liverpool [n.d.].

62i George Grossmith as "Ko-Ko," Barraud's of Liverpool [n.d.].

62j "Three Little Maids": Sybil Grey as "Peep-Bo," Leonora Braham as "Yum-Yum," Jessie Bond as "Pitti-Sing," Barraud, Oxford Street, London [n.d.].

62k Jessie Bond's Christmas card, "Xmas 1885." Lithographed.
11½ x 17½ cm.

> "One little maiden, all unwary,
> Fled from a ladies' seminary
> Changed to a sort of Jap'nese fairy
> By wizards of Savoy
>
> This little maid call'd Pitti-Sing
> Flies to you now on Fancy's wing
> And this is the message she would bring
> Peace, Happiness & Joy."

62l Currier & Ives. "Three Little Maids," lithograph, ca. 1885.
27 x 21½ inches.

During the "*Pinafore* craze" of 1879, ever topical Currier & Ives had three different comic lithographs based on that G. & S. opera. So, in 1885–1886, when "Three Little Maids" became a nationwide pirated "trademark" for every conceivable use, of course C. & I. was there with a large lithographed portrait of the three actresses who played in the first recognized American company: Kate Forster, "Pitti-Sing"; Geraldine Ulmar, "Yum-Yum"; and Geraldine St. Maur as "Peep-Bo."

CALIFORNIA BOUND:
"I WISH I COULD SEE A BUFFALO."

62m Sullivan. Als, pencil, written "on the train—just left Galesburg—(Chicago, Burlington & Quincy R.R.)," 13 & 14 July [1885], to [Mrs. Ronalds]. 6pp.

The only surviving letter from Sullivan to Mrs. Ronalds gave her an effete young Englishman's description of his Lewis and Clark rigors. "It isn't very easy to write in the train," he commented, as the Pennsylvania Railroad swirled him through the Alleghanies to Chicago, where "I drove about the town a little & saw that it was new, handsome & bustling, and from my point of view utterly uninteresting." En route, Chicago to Denver: "The dining car on this line is not so good as on the Pennsylvania Road, & the hours for meals barbaric. —Breakfast at 7. Dinner from 11.30 to 12.30! & supper 5 to 7. Oh Cadogen Place! [Mrs. Ronalds' flat] Oh Queen's Mansions! [A.S.'s flat]." Nebraska: "We have now got beyond the limit of dining cars & have begun to have meals at the eating stations. We have just had what they call a meal at Lincoln the capitol of Nebraska [there followed a horrendous description, closing with 'a glass of iced tea! At least they called it tea but it must have been made from prairie grass. We were in a temperance house again!'] . . . It is blazing hot, and we are passing over plains covered with corn . . . it is not the prairies proper, but it is very

The Eighteen Eighties

close to them . . . I wish I could see a buffalo." And near the close, a faint wisp of sentiment: "5000 miles from you, I am going 2000 further . . . I am quite homesick . . . God bless you all, Yr loving A." The closing instruction, "Give this letter to Smythe [his secretary]," accounts for its survival as well as for its lack of intimacy.

SULLIVAN'S CURTAIN SPEECH AT *THE MIKADO* GALA

62n Sullivan. Manuscript of a speech (made onstage in New York, *Mikado*, 1885), not signed nor dated, written on stationery with the initials "CS" [Charlotte Sullivan Hutchinson, sister-in-law to Sullivan]. 5 written pages on 3 double-folded leaves.

"Although I have made it a rule through my life, never to address the public when I appear before them in an artistic capacity, I am impelled to break through my rule tonight by the kind reception you have given to my friend Mr. Gilbert's and my work. . . ." He paid compliment to "the extraordinary energy of our good friend & colleague Mr. D'Oyly Carte" and to "the talented ladies and gentlemen who form this Company." He stressed that they brought the audience the authentic work and not "a spurious imitation . . . patched up from a pianoforte arrangement." "Tonight," he continued, "you see our work exactly as we intended it should be performed. The Company rehearsed for weeks in London at the Savoy Theatre, and then at 48 hours notice only, sailed for New York. . . ."

62o Cabinet photograph of Geraldine Ulmar as "Yum-Yum" taken by Falk, New York City, copyright 1886. 17 x 11 cm.

62p Cabinet photograph of "Three Little Maids": (l. to r.) Geraldine St. Maur as "Peep-Bo," Geraldine Ulmar as "Yum-Yum," and Kate Forster as "Pitti-Sing," taken by Falk, New York City (the first cast at the Fifth Avenue Theatre). 17 x 11 cm.

THE MIKADO IN TRADECARD ADVERTISING

62q In 1885–1886, *The Mikado* in America was ruthlessly exploited for countless advertisable products of every conceivable sort. The "Three Little Maids" became a universal trademark, in most instances using the actual likenesses of Misses Forster, Ulmar, and St. Maur. A random selection of tradecards of the day shows "Pitti-Sing," "Yum-Yum," and "Peep-Bo" advertising spool silk, dental cream, soap, cotton thread, Waterbury watches, and corsets. "Katisha" and "Ko-Ko" feature J. & P. Coats thread. "The Mikado" sold Lautz Bros. "Pure & Healthy Soap"; and he had a kerosene stove named after him. In many instances the *Mikado* cast members were accompanied by distortions of Gilbert's lyrics parodied to fit the crime.

62r "*The Mikado* Lancers," by P. Bucalossi, on airs from Gilbert & Sullivan's Opera, London: Chappell & Co., plate no. 18048.

62s "*The Mikado* Polka," by P. Bucalossi, on airs from Gilbert & Sullivan's Opera, London: Chappell & Co., plate no. 18041.

62t "*The Mikado* Valse," by P. Bucalossi, on airs from Gilbert & Sullivan's Opera, London: Chappell & Co., plate no. 18046.

THE "*EXHIBITION ODE*"

With the claims of the Leeds Festival for composing his *Golden Legend*, and with Gilbert impatiently awaiting some evidence of his creative interest in *Ruddigore*, all Sullivan needed was a command from H.R.H. The Prince of Wales that, of course, preempted his time. Sir Philip Cunliffe-Owen, representing the Prince, brought him a four-verse manuscript of words by Tennyson, an ode to be sung at the opening of the Colonial and Indian Exhibition on 4 May 1886 at Albert Hall. That the composer's schedule for this duty was a bit rushed may be apparent from the correspondence. First, there came the manuscript *Ode* from the Laureate, in the hand of someone other than either the poet or son, Hallam, with a few ink notations by Hallam at the top.

63a [Tennyson].   Manuscript for "Ode to be sung at the opening of the Indian & Colonial Exhibition," four verses, written on stationery of Farringford [n.d.]. 2pp.

Were Sullivan given to profanity, he might have had such recourse on receipt of a letter from Philip Cunliffe-Owen, dated 6 April 1886:

63b Cunliffe-Owen, Sir Philip, 1828–1894.   Ls, Royal Commission for the Colonial and Indian Exhibition (London, 1886), 6 April 1886, to Arthur Sullivan. 1p.

"Lord Tennyson would be very glad to be in communication with you in reference to the music that you are now setting his ode to.—(doubtless, though, this has occurred to you before, but I think it as well to remind you of it.)."

63c Sullivan. *Ode for the Opening of the Colonial and Indian Exhibition*. Words by A. Tennyson. Manuscript of the full score, signed and dated 19 April 1886. Brown paper wrappers. 27pp. 35 x 27 cm. (Published by Novello, 1886; first performed in Albert Hall, 4 May 1886.)

The manuscript was signed and dated by Sullivan on the last page. The date, 19 April 1886, is the same as Hallam Tennyson's last letter to the composer in which he asked for a check on the words closing the final verse. The score throughout has Tennyson's text written in Sullivan's hand.

THE GOLDEN LEGEND

"Ovation! nay, it was the greater triumph; such as once acclaimed the successful soldiers of Rome"—*The Mercury*, Leeds.

The instant plaudits aroused by Sullivan's *Golden Legend* transcended superlatives. Emma Albani, who was there in the leading soprano role, wrote afterward: "I have seen many new works produced at our English festivals, but I have never seen any one that has had such spontaneous and lasting success as 'The Golden Legend' . . . one could hardly believe the English public capable of showing so much."

64a Sullivan, and Joseph Bennett, 1831–1911. *The Golden Legend*, cantata. Full score, London & New York: Novello, Ewer and Co. [n.d.] The words adapted from the poem by Longfellow. On the title page is the presentation: "C. V. Stanford from Arthur Sullivan. 12 June 1888." Tan paper-covered boards with red cloth spine. Title, 3 bl., 1–345pp. 35½ x 28½ cm. Engraved, plate no. 7341.

It was appropriate that Sullivan inscribed this copy of his full score to Sir Charles Villiers Stanford (1852–1924), for Stanford shared the honors in 1886 at the Leeds Festival with *The Revenge*, his ballad for chorus and orchestra, which he himself conducted. With this copy of the cantata is page 1, Prologue, of Novello's proof sheets, with corrections, of the first 160 pages of engraving. On this page British "cornets" had to be returned to "Cornetti."

64b Sullivan, and Joseph Bennett. *The Golden Legend*. Vocal score, pianoforte arrangement by Berthold Tours, London & New York: Novello, Ewer and Co., also Chappell and Co., London. Novello's original octavo edition, first edition. Contemporary limp scarlet cover, gilt, with gilt edges, and gilt initials on the front: "E.L." [Edward Lloyd]. Title, bl., [i]–[xii], [1]–137pp. 26 x 17½ cm.

The presentation on the inside fly-leaf: "Edward Lloyd. in grateful acknowledgment Arthur Sullivan. Oct: 1886."

A second copy: in original boards, with title-page inscription, "*Jan: 1887* Fanette from Arthur Sullivan." "Fanette" was a pet name for Fanny (Ronalds) Ritchie.

A photograph postcard: Edward Lloyd, 1845–1927, famous English tenor, frequently associated with important works of Arthur Sullivan. Signed "Yours faithfully Edward Lloyd."

64c Word Book of *The Golden Legend:* "Novello's Series of the Words of Oratorios, Cantatas, &c. / The Golden Legend / adapted from the poem of / Longfellow / by / Joseph Bennett / and set to music by / Arthur Sullivan. Book of Words with Analytical Notes by Joseph Bennett." Novello, Ewer and Co. [1886] Title page [1], imprint [2], text [3]–40pp. 24½ x 18½ cm.

64d Sullivan. Als, Stagenhoe Park, Nr. Welwyn, 24 August 1886, to "Jo" [Bennett]. 5pp.

"Shall we call it 'The Golden Legend'?": As late as 24 August 1886, the date of this letter from Sullivan to Joseph Bennett, Longfellow's title had apparently not definitely been chosen. "I suppose there is no better title. It has the merit of being known. Will you write a few lines of 'Argument' to precede the libretto?" Evidently Bennett, critic, writer on music, and librettist—and overall a close friend of Sullivan—had not yet become involved in the Leeds Festival launching of his friend's *magnum opus*. Between late August and 16 October, Jo Bennett was to write the official analysis and word-book of this work. Meanwhile, Sullivan ran through a number of working points with Bennett on which he sought his reaction. In fact he hoped Bennett could join him at Stagenhoe Park, the place he had leased for the summer.

64e Albani, Emma (Mrs. Ernest Gye), 1847–1930. Als, Grand Hotel, Plymouth, Wednesday [n.d.], to Sir Arthur Sullivan. 1p. (On page 2 is a brief note signed: "Gee Gee" [George Grossmith].)

Praise from his leading lady: "I was delighted on Saturday and very glad to have witnessed your triumph!" So wrote Emma Albani, distinguished Canadian-born opera and concert soprano, whose husband Ernest Gye was lessee of Covent Garden. She had sung the role of "Elsie" in *The Golden Legend* at Leeds the preceding Saturday, but flattered the composer by writing: "I am longing to sing that beautiful prayer to Jehovah! – But must content myself with 'Christe Eleison', this evening anyhow [presumably at a Wednesday evening concert in Plymouth]." On the bottom of this page is "P.T.O." which, when obeyed, reveals a note from George Grossmith: "I suppose you have forgotten all about me. Why I could sing Oudin's & Ben Davies' heads off. Gee Gee."

64f Stainer, Sir John, 1840–1901. Als, 5 Amen Court [London], 26 October [1886], to Sullivan. 3pp.

Praise from a fellow-composer: John Stainer wrote his hearty congratulations "on your splendid success at Leeds." The rest of the letter concerned a performance of *The Golden Legend* that Stainer was about to conduct at Albert Hall, and for which he needed to borrow a set of bells. "All seemed to say they were in excellent tune. But how about the high pitch of the Albert Hall? I am rather fidgety about this... If they will not go with the organ, could you not drop the organ altogether at the performance and use the *Leeds* pitch? J.S."

64g Boïto, Arrigo, 1842–1918. *Mephistopheles*. English adaptation by Theo. Marzials, pianoforte arrangement by Michele Saladino. London: G. Ricordi & Co. (printed in Italy). Full tan morocco gilt. Engraved, plate no. 46855. 31 x 24½ cm. Presentation copy, signed and dated "Milan 28 Dec., 1893."

A New Year's gift from Boïto: For this splendid gift, to honor his fellow-composer, Boïto had a special four-page fold inserted before the title page. On page 3 of this fold is the name "Sir Arthur Sullivan," printed within an elaborately decorative box. On page 1 is his autograph inscription wishing all the best for the New Year: "A l'illustre Auteur de The Golden Legend j'offre cet exemplaire expressement tiré pour lui. Temoignage de vive admiration et reconnaisance."

RUDDIGORE

Gilbert started making changes in *Ruddygore* from the time the final curtain came down on opening night, 22 January 1887. The "y" in the title, which had provoked Victorian raised eyebrows, was changed to "i" from 2 February. The song by Grossmith in Act 2, to which Gilbert took strong exception in his letter of 23 January (the day after opening), was changed to the new words, finished and ready for the Savoy by the end of the week (his letter of 28 January). Luckily for Grossmith, an attack of peritonitis forced him off the boards for nearly a month, so he did not have to cope with these changes. But his replacement Henry Lytton, a young man about to become very famous in the G. & S. repertoire, had his baptism on 31 January.

65a Gilbert, W. S. 2 Als, 39 Harrington Gardens [London], 23 and 28 January 1887, to Sullivan. 3pp. and 2pp.

The song referred to as "A highly respectable man" in Gilbert's second letter, although printed in the earliest librettos, did not get into the vocal score. Its replacement, "Henceforth all the crimes that I find in the *Times*," was included in the first vocal scores, and in librettos after 2 February. But in modern productions even this second patter song has been omitted.

65b Sullivan, and W. S. Gilbert. *Ruddigore; or, The Witch's Curse*. Vocal score, arrangement for pianoforte by George Lowell Tracy (of Boston, U.S.A.), London: Chappell & Co., New York: William A. Pond. The copyright notice is in Tracy's name, 1887. Original red cloth boards gilt

(Chappell also issued standard printed grey wrappers). [i]–[iv], overture v–xii, [3]–129, 5 advt. pp. Plate no. 18,311. 28 x 22 cm.

No. 8, Duet for Margaret and Despard, appears on pages 112–113.

65c Cabinet photograph: Jessie Bond as "Mad Margaret" and Rutland Barrington as the reformed "Despard," posed in the second-act duet (No. 8 in the vocal score), "This is one of our blameless dances."

65d "*Ruddigore* Lancers," by P. Bucalossi, on airs from Gilbert & Sullivan's Opera, London: Chappell & Co., plate no. 18329.

65e "*Ruddigore* Quadrille," by P. Bucalossi, on airs from Gilbert & Sullivan's Opera, London: Chappell & Co., plate no. 18333.

THE "*INSTITUTE ODE*"

The direct concern of the royal family in musical matters often gave their selected tune-smiths and wordsmiths unconscionable deadlines. A good example was the timing of the plans for music to honor the laying of the foundation stone of the Imperial Institute by the Queen herself as part of the nation's Jubilee celebration.

66a Knollys, Sir Francis, 1837–1924. Als, Marlborough House [London], 5 June 1887, to Sullivan. 3pp.

In early June, 1887, Sir Francis Knollys had been in correspondence with Sullivan in behalf of the Prince of Wales regarding the musical program of this event at the Imperial Institute. In particular there was the choice of the poet who would write the words for the ode to be performed at the ceremony on 4 July. Even with a bit less than a month to work in, there still had to be concern for protocol: the fact that the poet-elect had never been presented to the Prince of Wales. Arrangements were set up by exchange of telegrams, so that the composer could meet the poet in London on 6 June. In a subsequent diary notation by Sullivan: "June 12. Mr. Lewis Morris called and discussed alteration in the words of the ode for the laying of the foundation stone of the Imperial Institute." In an earlier letter of 4 June, Knollys had called Sullivan's attention to the desire of the Queen "that some of the Pupils from the College [the Royal College of Music] could be included in the Musical Programme."

The Prince of Wales must have realized that he had called upon his unofficial musician laureate for unusually troublesome services, for on the very next day after the Imperial Institute ceremony he wrote Sullivan.

66b Albert Edward, Prince of Wales, 1841–1910. Als, Marlborough House, [London], 5 July 1887, to Sullivan. 2pp.

"I must write you a few lines to thank you most sincerely for all the trouble you took in composing the music for the Ode yesterday. It met with universal approbation & the Queen was especially delighted with it. All the musical arrangements thanks to you were admirable & I thought the whole ceremony went off admirably."

66c Sullivan, and Sir Lewis Morris, 1833–1907. *Ode*, written and composed expressly for the occasion of laying the foundation stone of the Imperial Institute by Her Majesty the Queen. Vocal score, London: Chappell & Co. [n.d.]. Tan paper wrappers. 11pp. Plate no. 18,384. 30 x 21 cm.

Chappell & Co.'s vocal score with pianoforte arrangement contained at least one passage calculated to gladden the royal heart: "First Lady of our English race." Unhappily the biography of Sullivan by Herbert Sullivan and Newman Flower (p. 171) attributed the *"Institute Ode"* to Tennyson as well as the preceding *"Exhibition Ode."* This error, fortified by use of the plural "Odes by Tennyson" in the index, may have caused Mr. Young (p. 148) to make the same attribution of the *"Institute Ode"* to Tennyson, even though both these biographies have the two odes correctly attributed in their chronological check-lists.

THE YEOMEN OF THE GUARD

The Yeomen of the Guard; or, The Merryman and his Maid was third and last of the only G. & S. operas with a full published score. Like its predecessors *H.M.S. Pinafore* and *The Mikado*, the publishing interest was Germanic, Joseph Weinberger of Vienna. And, like *Pinafore* with its published title *Amor an Bord*, the *Yeomen* was equally unrecognizable as *Capitän Wilson*. The two also shared the similarity of a lithographic process which had a German text, not in type, but in cursive characters. The text was the translation of Victor Léon and Carl Lindau, 1889. In the same year Berlin had a production of *Yeomen*, with the more readily recognized title *Die Königsgardist*, by Zell and Genée, published by Bosworth. And still a third translation, as recent as 1972, was played in the Staats Theater in Kassel: libretto in German by Charles Lewinsky, with the title, *Der Gaukler von London*, stemming from the G. & S. subtitle. (The word "Gaukler," buffoon or Merry Andrew, i.e., "The Merryman," an interesting deviation.)

67a Sullivan (libretto by W. S. Gilbert). *Capitän Wilson*. Operette in 2 Akten, nach W. S. Gilbert frei bearbeitet von Victor Léon u. Carl Lindau, Instrumentirt von Julius Stern. Partitur. Wien: Jos. Weinberger & Hofbauer [n.d.]. Original printed grey wrappers. ii–xx, 1–289pp. 34 x 26 cm.

In this copy of *Capitän Wilson*, the Double Chorus, a Sullivan essential, "Volk und Gardista," is found on pages 20–21. In a diary note Sullivan recorded (1889): "Feb. 1. Wrote to Vienna 'New Free Press' protesting against pirated & mutilated production of the 'Yeomen' at the Carl Theatre under the title of 'Capitain [sic] Wilson.' "

67b "Lied Des Wilson," aus *Capitän Wilson*, "Wenn Leben Gluck, kommt stets der Tod zu früh." Plate no. W. & H. 107.

67c "Lied Der Mary," aus *Capitän Wilson*, "Wenn Braut ich wär', Wie wär an Liebe ich so reich, An Zärtlichkeit mir keine gleich, wenn Braut ich wär.' " Plate no. W. & H. 109.

Both the above sheet-music printed by Jos. Weinberger & Hofbauer, Wein. I Kärntnerstrasse 34. Leipzig. Fr. Hofmeister.

Publisher Weinberger, who was responsible for the full score of *Yeomen of the Guard*, disguised as *Capitän Wilson*, even printed separate sheet-music with colorful pictorial covers of six different numbers. Two examples, the beautiful tenor aria, "Is life a boon?", and its equally lyrical counterpart for mezzo, "Were I thy bride," show the *echt* Gilbert.

67d Sullivan (libretto by W. S. Gilbert). *Der Königsgardist*. Vocal score (the more readily recognizable *Yeomen*), translation by F. Zell and Richard Genée, Leipzig: Bosworth & Co., copyright 1888 (London: Chappell & Co. and New York: W. A. Pond & Co. share the imprint.) Without the front paper wrapper. 151pp. Plate no. B. & Co. 2. 27½ x 22½ cm.

On pages 30–31 of this copy is No. 6, Lied (Wolski) [the name of Captain Fairfax in this version], "Wem Leben Glück."

67e Gilbert, W. S. Als, 39 Harrington Gardens [London], 3 October 1888, to Sullivan. 3pp.

On the very day of the first performance, in this temperate, clear-thinking letter, Gilbert explained the importance of cutting the song for Sergeant Meryll near the start of Act 1. ("A laughing boy but yesterday" was sung on opening night and then was cut.) "The Act commences with Phoebe's song—*tearful in character*. This is followed by entrance of Warders—*serious & martial in character*. This is followed by Dame Carruthers 'Tower' Song—*grim in character*. This is followed by Meryll's song, *sentimental in character*. This is followed by Trio for Meryll, Phoebe & Leonard *sentimental in character*. Thus it is that a professedly comic opera commences." Gilbert continued, suggesting reducing ("by one half") the length of the Warders' couplets in the Finale. (They were.) "This you will observe is not 'cutting out your music', but cutting out a *repeat* of your music. And I may remind you . . . my words." It is manifest that author and composer were on the ragged edge of strife, which Gilbert was seeking to avoid—"I write, not as an author but as an expert in stage-management."

67f Sullivan. Musical quotation, signed, from "I have a song to sing, O!", [n.p.], July 1897, to Lady Campbell Clarke. 1p.

"I have a song to sing, O!" was a popular number for ladies to request when approaching Sullivan with their autograph albums. This time it was written for Lady Campbell Clarke "from her old friend Arthur Sullivan July 1897." Thirty-five years earlier, Campbell Clarke's signature had appeared on young Sullivan's application for a pass to the British Museum Reading Room [see No. 2b].

PHOTOGRAPHS OF THE "TOWER" TRIANGLE

67g George Grossmith as "Jack Point" (the merryman), by Barraud.

67h Geraldine Ulmar as "Elsie Maynard" (his maid), by Barraud.

67i Courtice Pounds as "Colonel Fairfax" (his rival), by London Stereoscope Co.

"INDULGENCE SLIP"

67j A printed leaflet of apology, frequently found in programs of this period if the management had anything to explain to the audience. This example from the first night of *Yeomen of the Guard* (3 October 1888) explained that anything unpleasant emanating from the tenor (Courtice Pounds) that night was not his fault since he "is suffering from a severe cold." The press had nothing but praise for his performance.

67k "*The Yeomen of the Guard* Quadrille," by P. Bucalossi, on airs from Gilbert and Sullivan's Opera, London: Chappell & Co., plate no. 18610.

67l "*The Yeomen of the Guard* Waltz," by P. Bucalossi, on airs from Gilbert and Sullivan's Opera, London: Chappell & Co., plate no. 18611.

MACBETH—WITH IRVING, TERRY, AND SULLIVAN

On Saturday, 29 December 1888, Henry Irving and Ellen Terry launched a new production of *Macbeth* at the Lyceum Theatre (London). This was important musically as well as theatrically, for Irving had engaged Sullivan to compose the incidental music. But, in the words of biographer Percy Young, "Henry Irving had neither required nor expected music of such complexity. . . ." The *Macbeth* music showed "the facets of Sullivan's music that are least generally known," and how (Young maintains) "perhaps he could have succeeded in the field of serious opera if he had lived in the right kind of climate." In the Overture, "so far as motif material is concerned there is enough here to furnish the framework of an opera."

68a The First Night program: Royal Lyceum Theatre, 29 December
1888. 4pp.

Overture, Incidental Music, and Preludes composed expressly by Arthur Sullivan.

68b Cabinet photograph of Ellen Terry as "Lady Macbeth": "Why did you
bring these daggers from the place?" (Act III, Scene 1). Taken by
Window & Grove [London] [n.d.]. 35½ x 28 cm.

MACBETH LETTERS TO SULLIVAN—*HIS* AND *HERS*

68c Irving, Sir Henry, 1838–1905. Als, Lyceum Theatre [London], [n.d.],
to Sullivan. 3pp.

In *staccato* sentences, the great actor-producer collaborated with his composer on instrumentation: "Trumpets & drum are the King's *behind scenes*. Entrance of Macbeth *only drum*. 'A drum a drum Macbeth doth come.' Distant march would be good for Macbeth's exit in 3rd scene—or drum & trumpet, as you suggest. In the last Act there will be several flourishes—trumpets—'Make all our trumpets speak' &c. & roll of drum sometimes. Really anything you can give of a stirring sort—can be easily brought in. As you say you can dot these down at rehearsal—but one player would be good to tootle tootle, so we can get the exact time."

68d Terry, Dame Ellen, 1848–1928. Als, 22, Barkston Gardens, Earls
Court [London], 17 March 1889, to Sullivan. 2pp.

"Dear Sir Arthur, I fear you may forget you promised me one of the very first copies of the *Piano* score of the Macbeth music. – You, most like [sic], will get them before anyone else knows they are even ready . . . I hope you are quite well now, & writing with happiness more splendid music for the *general* happiness. I wish we were doing another big play, & that you were writing the music for it. – It was *lovely* [triple underline] to have you at the Theatre." (It does not seem that Chappell published a piano score. There was a full score and an arrangement for military band published of the *Macbeth* Overture.)

QUARREL TWO—1889

69a Sullivan.   Al draft, 12 March 1889, to Gilbert. 8pp.

"I confess that the indifference of the public to the 'Yeomen of the Guard' has disappointed me greatly . . . if the result means a return to our former style of piece, I must say at once, and with deep regret, that I cannot do it. I have lost the liking for writing Comic opera, and entertain very grave doubts as to my power of doing it . . . You say that in a serious opera, you must more or less sacrifice yourself I say that this is just what I have been doing in all our joint pieces . . . bear in mind that in Sept: there will be very little of the old Savoy Comp: left . . . Jessie, Brandram, Pounds & Denny. . . ."

69b Gilbert.   Als, 39 Harrington Gardens [London], 19 March 1889, to Sullivan. 2pp.

"Your letter has filled me with amazement & regret . . . You are an adept in your profession & I am an adept in mine. If we meet, it must be as master & master—not as master & servant."

69c Sullivan.   Als "copy," Venice, 27 March 1889, to Gilbert. 3pp.

"I was so annoyed at your abrupt letter . . . I thought it wiser not to answer it without a few days delay . . . it seems . . . a silly & unnecessary thing for you & I to quarrel over a matter that can really be so easily arranged; and, that I really don't think my requests are unreasonable." They were: 1) decision in "laying out of the *musical situation*" and alterations, 2) "important share in arranging the attitudes and business in all the musical portions," and 3) rehearsals—not to weary the voices or cause careless singing.

69d Gilbert.   Als, 39 Harrington Gardens [London], 31 March 1889, to Sullivan. 8pp.

"The requirements contained in your letter of the 27th are just & reasonable in every way . . . It is true that I expostulated, last August, at being required to entirely reconstruct the second act, (which had been in your possession since June) *just as we were about to enter upon rehearsals*, but I did not question . . . your abstract right . . . I confidently challenge you to name a single instance in our 12 years collaboration in which a wish, expressed by you in connection with the musical portions of the piece, has not been unhesitatingly acted upon . . . [re rehearsals] how am I to know that you object . . . unless you tell me so? . . . why not take the acting rehearsals & the singing rehearsals separately, until, say, the last week? . . . I say that when you deliberately assert [in a letter to Carte] . . . that you have submitted silently & uncomplainingly for 12 years to be extinguished, ignored, set aside, rebuffed & generally effaced by your librettist, you grievously reflect, not upon him, but upon yourself & the noble art of which you are so eminent a professor."

69e Sullivan.   Letter (in the hand of Walter Smythe, secretary to Sullivan),
 24 April 1889, to Gilbert. 2pp.

". . . I am quite prepared to set to work at once upon a light or comic opera with you, (provided of course that we are thoroughly agreed about the subject) and to think no more of our rather sharp discussion. I am enabled to do this all the more willingly since I have now settled to write an opera on a grand scale . . . to be produced next Spring . . . I can realize the great desire of my life, and at the same time continue a collaboration which I regard with a stronger sentiment than that of pecuniary advantage."

69f Sullivan.   Al draft, 8 May 1889, to "G" [Gilbert]. 4pp.

"I understand from him (Carte) sometime ago that you had some subject connected with Venice & Venetian life, and this seemed to me to hold out great chances of bright colour and taking music. Can you not develop this into something that we can both go into with warmth & enthusiasm. . . ." Thus *The Gondoliers* was born.

CALM INTERLUDE—1889

GILBERT TO "S":

70a Als, 31 May 1889, 39 Harrington Gardens. 1p.

". . . Struggling with the difficulties of Act I—which are gradually succumbing to the intellectual hammering of my Titanic brain."

70b Als, 5 June 1889, 39 Harrington Gardens. 2pp.

Gilbert asked if Sullivan would meet him on Friday to hear the new plot.

70c Als, 21 June 1889, Breakspears. 2pp.

Gilbert was getting on with Act I and, if convenient, would read it to Sullivan the next Wednesday when he came to town. "The first nine pages of MS are *all music*, & no dialogue."

70d Als, 10 August 1889, Breakspears. 3pp.

Gilbert was still working on the plot, trying to make Act I intelligible with the "growling chorus." Act II was also progressing.

70e Als, 11 September 1889, Breakspears. 2pp.

Gilbert asked Sullivan to send a copy of "In a contemplative fashion" so it could be altered. He added "I think I had better leave the absolute end of Act I until I see you. I *have* done something that might do."

70f Als, 22 September 1889, Breakspears. 3pp.

"I have altered the 'In a contemplative fashion' as you suggested."

70g Als, 11 October 1889, Breakspears. 6pp.

"I have found it necessary to make a few alterations & modifications, but none of them, I think & hope, will give you any trouble . . . I couldn't consult you about this as you were away in Leeds . . . I have done without Brandram's song 'In the days when I was wedded'— because it stopped the action of the piece (already too long) . . . I can come up to town on Tuesday to read the piece to you—& if you approve of it in its existing form, I can read it to the company on Wednesday."

70h Als, 25 October 1889, 39 Harrington Gardens. 2pp.

"I very much want to rewrite 'Now I'm about to kiss your hand'—making it more musically rhythmical—& ending with a minuet . . . Wyatt & Barrington are both such excellent dancers that it seems a pity to miss so good a chance of utilizing them. What do you think?"

70i Als, 9 November 1889, 39 Harrington Gardens. 2pp.

"If I remember rightly, you expressed some doubt as to whether Gianetta's song ('Kind sir, you cannot have the heart'[)] was not too long . . . I have come across a song which I wrote for the same situation . . . if you don't like it as well as the other, tear it up—. . . Don't trouble to answer this."

THE GONDOLIERS

TO "DEAR S."—Before and After: The first of these shows Gilbert at his creative and co-operative best. The second, a rare example of his letting himself go in generous warmth of expression:

71a Gilbert.   Als, 39 Harrington Gardens, 8 August 1889, to Sullivan. 3pp.

In this, Gilbert wrote that he enclosed "(1) Another verse to 'Thank you Gallant Gondolieri' (one for each girl, now) (2) Expostulatory song for either of the girls, when Grand Inquisitor informs them that they must be separated from their husbands. (3) Farewell duet, addressed by Tessa & Gianetta to their husbands—before the final chorus. (I have not written the final chorus because you said you thought it had better wait until you had decided on a rhythm.[)] I hope you will like the numbers." He then took exception to the decision of Sullivan and Carte for the choice of Grossmith's replacement, "but as I am in the minority I must give in."

71b Gilbert.   Als, 39 Harrington Gardens, 8 December 1889, to
Sullivan. 2pp.

This second letter closed with these two sentences: "I must again thank you for the magnificent work you have put into the piece. It gives one a chance of shining right through the twentieth century with a reflected light. Always sincerely yours W. S. Gilbert."

71c Sullivan, and W. S. Gilbert.   *The Gondoliers; or, The King of Barataria.*
Vocal score, arrangement for pianoforte by J. H. Wadsworth (of Boston,
U.S.A.), London: Chappell & Co. and Cincinnati, Ohio: The John
Church Company, copyright by J. H. Wadsworth, 1890. Grey printed
wrappers. [i]–[iv], overture [v]–xii, [1]–185pp. 28 x 22 cm. Plate
no. 18,844.

71d Castanets, from the original production of *The Gondoliers*, dated in ink,
1890. These belonged to Charles Rose, in the role of Gondolier,
"Francesco."

71e "*The Gondoliers* Quadrille," by P. Bucalossi, on airs from W. S. Gilbert
and Arthur Sullivan's Opera, London: Chappell & Co. [n.d.], plate
no. 18864.

71f *"The Gondoliers* Waltz," by P. Bucalossi, on airs from W. S. Gilbert &
Arthur Sullivan's Opera, London: Chappell & Co. [n.d.], plate
no. 18861.

THE CHARLES DANA GIBSON CARTOON

72 Gibson, Charles Dana, 1867–1944. Original ink over pencil sketch on
white card, signed, drawn for *Puck*, on the reverse is written in pencil the
short dialogue used as a caption in the issue of 11 January 1888. Also on
the reverse is an identification sheet for *Puck*: "No. 4616, Size, 4 inches,
Return Dec. 30th 1887." Ca. 32½ x 29 cm. [detail, see cover illustration].

The sketch of top-hatted Arthur Sullivan appeared in the comic magazine *Puck*, the issue
of 11 January 1888. The artist was twenty-one-year-old Charles Dana Gibson, drawing in
the manner of the British weeklies of the period, before he had evolved the Gibson style
soon to be his trademark. He was illustrating one of many versions of a true story told by
Arthur Sullivan which occurred on his trip back East from visiting California in the summer of 1885, a time when the name of Sullivan in a small western community could mean
only John L., "the slogger":

> "New Arrival – Are the rooms ready I wired for last night?
> English Hotel Clerk – What's the name?
> Arrival: Sullivan!
> Clerk: Oh, ya-as, your honor. Boots, show Mr. Sullivan to the first suite of drawing-
> rooms. You'll find heverything ready, Mr. Sullivan.
> Arrival: Sir Arthur, sir! Not mister. I'm Sir Arthur Sullivan, the composer.
> Clerk: Tenth floor, back Boots! (to himself) I *thought* he was a little stubby for John
> Hel!"

THE MILLAIS PORTRAIT

73 Sullivan. Als, 1, Queen's Mansions [London], 30 April 1888, to "My
dear John" [Sir John Everett Millais, 1829–1896]. 3pp.

"I was so moved yesterday when I saw my portrait for the first time, that even had you not
enjoined me not to speak, I could have said very little." Thus Sullivan began his letter of
appreciation and gratitude to the artist, for the work itself and for the work as Millais'
"splendid and princely gift." They had known each other since 1863, according to a note of
recollection Sullivan sent to Millais' daughter, Mrs. Stuart-Wortley, after his death in
1896. "Millais was a man who inspired those who knew him with greatest personal affection. There was something exceptionally lovable in his nature. . . ." It is likely that the art-

ist could have written the same of his friend, the composer . . . they were *simpatico*. The Millais portrait was willed by Sullivan to the National Portrait Gallery, where it now hangs.

LETTERS FROM MUSICIANS

74a Barnby, Sir Joseph, 1838–1896. Als, Eton College, 7 October 1880, to Sullivan. 2pp.

His friend and fellow-composer from earliest days wrote Sullivan "warm and hearty congratulations on the achievement of a great work." The reference was to *The Martyr of Antioch*, and was signed "your devoted friends," by both Joseph Barnby and his wife, Edith Mary.

74b D'Albert, Charles, 1809–1886. Als, 14 Alexander Square [London], 10 June 1880, to Sullivan. 3pp.

Dance-music arranger D'Albert placed great value in Sullivan's opinion with regard to his musician-son's career. Conductor Augustus Manns wanted young Eugene D'Albert to play the Schumann Concerto at the Crystal Palace; and D'Albert, senior, sought Sullivan's approval, "as I should be very sorry that my son should do anything contrary to your views." Eugene D'Albert had been at the National Training School under Sullivan.

74c Liszt, Franz, 1811–1886. Als, Westwood House, Sydenham, "mercredi" [n.d., probably 14 April 1886]. 1p.

The venerable Abbé's last visit to London was solidly scheduled by his British musical elite admirers, including his pupil (and Sullivan's fellow-student at Leipzig) Walter Bache. In this note to Sullivan, he regreted that all his days were taken, so he could not accept Sullivan's invitation. One can almost pinpoint the date. He arrived on Saturday, 3 April, and left on Tuesday, 20 April. This permitted only two "mercredi"s, and on Wednesday, 7 April (according to *Grove*), he spent the day at Windsor playing for the Queen. Therefore, the date of this note was almost certainly Wednesday, 14 April 1886.

74d Mackenzie, Sir Alexander Campbell, 1847–1935. Als, Garden Cottage, Maidenhead, Berks., 19 December 1886, to Sullivan. 1p.

Quite a different composer-personality than his friend Sullivan, Mackenzie "willingly will endeavour to represent [him, Sullivan] on the occasion in question. I only hesitated at first on account of my strong desire not to make myself prominent and also because I am always terrified when I have to speak." A.S. had no such qualms.

74e Massenet, Jules, 1842–1912. Als, Paris, 27 December 1886, to Sullivan. 2pp.

Addressing "Cher Maitre," Massenet was enchanted to have the opportunity to introduce to Sullivan "M. Borelli, *un excellent musicien* [triple underline] qui merite votre accueil favorable." Massenet had been following all Sullivan's successes, and, facetiously, if it would gratify Sullivan, he would send him congratulations after each work.

74f Randegger, Alberto, 1832–1911. Als, 17 Duke Street, Manchester Square [London], 21 September 1880, to Sullivan. 1p.

Composer-conductor Randegger had two favors to ask: Might he attend the London band rehearsals of the new work for the Leeds Festival (*The Martyr of Antioch*)? And, 'Will you grant me your permission to include this new work of yours in my Norwich Festival scheme. I hope you will say 'yes' to both, & oblige your old friend. . . .'"

74g Saint-Saëns, Camille, 1835–1921. Letter signed, [n.p., probably Paris], 28 October 1886, to Sullivan. 2pp.

Like his compatriot-composer Massenet, Saint-Saëns was also interested in furthering the career of Monsieur Borelli: "Mon cher ami . . . C'est un musicien de talent . . ." whom he recommended "de chaudement" [see No. 74e].

74h Sarasate, Pablo de, 1844–1908. Als, Hotel Dieudonne, London, 15 June 1885, to Sullivan. 2pp.

The great Spanish violinist desired to interest Sullivan, "Cher Maestro," in Madam Roger Miclos, "one of the great pianists of the French school" [translated from the original French]. She would be happy if Sullivan could arrange to have the Prince of Wales hear her at a Sunday recital at Marlborough House. Sarasate wished Sullivan a good voyage and a prompt return (from his second trip to America, summer 1885).

LETTER FROM AN AMERICAN AUTHOR

74i Harte, Bret, 1836–1902. Als, 15 Upper Hamilton Terrace [London], 11 January 1883, to Sullivan. 2pp.

Apparently in 1883 Bret Harte was still hopeful he could interest Sullivan in one of his stories. "I send you by book post, today, a copy of 'The Pictorial World' containing my story entitled 'At the Mission of San Carmel.' It is the revised plot of the opera I submitted to you last summer—recast in a narrative form."

THE FAN-TASTIC FAN

75 Fan of twenty-four sandalwood sticks, bearing autographs on both sides, some as many as three to a side. Total number of autographs—80.

This extraordinary fan was the collection and creation of the George Henschel family, probably of Mrs. Henschel. Its splendid array of American literary names attests that its owners were still in Boston shortly after it was begun (ca. 1879), for Henschel was the first conductor of the Boston Symphony Orchestra.

Some artist signers included a sketch in ink or colors along with their signatures. Some musicians included a phrase or two of music. Some poets, a verse of their own. One side of one stick bears the signatures of: Mark Twain, J. R. Lowell, and W. D. Howells; another, Henry James and John S. Sargent; another, Adelina Patti and Nellie Melba. P. Tschaikovsky and Henry W. Longfellow share one stick, the latter added on an adjoining stick: "Full of the name and the fame of the Puritan maiden Priscilla."

Of course, one side led off with Arthur Sullivan on stick No. 1, dated on his birthday, 13 May 1880; and, the reverse side of stick No. 1 (the back of Sullivan's) was signed by George Henschel, dated London 1879.

SONGS—PIANOFORTE ACCOMPANIMENT

Sullivan composed only six songs of which these two by the Laureate are examples.

76a "Edward Gray," words by Lord Tennyson, London: J. B. Cramer & Co., Ltd. (1880), plate no. J.B.C. & Co. 11,184.

76b "The Sisters," duet for female voices, words by Alfred Tennyson, London: Stanley Lucas, Weber & Co. (1881), plate no. S.L.W. & Co. 1525.

Also: Agreement for publishing a vocal duet, "The Sisters," Arthur S. Sullivan, Esq., and Messrs. Stanley Lucas & Co., 9 May 1881. 3pp.

HYMNS AND ANTHEMS

77a "The Dominion Hymn," music by Arthur Sullivan (words anon.), dedicated to the "People of Canada," London: Chappell and Co. (1880), plate no. 17062.

This was first published by de Zouch & Co., Montreal (1880), in which form it was presented by the composer to Queen Victoria.

77b Ponsonby, Sir Henry F. Als, Balmoral, 29 October 1880, to
Sullivan. 2pp.

"Sir – I am commanded by The Queen to return you many thanks for your kindness in presenting Her Majesty with the 'Canadian Hymn'. The Queen will be very glad to accept a copy of your new Sacred work 'The Martyr of Antioch'. I have the honour to be, Sir, your obedient Servant Henry F. Ponsonby."

77c "Hark! What mean those holy voices?", Christmas carol, for voices with
organ accompaniment, *Lute*, No. 12, London: Patey & Willis (1883),
plate no. P. & W. 927.

77d "Who is like unto Thee?", anthem for solo and chorus, No. 264:
Novello's Anthems, dedicated to Walter Parratt, Esq., Mus. Bac.,
London: Novello, Ewer & Co. (1883).

Sullivan's presentation cup to Gilbert. (55j)

Gilbert's letter of appreciation (hand of Nancy McIntosh). (55k)

The Boltons
South Kensington GRIM'S DYKE.
HARROW WEALD.

3rd Dec 1880

Dear Sullivan

It always seemed to me that my particularly humble services in connection with the Leeds Festival had received far more than their meed of acknowledgement in your preamble to the libretto — & it most certainly never occurred to me to look for any other reward than the honour of being associated, however remotely & unworthily, in a success which, I suppose, will endure until music itself shall die.

Pray believe that of the many

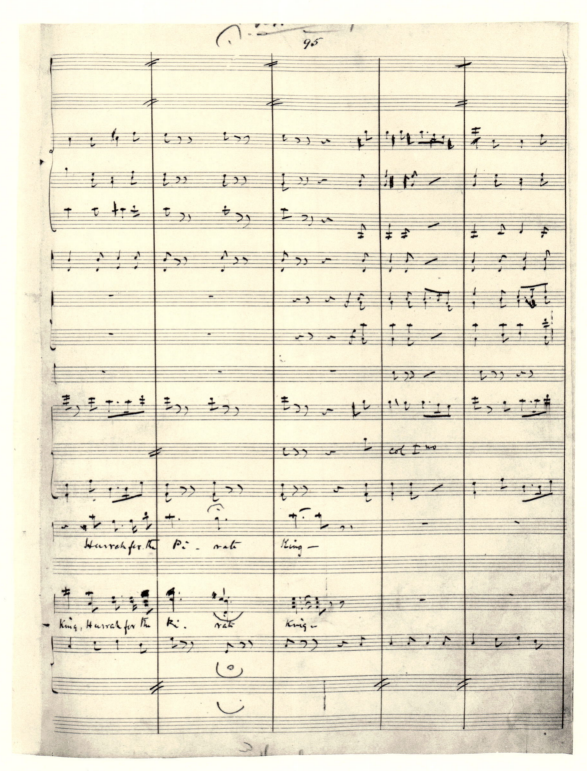

The Pirates of Penzance, Act I (1879). (53c)

The Pirates of Penzance

Silk program, New York opening. (53e)

OPERA COMIQUE, STRAND.
LONDON. W.C.

...May 12th. 18 80

Gilbert and Sullivan

I agree to the terms and conditions of your note and assignment of yesterday, namely to pay to you two thousand nine hundred pounds (£= 2,900) (one half to be paid at Christmas 1880 and the remaining half at Midsummer 1881) you assigning to me in consideration thereof the sole right of representation

if you represent the Pirates of Penzance, the Pinafore and the Sorcerer in Great Britain and Ireland out of London from now to Christmas 1881, it being understood that I do not license the Pirates of Penzance for performance by amateurs. This cancels the existing agreement for the Pinafore and Sorcerer for the provinces for the current year.

To Messrs W S Gilbert and Arthur Sullivan

The Triumvirate's first agreement, 1880. (54d)

Patience

> **OPERA COMIQUE.**
>
> Licensed by the Lord Chamberlain to Mr. Barker, 299, Strand.
>
> Lessee and Manager - - - - Mr. D'OYLY CARTE
>
> On SATURDAY, APRIL 23rd,
>
> And Every Evening, an entirely New and Original Æsthetic Opera, in Two Acts, entitled
>
> # PATIENCE;
>
> OR,
>
> ## BUNTHORNE'S BRIDE.
>
> Written by W. S. GILBERT.
>
> Composed by ARTHUR SULLIVAN.
>
> PRICES OF ADMISSION :—Orchestra Stalls, 10s.; Balcony Stalls 5s. and 4s.; (Front Row, 6s.); Private Boxes, £1 1s. to £3 3s.; First Circle, 2s. 6d.; Amphitheatre, 1s. 6d.; Gallery, 1s.
>
> Refreshment Department under the Management of Mr. H. Dodsworth.
>
> **Box Office open daily from 11 to 5.   No Booking Fees.**

First night, Opera Comique. (56b)

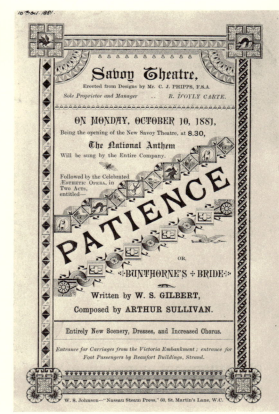

> **Savoy Theatre,**
> Erected from Designs by Mr. C. J. PHIPPS, F.S.A.
> Sole Proprietor and Manager .. R. D'OYLY CARTE.
>
> ON MONDAY, OCTOBER 10, 1881,
> Being the opening of the New Savoy Theatre, at 8.30,
>
> **The National Anthem**
> Will be sung by the Entire Company.
>
> Followed by the Celebrated ÆSTHETIC OPERA, in Two Acts, entitled—
>
> # PATIENCE
> OR,
> BUNTHORNE'S + BRIDE
>
> Written by W. S. GILBERT,
> Composed by ARTHUR SULLIVAN.
>
> Entirely New Scenery, Dresses, and Increased Chorus.
>
> Entrance for Carriages from the Victoria Embankment; entrance for Foot Passengers by Beaufort Buildings, Strand.
>
> W. S. Johnson—"Nassau Steam Press," 60, St. Martin's Lane, W.C.

Opening night of The Savoy Theatre. (56c)

Oscar Wilde to George Grossmith – *Patience* (early April 1881). (56e)

A dance arrangement of music from *Iolanthe*, ca. 1883. (57e)

"Exhibition Ode." (63c)

10. Downing Street,
Whitehall.

May 3. 83

Dear Mr. Sullivan

I have the pleasure to inform you that I am permitted by Her Majesty to propose that you should receive the honour of Knighthood, in recognition of your distinguished talents as a Composer and of the services which you have rendered to the promotion of the art of

Gladstone to Sullivan, 3 May 1883. (59a)

Arthur Awdach, Lord of Penzance

Oct. 22. 1880

Cartoon by George Henschel, 1880. (55g)

Memorandum of Agreement made

the eyght day of February one thousand eight hundred and eighty three **Between** William Schwenck Gilbert of N° 24 The Boltons South Kensington London and Arthur Seymour Sullivan of N° 1 Queens Mansions Victoria Street London of the one part and Richard D'Oyly Carte of the Savoy Theatre Strand London of the other part **Whereas** the parties hereto some time since entered into Agreements by which the said Richard D'Oyly Carte became the sole licensee in London for the performances of certain operas written and composed by the said William Schwenck Gilbert and Arthur Seymour Sullivan upon the terms of certain payments to the said William Schwenck Gilbert and Arthur Seymour Sullivan of amounts equal to certain proportions of the profits arising from such performances after deducting certain payments and expenses as in the said Agreements more particularly mentioned **And whereas** the said Richard D'Oyly Carte is the Owner of a Theatre called the Savoy Theatre **And whereas** the said William Schwenck Gilbert and Arthur Seymour Sullivan have written and composed an Opera called 'Iolanthe or the Peer and the Peri' which was produced by the said Richard D'Oyly Carte at the said Savoy Theatre on the twenty fifth day of November last **Now it is hereby agreed** between the parties hereto as follows The said William Schwenck Gilbert and Arthur Seymour Sullivan hereby grant to the said Richard D'Oyly Carte for the term of five years and thirty one days from and including the said twenty fifth day of November one thousand eight hundred and eighty two expiring on the twenty fifth day of December one thousand eight hundred and eighty seven the sole right of representation and performance of the said Opera called 'Iolanthe' and also of each and every Opera heretofore written and composed and which shall be hereafter written and composed jointly by the said William Schwenck Gilbert and Arthur Seymour Sullivan during the said term

The said Richard D'Oyly Carte agrees to pay to each of them the said William Schwenck Gilbert and Arthur Seymour Sullivan one third of the net profits earned by the representations after deducting all expenses and charges of producing the said operas and of all the performances of the same including in such expenses a rental of Four thousand pounds per annum for the said Savoy Theatre and all rates taxes expenses of lighting repairs incidental to the performances and rendered necessary from time to time by ordinary wear and tear premiums for insurance of costumes music properties and other moveable effects in and about the said Theatre All premiums for insurance of the said Theatre and scenery therein to be defrayed by the said Richard D'Oyly Carte as also all expenses of substantial repairs

All scenery which may be in and about the said Theatre from time to time shall remain in the said Theatre and shall not be removed therefrom without the consent of the said Richard D'Oyly Carte.

/

Gilbert – Sullivan – D'Oyly Carte: First contract, 1883. (58)

Princess Ida

Poster, Leeds (1891). (60g)

Gilbert to Sullivan, 22 September 1883. (60c)

Italian prompt-book. (62d)

The Mikado

Currier & Ives, "Three Little Maids,"
ca. 1885. (62l)

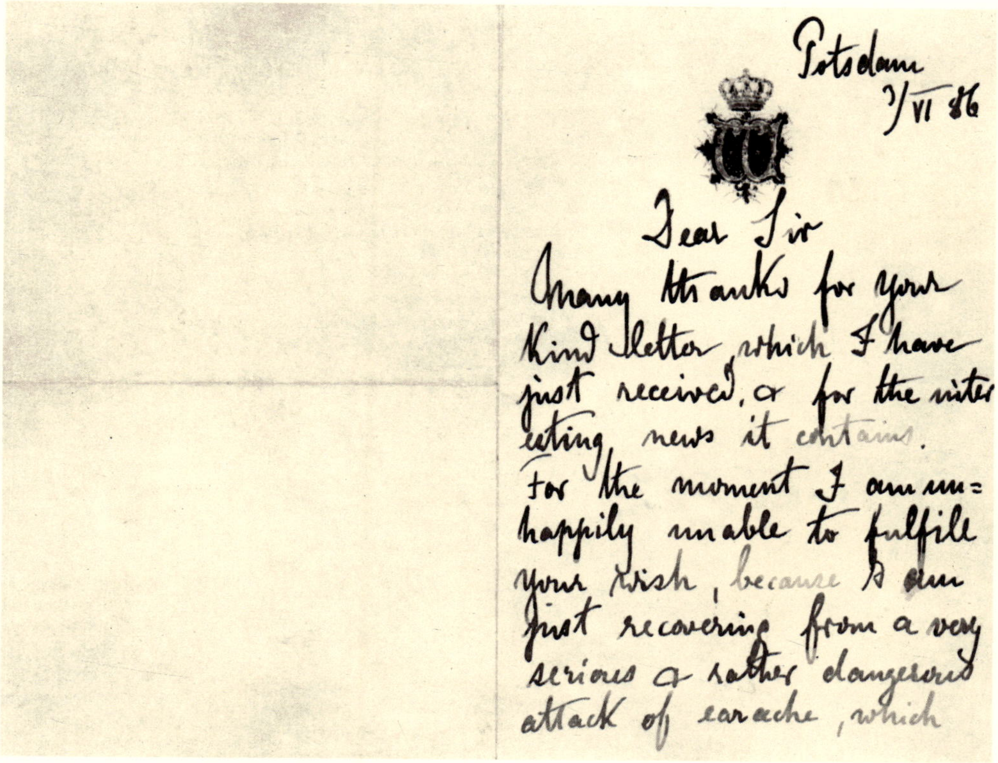

Potsdam
2/VI 86

Dear Sir

Many thanks for your kind letter, which I have just received, & for the interesting news it contains.

For the moment I am unhappily unable to fulfill your wish, because I am just recovering from a very serious & rather dangerous attack of earache, which of which I heard & read so much in the English press. I hope that for the arrival of the Crown Prince they will have "polished up the handle of the big front door", for he might have been a "roosiān" etc. but he is a "Proosiān". I often think of our nice evenings at Kiel & the charming musik on the yacht, which gave me the lucky oppotunity of making your acquaintance. Your truly
William Prince of Prussia

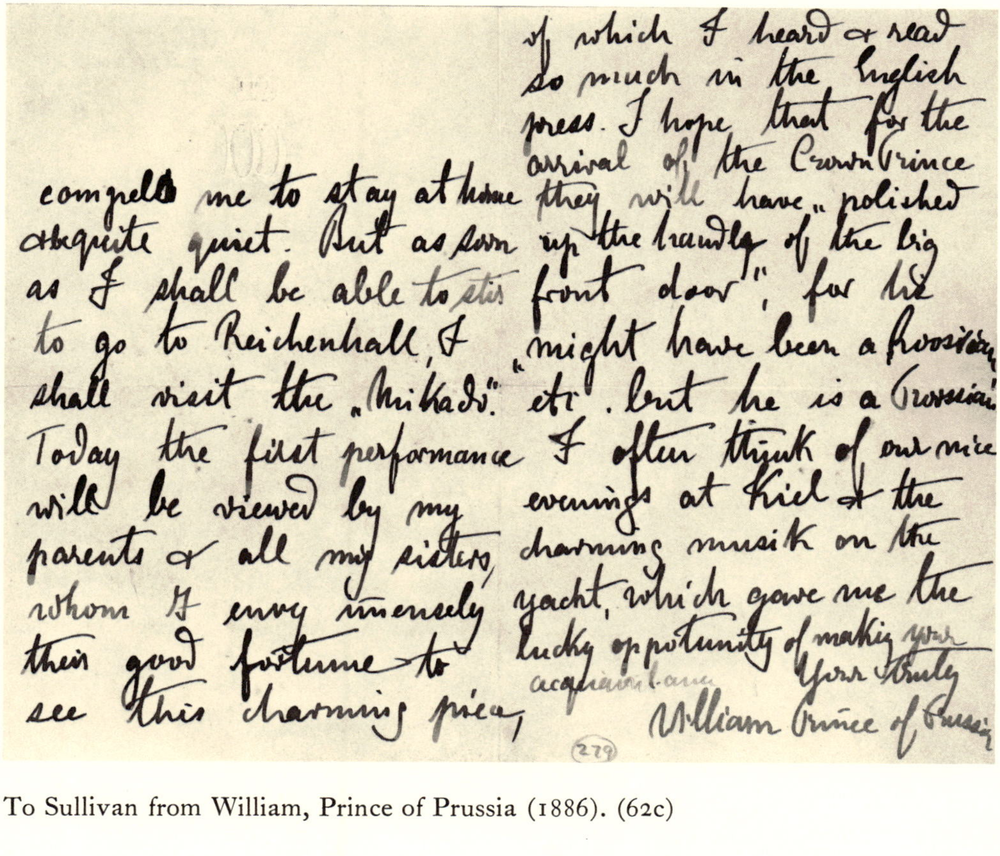

compells me to stay at home & quite quiet. But as soon as I shall be able to etc. to go to Reichenhall, I shall visit the "Mikado". Today the first performance will be viewed by my parents & all my sisters, whom I envy immensely their good fortune to see this charming piece,

(279)

To Sullivan from William, Prince of Prussia (1886). (62c)

MISS JESSIE BOND & MR. BARRINGTON in "RUDDIGORE."
COPYRIGHT.
Barraud, 263 Oxford St London.
A few doors West of "The Circus"

Jessie Bond & Rutland Barrington. Act 2
(1887). (65c)

Gilbert to Sullivan, 23 January 1887. (65a)

This is followed by Dame Carruthers' "Tower" song: — grim in character.
This is followed by Meryll's song: — sentimental in character.
This is followed by trio for Meryll, Phœbe & Leonard: — sentimental in character

Thus it is that a professedly comic opera commences.

I wish, moreover, to accentuate the hint I gave you on Friday; — that the Warders' couplets in the finale are too long, & should be reduced by one-half. This, you will observe, is not "cutting out your music", but cutting out a repeat of your music. And I may remind you that I am proposing to cut, not only your music, but my words. Also, that I write, not as an author but as an expert in stage management.

39, HARRINGTON GARDENS,
SOUTH KENSINGTON.
3rd Oct. 1888.

Dear Sullivan,

I desire, before the production of our piece, to place upon record the conviction that I have so frequently expressed to you in the course of rehearsal — that unless Meryll's introduced & wholly irrelevant song is withdrawn, the success of the first Act will be most seriously imperilled.

Let me recapitulate: —

The Act commences with Phœbe's song — tearful in character
This is followed by entrance of Warders — serious & martial in character

Gilbert to Sullivan – opening day of *The Yeomen of the Guard*. (67f)

Gilbert to Sullivan – *The Gondoliers* in preparation. (71a)

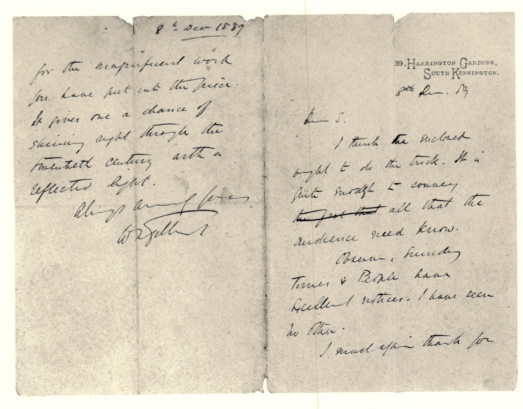

Gilbert to Sullivan – after the opening of *The Gondoliers*. (71b)

The Eighteen Nineties

Arthur Sullivan, July 1899, age 57. (99e)

As in the 1880's, Sullivan's final creative decade was devoted mainly to major works. The 1890's led off with his one grand opera. There followed seven in the light and comic opera field (including his last two with Gilbert), one ballet, two incidental music settings, and his "Victory *Te Deum*." There were only three hymns composed in this period, including the Jubilee Hymn, one march (the "Imperial"), three songs—two inevitably by Tennyson—and three other songs to words by Disraeli, Jean Ingelow, and Poe that were not published until four years after the death of the composer.

IVANHOE—SULLIVAN'S GRAND OPERA

78a Sullivan. Manuscript of his diary for 1891. One volume, 8vo. Original black morocco with brass locks. (One of the 20 volumes, 1881–1900.)

Loaned by the Beinecke Library, Yale University.

31 January 1891: "Lovely day—stayed at home—3 letters from Gilbert [one of these, see No. 81]; . . . his last a rough & insolent refusal to come to the performance of 'Ivanhoe' . . . At 8. Prince & Princess of Wales with Pcs Victoria & Maude & Duke & Duchess of Edinburgh entered their box. 'God save The Queen' played by the orchestra, Cellier conducting. At 8.5 I entered. Tremendous reception by a brilliant and packed house . . . Began 'Ivanhoe' . . . went splendidly, without a hitch from beginning to end. All sang well . . . Great enthusiasm at the end, everyone called. I went on with Sturgis . . . home at 4."

Sullivan was not wholly in sympathy with Wagner's music, and was jealous of Wagner's success, especially the existence of the Festspielhaus. But in 1876, when Bayreuth opened, Wagner's entire thirty-five-year repertoire of operas (everything except *Parsifal*) was available for scheduling. When D'Oyly Carte's Royal English Opera opened in 1891, Sullivan had been writing grand opera for only seven months and had a repertoire of one. If for no other reason, this basic factor made Cambridge Circus no match for Bayreuth.

78b Sullivan, and Julian Russell Sturgis, 1848–1904. *Ivanhoe*, a romantic opera. Manuscript of the full score, signed and dated 11 December 1890. Green half morocco gilt. 708 written pages. 40 x 34 cm.

Loaned by John Wolfson.

Ivanhoe opened on 31 January 1891. Carte had double-cast six principal roles, and as he had failed to grasp the essential difference between producing grand opera and light opera, *Ivanhoe* was played nightly through July of that year for an unbelievable 160 consecutive performances, a feat matched by no grand opera before or since. The production was a *succès d'estime* for Sullivan, a financial disaster for Carte, and a potential suicide for the opera itself. There is little question that its initial overexposure, plus the failure of the Royal English Opera, cast a shadow over *Ivanhoe* which has continued to keep the work from the public. It was produced by Thomas Beecham in his 1910 season at Covent Garden, and has served as the model for the English operas of Vaughan Williams and others in the first quarter of this century. The score contains much very fine music, and is well worthy of re-appraisal. John Wolfson, owner of the *Ivanhoe* manuscript, considers that it exemplifies one quality that Sullivan shared with Wagner, intense nationalism, and that it is as passionately English a work as *Die Meistersinger von Nüremberg* is German.

78c Sullivan, and Julian Sturgis. *Ivanhoe*, a romantic opera. Full score, London: Chappell & Co. [n.d.]. Printed by G. G. Röder, Leipzig. Half blue morocco with marbled papers. 447pp. Plate no. 19074. 35½ x 27 cm.

On the title page is a presentation: "François Cellier from his old and attached friend Arthur Sullivan 1891." On page [iii]: "Dedicated by special permission to Her most Gracious Majesty The Queen, at whose suggestion this work was written, in grateful acknowledgment of Her Majesty's kindly encouragement, by her humble and devoted Subject and Servant, Arthur Sullivan."

78d Gilbert, W. S. Als, 39 Harrington Gardens [London], 20 February 1889, to "S" [Sullivan]. 8pp.

Librettist advice from an expert: In this long, carefully written letter Gilbert tried to argue that Sullivan could enjoy the best of both worlds. "I have thought carefully over your letter, & while I quite understand & sympathize with your desire to write . . . 'Grand Opera', I cannot believe that it would succeed, either at the Savoy or at Carte's new theatre, unless a much more powerful singing & acting company were got together than the company we now control . . . I can quite understand your desire to write a big work—well, why not write one? But why abandon the Savoy business? Cannot the two things be done concurrently? If you can write an oratorio like The Martyr of Antioch, while you are occupied with pieces like Patience & Iolanthe, can't you write a grand opera, without giving up pieces like the Yeomen of the Guard? . . . From me, the press & the public will take nothing but what is, in essence, humorous. The best serious librettist of the day is Julian Sturgis. Why not write a grand opera with him? *My* work in that direction would be, deservedly or otherwise, generally pooh-poohed."

78e Two programs: *Ivanhoe*, first night, 31 January [1891], The Royal Opera, proprietor and manager, R. D'Oyly Carte. With color-lithograph covers, two designs, one with neo-classic woman's figure, signed "Alice Havers"; another with a bridal figure, unsigned. Double-leaf card with gilt edges. 18½ x 11½ cm.

Even though the first-night program does not indicate that the composer conducted, Sullivan in his diary confirms that he did indeed. And on the two subsequent performances (2 and 4 February) that launched the two alternate casts, the familiar line appeared in both programs stating that the composer was conducting.

78f Ticket: *Ivanhoe*, first night, 31 January 1891, Royal English Opera, Royal Tier Stall, Row E 11. A pink coupon.

78g *A Souvenir of the One Hundredth Performance of Ivanhoe*, by Lewis Hind, with twenty-one illustrations from drawings by Maurice Greiffenhagen, and others. Published for the proprietor of the Royal English Opera by J. S. Virture & Co., Limited, Monday, 24 May 1891. Original printed boards. 32pp. 17 x 24 cm.

78h H.R.H. Princess Louise, 1848–1939. Als, Osborne, 2 February 1891, to Sir Arthur. 5pp.

"The Queen wishes me to write & tell you, with what pleasure she sees in the papers of to-day, that your opera met with such a great success on Saturday." The Princess (the Marchioness of Lorne, who had entertained Sullivan in Ottawa on his first American trip) went on to say: "It is a particular satisfaction to her [the Queen], as she believes that it is partly owing to her own instigation, that you undertook this great work."

78i Sullivan. Letter, 1 Queen's Mansions, 4 February 1891, to "Madame" [H.R.H. Princess Louise, Marchioness of Lorne]. 3pp.

As could be expected Sullivan wrote effusively of his pride and pleasure "to receive such a gracious message from his Sovereign." In asking Princess Louise to return his profound gratitude to the Queen, he asked that she assure the Queen "that it was indeed in deference to Her Majesty's expressed desire and gracious encouragement" that he began and completed his first grand opera. But this was not an opportunity for the ambitious Sullivan to miss. He closed his letter with the request that he be allowed to dedicate the opera to the Queen, "and if Her Majesty would graciously accept this tribute of my devotion and respect, I should look upon it as the crowning point of my career." Her Majesty assented.

PALACE PROGRAMS

79a Balmoral Castle, 4 September 1891, *The Mikado* "By Royal Command."

D'Oyly Carte's Opera Company from Her Majesty's Theatre, Aberdeen, performed *The Mikado*. It was D'Oyly Carte's Touring Company "C," after five performances in Aberdeen. The program, with such cast names as George Thorne, Fred Billington, and Kate Forster, was a spectacular white fringed-silk affair, printed in blue, with the opera title in bright red as well as the reproduction of Balmoral Castle. And from the two lower corners dangled white pom-poms! (The Grand Inquisitor's reaction might have been: "Distinctly jimp!"—*The Gondoliers*.)

79b Windsor Castle, Sunday evening, 5 July 1891.

A concert held on the night before the wedding of Princess Marie Louise of Schleswig-Holstein (1872–1956) which was to take place in St. George's Chapel. Sir Walter Parratt (1841–1924), friend of Sullivan's, organist at St. George's (soon to be made Master of the Queen's Musick), was in charge of this concert. Emma Albani was the principal soloist. The program included Sullivan's "O Gladsome Light" (*Golden Legend*), in which the composer conducted the (unaccompanied) choir of St. George's Chapel. The white and silver lace design of the program well suited the Royal Princess' wedding.

BLENHEIM HOUSE-PARTY

80 Sullivan.   Photograph of a house-party at Blenheim Palace [n.d., 16 and 17 May 1891] 22½ x 34 cm. (The original is contained in a large album.) A separate page of signatures, including Arthur Sullivan and Mary Frances Ronalds, Blenheim, 16 and 17 May 1891. 36 x 24½ cm. (The original is contained in the same album, three pages before.)

The original is the only photograph yet discovered showing both Arthur Sullivan and Mary Frances Ronalds. The house-party at Blenheim Palace, over a mid-May weekend, was sixteen strong, all signing in the album, including the Duke and Duchess of Marlborough. Among their guests: Lord and Lady Brougham & Vaux, Hermann and Mary Halzfeld, Dorothy Musgrave, H. Plunket Greene, J. Frederick Bridge, Madison Jones, M. F. Ronalds, Arthur Sullivan.

THE BIG QUARREL: 1890–1891

81a Sullivan.   Memorandum, in Walter Smythe's hand, 1 Queen's Mansions. 5pp.

"Interviews & correspondence relative to the dispute between W. S. Gilbert, R. D'Oyly Carte and Arthur Sullivan." Monday, 21 April – Saturday, 3 May 1891.

81b Gilbert.   Letter "copy," 39 Harrington Gardens [London], 5 May 1890, to R. D'Oyly Carte. 1p.

". . . [A]fter Xmas 1890 I revoke your license to produce and perform in the provinces or elsewhere the following libretti. . . ."

81c Carte, Richard D'Oyly, 1844–1901. Letter "copy," Savoy Theatre, 6 May 1890, to Gilbert. 1p.

". . . I must remind you that the agreement . . . was made for two years expiring at Christmas 1891, that that agreement is binding upon all parties until after that date. . . ."

81d Gilbert. Als, 39 Harrington Gardens, 8 May 1890, to Sullivan. 3pp.

"You accuse me of having groundlessly charged you with marked discourtesy toward me. Allow me to explain myself . . . in the case in question it was I, & not you, who had been insulted by Carte & it was consequently for me, & not for you, to say what terms I would continue in association with him . . . from a letter which I received from you [9 December 1889] '. . . Don't talk of reflected light – In such a perfect book as "The Gondoliers" you shine with an individual brilliancy which no other writer can hope to attain. If any thanks are due anywhere, they should be from me to you for the patience, willingness & unfailing good-nature with which you have received my [Sullivan's] suggestions, & your readiness to help me by acceding to them.' "

81e Sullivan. Als "copy," [n.p.], 9 May 1890, to Gilbert. 1p.

"I neither desire nor intend to continue a correspondence which, with argument & counter-argument can result in no practical good . . . they were written in all good faith & sincerity [words written in a letter of 9 December 1889]."

81f Gilbert. Als, and a "copy" Als to Mrs. R. D'Oyly Carte, Breakspears, Uxbridge, 6 September 1890, to Sullivan. 6pp.

". . . I can't bear the thought of prolonged hostilities against people with whom I have been on good terms for so many years . . . I have been miserable since this wretched affair began & would gladly end it. The notion your being a defendant in a suit in which I am a plaintiff has thoroughly upset me. . . ."

"Madame . . . an overture of reconciliation . . . I am not prompted to write this letter by any belief that my case is a weak one, but simply because it distresses me that associations . . . of so many years . . . should be exchanged for feelings of lasting antipathy and resentment . . . I am prepared to meet you and your husband [as one party] . . . and Sir A. Sullivan at Beaufort House (without lawyers on either side) to discuss a means whereby the differences between us may be amicably & finally adjusted. . . ."

81g Sullivan. Als "copy," Grove House, Weybridge, 8 September 1890, to "G" [Gilbert]. 8pp.

"If there is to be a reconciliation let it be a thorough one with confidence restored all round, not merely a patched up truce. But confidence cannot be restored whilst you still contend that no other course was open to you [suit and court appearance the previous Wednesday] . . . as if you cared one rap for a few hundred pounds—its not your nature . . . Don't think me exaggerating when I tell you that I am physically & mentally ill over this wretched business . . . I am tempted to make a suggestion . . . you should withdraw your action at law against Carte and let the disputed matter be settled by a friendly arbitration, (not a legal one of course). . . ."

81h   Gilbert.   Als (partial signature as the letter is damaged), Breakspears, 9 September 1890, to Sullivan. 3pp.

"The tone of your letter causes me to regret that I should have allowed a sentimental recollection of our long alliance to outweigh all consideration of the bewilder[ing] treatment I have received at your hands . . . And I must add that if he [Carte] had not deliberately & arbitrarily withheld from me . . . money which you knew to be absolutely my own, I should never have taken the steps which caused you to array yourself [pu]blicly against me . . . I acted as I did simply because (as you had declined to interfer) I had no alternative . . . I deeply regret that I should have exposed myself to the magisterical reproof contained in your letter. I wrote in the afterglow of many memories & I am old enough to know that a man [illegible] distrust himself when he is under such influences."

81i   Sullivan.   Als, 1 Queen's Mansions, 14 November 1890, to Mr. [deleted]. 22p.

"It is quite true that Gilbert & Carte met at the latter's house last Tuesday & settled their dispute amicably. Gilbert withdraws his action & everything is now (between Gilbert and Carte) as it was seven months ago before the row began. It has been a pitiful business altogether." (The letter was possibly written to a lawyer involved in the dispute.)

81j   Gilbert.   Als, Græme's Dyke, Harrow Weald, 30 January 1891, to Sullivan. 5pp.

This letter concerned profit shares withheld from Gilbert pending settlement of outstanding legal expenses "in an action which I had authorized," and concerned Sullivan's affidavit. Gilbert added, "In reply . . . I shall be happy to accept your invitation [for the opening night of *Ivanhoe*], if before tomorrow evening, I receive from you an admission that the statements of which I complain were made under misinformation."

81k   Sullivan.   Letter "copy," in Walter Smythe's hand, 1 Queen's Mansions, 4 February 1891, to Gilbert. 2pp.

"Little did I think that in asking you to come . . . on Saturday, I was reopening an unhappy controversy, which I firmly believed was settled and forgotten. We look at things from such different points of view, that I fear neither will ever be able to convince the other."

81l   Gilbert.   Als, Graeme's Dyke, 5 February 1891, to Sullivan. 4pp.

"I was reluctant to prolong an unpleasant correspondence while you were engaged in the arduous task of producing your new Opera –." Gilbert quoted from a letter of 10 October from Mrs. Carte and also mentioned Sullivan's affidavit of 3 September. "I am heartily sorry that the attitude you have assumed appears to preclude all possibility of a complete reconciliation."

81m   Gilbert.   Als, Graeme's Dyke, 5 October 1891, to Sullivan. 4pp.

Gilbert mentioned that he had replied to Chappell that there was no prospect he and Sullivan could work together again. To Sullivan he continued, "It is perhaps unnecessary to assure you that all feeling of bitterness has long since passed from my mind, but there remains a dull leaden feeling . . . if you can suggest any reasonable means whereby this cloud can be removed. . . ."

81n   Sullivan.   Letter "copy," in Walter Smythe's hand, 1 Queen's Mansions, 6 October 1891, to Gilbert. 2pp.

"Let us meet & shake hands, and if you still wish to discuss the question of the affidavit (which was also the point upon which I felt aggrieved) we can do so later. We can dispel the cloud hanging over us by setting up a counterirritant in the form of a cloud of smoke."

81o   Sullivan.   Als draft, 1 Queen's Mansions, 2 November 1891, to Gilbert. 2pp.

"I have accordingly this morning agreed to set work at once upon it [probably *Haddon Hall*]. I look upon our [illegible] joint collaboration as merely postponed for a little time, & hope that we shall soon have another success together."

81p   Gilbert.   Als, Graeme's Dyke, 3 November 1891, to Sullivan. 1p.

"All right. I am writing by this post to close in another direction [probably *Haste to the Wedding*]."

THE FORESTERS—INCIDENTAL MUSIC

82a   Sullivan, and Alfred Lord Tennyson, 1809–1892. *The Foresters*, incidental music. Manuscript, signed, partially in Sullivan's hand, partially in a copyist's hand (1892). (Note on page 1: "Copy No. 3 complete without voice parts.") 48 leaves (83pp.). 33½ x 27 and 34½ x 27 cm.
Loaned by Stanford University Libraries, A Memorial Library of Music.

This manuscript of *The Foresters*, as noted on its first page, is "Copy No. 3 complete without voice parts"; in other words, it contains only the incidental music, cued to the libretto. Not surprisingly, much of the autograph is not Sullivan's but probably that of Henry Widmer, Augustine Daly's musical assistant who must have worked closely with Sullivan. The score reveals the notation of each. The musical numbers 34 through 39 [see page xiii], are in Act IV, scene 1 (pages 113–141 of the libretto published by MacMillan in book form). At Robin Hood's "Strike up our music, Little John," there is a tune by Sullivan to which the "Abbot" and the "Justiciary" are forced to dance.

Chappell (London) and Novello, Ewer & Co. (New York) published the vocal score the same year it was first produced (Daly's Theatre, New York, 17 March 1892). It was arranged from the full score by Ernest Ford (co-conductor with F. Cellier of *Ivanhoe*) though his name was omitted from the first edition.

82b Program: *The Foresters*, Lyceum Theatre [London], Henry Irving, manager, "special performance," 17 March 1892. 4pp. 25½ x 19 cm.

"Performed once only (in private) at the Lyceum Theatre, March 17, 1892." Although apparently unrecorded elsewhere, this Lyceum "special performance" of *The Foresters*, stressing the date and "for the first time," was listed by Clement Scott in his work on the Lyceum repertoire (*From "The Bells" to "King Arthur"*) from which the opening quotation was taken. This suggests a copyright safeguard to precede the New York public first-night performance, rather like the Paignton performance of *The Pirates of Penzance* [see No. 53d]. It was probably for Tennyson's text alone. The music, in fact even Sullivan's name, was not mentioned. In this lone performance, Irene Vanbrugh played "Maid Marian," and Acton Bond, "Robin Hood."

82c Program: *The Foresters*, Daly's Theatre, New York, 5 April 1892. 4pp. 36 x 27 cm.

The New York opening of *The Foresters* at Daly's Theatre was described by ever-vivid George Odell (*Annals of the New York Stage*): "The eagerly awaited night arrived, March 17, 1892, and the audience sat in a dream world . . . This was a momentous production. The union of Tennyson, Arthur Sullivan, Daly, Ada Rehan, and John Drew seems like a gift from the Fairyland involved in *The Foresters*." Unaccountably all of Sullivan's biographers have used 25 March as the first-night date. The performance for the program of 5 April 1892 fell in the middle of the run.

82d Program: *The Foresters*, Daly's Theatre, Leicester Square [London], 3 October 1893. 4pp. (with newspaper clipping insert). 18½ x 24 cm.

Although the fact that Daly's *Foresters* production was performed in London has eluded some, it was played at Daly's Theatre, Leicester Square, opening 3 October 1893. Ada

Rehan again was "Maid Marian;" Arthur Bourchier was "Robin Hood." They had been in Daly's second New York season's production, January 1893.

82e Daly, Augustine, 1838–1899. Als, Daly's Theatre, Leicester Square, London, 18 July 1896, to "Dear Sir" [Bendall?]. 1p.

Since this letter was in Sullivan's files, it was probably addressed to his musical assistant, Wilfred Bendall, who succeeded Walter Smythe as secretary in 1896. Daly wrote "the music of 'The Foresters' is at my theatre in New York." He would return it to Sir Arthur on his arrival in New York.

COMIC OPERA WITHOUT GILBERT—*HADDON HALL*

83a Sullivan, and Sydney Grundy, 1848–1914. *Haddon Hall*, an original light English opera. Vocal score, first edition, London: Chappell & Co., copyright 1892. Original printed grey wrappers. [i]–[ii], [1]–169, 3 advt. pp. Plate no. 19,348. 28 x 22 cm.

On the title page is the presentation: "This first copy published to Mrs. Ronalds from Arthur Sullivan 19 Nov: 1892."

Sullivan's collaboration with Sydney Grundy came at a period of pressures of two kinds; the last salvos of Gilbert at the closing months of their "big quarrel," and the recurring first salvos of serious and painful worsening of his kidney condition. Although the public at the time gave praise and support to this first comic opera effort without Gilbert since *Trial by Jury*, still Grundy was no Gilbert. Even so, *Haddon Hall* had a run of 204 performances at the Savoy.

83b Program: *Haddon Hall*, Savoy Theatre, 24 September 1892 (first night). With colored lithographs by [Alice] Havers. 4pp. 13 x 17 cm.

This colorful lithographed four-page program, with neo-classic figures flanking a Grecian altar, was standard for the Savoy Theatre at this time (vide *The Gondoliers* and *Utopia, Limited*). Near the bottom of page 2 is the line, "On this occasion the Opera will be conducted by the Composer." It will be noted that the cast included all the Savoy regulars one might have expected: Rutland Barrington, Courtice Pounds, *et al*.

83c Publisher's agreement: Rights to publish *Haddon Hall*, Sir Arthur Sullivan and Messieurs Chappell and Co., 16 December 1892, signed by Chappell & Co. and Walter Smythe (secretary to Sir Arthur), of 2 Queen's Mansions S.W. 4pp.

"Agreement: An original Light English Opera in Three Acts entitled 'Haddon Hall' . . . For the Vocal Score the sum of one shilling per copy. For the pianoforte arrangements; and for every Song or separate piece being part of said opera; and for all arrangements Dance Music &c. from said opera, the sum of sixpence per copy. . . ."

83d "*Haddon Hall* Quadrilles," by P. Bucalossi, on airs from Sydney Grundy & Arthur Sullivan's Opera, London: Chappell & Co., copyright 1892, plate no. 19367.

83e "*Haddon Hall* Waltz," by P. Bucalossi, on airs from Sydney Grundy & Arthur Sullivan's Opera, London: Chappell & Co., copyright 1892, plate no. 19374.

83f *Haddon Hall* poster: 30 x 20 inches.

This poster, derived from a photograph by Alfred Ellis, London, figures Nita Cole as "Nance" and W. H. Denny as "The McCrankie." *Haddon Hall* was in the repertoire of D'Oyly Carte "E" Company which played Leeds for the week beginning Monday, 16 October 1899.

DINNER AT THE SAVOY

84 Menu: Savoy Hotel, 21 July 1893. Double-leaf card with twelve autographs in pencil on the cover page.

This "Dinet du 21 Juillet, 1893" must have related to a very special occasion to have brought together such an array of guests. The twelve who signed included Mascagni, Christine Nilsson, John Everett Millais, Nellie Melba, Arthur Sullivan, and M. F. Ronalds.

UTOPIA, LIMITED

85a Sullivan. Saturday, 7 October, from his diary, 1893. [See No. 78a.]

Photograph by The Beinecke Library, Yale University.

In Sullivan's diary entry for Saturday, 7 October 1893, at the production of *Utopia, Limited*, the composer admitted to being "shockingly nervous as usual—more than usual," but on his entering the orchestra pit he was not too nervous to note "my ovation lasted 65 seconds!" (He had written "minutes" which he deleted.) "Piece went wonderfully well—not a hitch of any kind, & afterwards G. & I had a *double call*. Supped at the Savoy Hotel afterwards G. Carte & myself, each asking about 8 friends each—Miss Macintosh [sic] in the chair!" (Nancy McIntosh had sung the leading role that night.)

85b Photograph of Nancy McIntosh as "Zara," *Utopia, Limited*, taken by Alfred Ellis & Walery, London [n.d.]. 16½ x 11 cm.

This was the role in which Nancy McIntosh made her debut. Born in Ohio, she went to London to study with George Henschel; later she became the adopted daughter of W. S. Gilbert.

85c Gilbert, W. S. *Utopia, Limited*. Manuscript of lyrics, Act I, not signed nor dated [1893]. 69pp.

The Sullivan archive contains an amazing wealth of manuscript material for Act I, evidently sent to Sullivan by Gilbert for his consideration and, perhaps, for setting. This may have reflected a new posture for Gilbert, very much on his cooperative best after the long "big" quarrel. Among these sixty-nine pages of his manuscript is the opening chorus of Act I [see page xiii], together with the Alfred Ellis cabinet photograph that so exactly, and entertainingly, followed the dramatist's scene direction: "Scene—a Tropical Landscape. Girls discovered lying about lazily—some in hammocks. . . ."

85d Photograph: Two ladies of the chorus in costume for *Utopia, Limited*, taken by Alfred Ellis, London [n.d.]. 17 x 11 cm.

85e "*Utopia, Limited* Lancers," by F. R. Kinkee, on airs from W. S. Gilbert & Arthur Sullivan's Opera, London: Chappell & Co., plate no. 19565.

85f "*Utopia, Limited* Polka," by Paul Duprêt, on airs from W. S. Gilbert & Arthur Sullivan's Opera, London: Chappell & Co., plate no. 19567.

85g "*Utopia, Limited* Quadrille," by Frank Leslie, on airs from W. S. Gilbert & Arthur Sullivan's Opera, London: Chappell & Co., plate no. 19558.

THE CHIEFTAIN

86a Sullivan. Als, 1 Queen's Mansions, 7 July 1894, to "Frank" [Burnand]. 2pp.

Sullivan, for once with time on his hands—"five or six weeks *free*"—followed through in this letter on Burnand's suggestion that they rewrite and revive *The Contrabandista* [see No. 15a]. It was a commendable mistake in judgement. He was trying to help an old friend, who (perhaps not unknown to Sullivan) was trying to "cash in" on the fragile relations of the composer with Burnand's arch-rival, Gilbert. And so *The Chieftain* was born, ill-starred, 12 December 1894.

86b Sullivan, and F. C. Burnand, 1836–1917. *The Chieftain*, an original comic opera. Vocal score, London: Boosey & Co., copyright 1895. Original printed grey wrappers. [i]–[ii], [1]–162pp. Plate no. H.1242. 28 x 22 cm.

86c Program: *The Chieftain*, Savoy Theatre, 12 December 1894. 4pp.

The first-night program was a modest affair containing the important assurance that "On this occasion the Opera will be conducted by the Composer." With it, apparently D'Oyly Carte—not without prodding by the librettist and composer, one can feel sure—included a leaflet that was an effort to make a virtue out of the rewriting of this warmed-over *Contrabandista* from 1867. The composer was riding high on the wave of success; his librettist of twenty-five years before was not so successful.

86d Sullivan. Als, Hotel de Paris, Monte Carlo, Monday 29 January [1895], to "Frank" [Burnand]. 4pp.

After the opening of *The Chieftain*, Sullivan had slipped off to Monte Carlo. But when he learned how badly the opera was doing, he began writing new songs and dances which he scored and rushed back to the Savoy. The first part of this letter is a fascinating exposition of the composer's grasp of the librettist's task as well as his own. Here he virtually wrote a lyric for Burnand, supplying mock words and music. But all this creative enthusiasm was for naught. *The Chieftain*, after only ninety-six performances, was withdrawn on 16 March.

86e Poster: *The Chieftain*. A striking figure of a Spanish brigand against a bright red background. By Dudley Hardy, Waterlow & Sons Ltd., Lith., London Wall. Copyright Rgd. 30 x 20 inches.

A SULLIVAN SONG FOR *THE LADIES' HOME JOURNAL*

87a Sullivan, and Sydney Grundy, 1848–1914. "Bid me at least good-bye!", song. London: Chappell & Co., copyright 1894. Plate no. 19774.

The year after Sullivan had collaborated with Sydney Grundy on *Haddon Hall*, the librettist wrote a play for which he apparently asked his recent colleague to compose an incidental song. The play, *An Old Jew*, opened at the Garrick Theatre on 6 January 1884, described as "A Comedy in five acts." The uninviting review it received in *The Theatre* magazine was in keeping with the passé ballad poetry of this song which began: "Tis twenty years since our last meeting, / Hush'd is anger, numb'd is pain; / dead is love, and friendship's greeting, / We shall ne'er exchange again. ..." But, so important was Sullivan's name, that *The Ladies' Home Journal* contracted with him for the United States rights for a three-month period, to run this song in their issue of December 1894. Its publication must have been a success because two years later the *Journal* came back for more—"The Lost Chord" [see No. 93a and b].

87b Poster: "*The Ladies' Home Journal* for December. Sir Arthur Sullivan's New Ballad." ("Bid me at least good-bye!", December 1894.) 39 x 28 cm.

This counter-card-size poster gave no title for the "New Ballad," but displayed a large oval portrait photograph of Sullivan. *He* was the attraction.

87c Memorandum of Agreement: The Curtis Publishing Company and Arthur Sullivan, signed and witnessed by Walter Smythe, 29 May 1894. 2pp.

This contract indicated that the song "Bid me at least good-bye!" was copyrighted in the United States by *The Ladies' Home Journal*.

KING ARTHUR—INCIDENTAL MUSIC

88a Sullivan. *King Arthur* (libretto by J. Comyns Carr). Manuscript of the full score, signed and dated 6 January 1895. Unbound. 90pp. 27 x 35 cm. (First performed at Lyceum Theatre, 12 January 1895.)

The manuscript of *King Arthur* was willed by Sullivan to Wilfred Bendall (1850–1920), who served as his musical assistant and secretary following the death of Walter Smythe in 1896. It was published in 1903, after Sullivan's death, as a pianoforte score, arranged by Bendall for concert performance. Sullivan apparently had rewritten the Finale of the Prologue (Act I) in a single night, only two days before the opening. There are fifteen pages of music in Sullivan's hand, solely for strings, that appear to relate to the Prologue, but are not in the published score. It is difficult to determine from the manuscript what relates to the original Lyceum production, before or after Sullivan's changes, and what may relate to Bendall's rearrangement. Quite possibly the fifteen pages for strings alone are the product of Sullivan's midnight oil, ca. 10 January.

88b Program: *King Arthur*, Lyceum Theatre, 12 January 1895.

The first-night program for *King Arthur* announced "This Evening, Saturday, January 12, 1895 . . . for the first time," and then listed the Royal Lyceum's artist royalty that included Henry Irving, Ellen Terry, J. Forbes-Robertson, Arthur Sullivan, and Burne-Jones. In addition to giving Sullivan credit for the choral and incidental music "composed expressly for the play," the program stated that "The Entr'actes will be selected from Instrumental Works of the same Composer." Although it did not so indicate, according to his biographers Sullivan and Flower (*Sir Arthur Sullivan*, London, 1927), the composer conducted on the first night.

88c Memorandum of Agreement: Arthur Sullivan and Henry Irving, 189–. 3pp.

A draft with pencil additions, signed: "A.S.", concerning the incidental music to the play *King Arthur*.

THE GRAND DUKE

89a Sullivan. Saturday, 7 March, from his diary, 1896. [See No. 78a.]

Photograph by the Beinecke Library, Yale University.

Arthur Sullivan's diary entry for Saturday, 7 March 1896, rather gave the show away—it was so lacking in life and anticipation. "Busy all day, shopping &c. Auntie [Mrs. Ronalds] called for Bertie [Herbert Sullivan, Arthur's nephew and adopted son] & me at ¼ to 8 to go to theatre. Began new Opera 'Grand Duke' at ¼ past 8—usual reception. Opera went well —out at 11.15. Parts of it dragged a little—dialogue too redundant but success great and genuine I think. Supped at Savoy with Oppenheim &c—then home. Thanks God Opera is finished & out."

89b Sullivan (libretto by W. S. Gilbert). *The Grand Duke*. Manuscript of the full score, not signed nor dated. Half green morocco gilt. 440 written pages (including the title to the overture). 27 x 36 cm.

Loaned by John Wolfson.

Gilbert and Sullivan's final opera, *The Grand Duke*, was set in the tiny Duchy of Pfennig Halbpfennig in a very Gilbertian Germany. The librettist took pleasure in satirizing the German background of the nineteenth-century British Court as far as he dared, and further, for cuts were made before the opera opened. "Hesse" had preceded the name of the Duchy, but was removed. And the second line of the Chorus of Chamberlains, "The good Grand Duke of Pfennig Halbpfennig / Though he may be of German Royalty a sprig," was bowdlerized to, "Though, in his own opinion, very very big." There were many "sprigs" of German royalty very, very close to the British royal family. How Sullivan must have squirmed through some of these satirical sallies! On his side, he provided a mock-German score which alternated between music reminiscent of Wagner and of Johann Strauss. In the manuscript, the passage that stopped the show on the first night was the entrance of the Prince's Herald, well along in Act 2. This manuscript contains the only existing orchestral parts to three numbers that were cut from performance and from the published score shortly after the first night: (vocal score) No. 21, "The Brindisi" sung by the Baroness, "Come, bumpers—aye, ever-so-many"; No. 27, "The Roulette Song" sung by The Prince of Monte Carlo, "Take my advise—when deep in debt"; No. 28, patter song sung by The Grand Duke, "Well, you're a pretty kind of fellow."

89c Sullivan. Als, River House, Walton-on-Thames, 10 August 1895, to Gilbert. 4pp.

"I have read the sketch plot again, & like it even better than I did yesterday . . . I have written to Carte . . . to say that I am quite ready to begin, as soon as you have anything ready for me. . . ." In mid-letter Sullivan made a radical suggestion for change: "which . . . I am sure you will not reject without considering it, as it is from a purely musical reason that I make it." The idea was to give the principal soprano part, "Lisa," to Ilka von Palmay, and make Rosina Brandram (a contralto), "Elsa." "Then see what an advantage this is to me. In all the concerted music we shall have a Soprano & Contralto, instead of two Sopranos, and in all concerted pieces where Countess Krakenfeld is the only female, we get a Soprano instead of a Contralto." Smooth and reasonable as that might have appeared, Gilbert did not yield insofar as Brandram was concerned. Palmay kept her role as "Julia," for whom the rival female part was—not "Elsa," but "Lisa"—to be sung by Florence Perry, another soprano.

89d Sullivan, and W. S. Gilbert. *The Grand Duke; or, The Statutory Duel.* Vocal score, arranged from the full score by Wilfred Bendall, London: Chappell & Co., copyright 1896. Original maroon cloth boards gilt. [i]–viii, [1]–166, 2 advt. pp. Plate no. 20,079. 28½ x 22 cm.

Presentation on title page: "Mrs. Ronalds from Arthur Sullivan 1896."

89e Sullivan. Als, Le Grand Hotel, Monte Carlo, 12 and 13 March 1896, to "Frank" [Burnand]. 2pp.

It is easy to imagine the anti-Gilbert letter Burnand wrote to his composer friend immediately after the tepid notices and cool word-of-mouth accorded *The Grand Duke.* Sullivan replied, "Why reproach me? I didn't write the book!!" But somehow or other he must have dragged in mention of *The Chieftain,* for which Sullivan certainly did not write the book, either. The close showed Sullivan as able to laugh at himself even in such trying conditions: "Another week's rehearsal with W.S.G. & I should have gone raving mad. I had already ordered some straw for my hair."

89f "*The Grand Duke* Lancers," by Warwick Williams, on melodies from W. S. Gilbert & Arthur Sullivan's Opera, London: Chappell & Co., copyright 1896, plate no. 20095.

89g *"The Grand Duke* Waltz," by P. Bucalossi, on melodies from W. S.
Gilbert and Arthur Sullivan's Opera, London: Chappell & Co.,
copyright 1896, plate no. 20103.

1896—A BAD YEAR FOR "AUNTIE" AND ARTHUR

90a Sullivan. Als, St. Moritz, 31 August 1896, to "Bertie" [Herbert
Sullivan]. 5pp.

Writing his nephew Bertie on his birthday, Uncle Arthur confessed: "I made a mess of
Auntie's [birthday]. I thought it was the 29th & it is the 23rd unfortunately. I am not good
at birthdays."

90b Sullivan. Als, St. Jean-Villefranche, 30 December 1896, to "Bertie"
[Herbert Sullivan]. 4pp.

"I think we all touched the bottom of misfortune and unhappiness this past year. . . ." On
pages 2 and 3, Sullivan went into the subject of trouble and unhappiness caused by Auntie
[Mrs. Ronalds], and how he hoped Bertie would "be a friend & guide to her. You see, my
dear Bertie, it is a very trying period of life for her."

90c Sullivan. Als, St. Jean-Villefranche, 13 January 1897, to "Dearest Ida"
[American-born Mrs. Sam Newhouse]. 3pp.

At the close of a gossipy, sociable letter, Sullivan asked: "How is Fanny R.? if you have ten
minutes write & tell me how things go on, & whether she is better & more reasonable now.
I hear *once a week* from her (according to my arrangement) & the letters are calm & sensible."

90d Newhouse, Ida. Als, Beverly Hills, California, 21 December 1943, to
Reginald Allen. 3pp.

Ida Newhouse, who moved easily in the Prince of Wales' set and knew Sullivan well, was
requested to write her recollections of Mrs. Ronalds. Although in her seventies in 1943, she
drew a vivid picture with a strong hand: "Mrs. Ronalds was his friend for many years, too
many, in fact, as she became so exacting and jealous of him . . . and when he became very
interested in a pretty and fascinating young woman, Mrs. Ronalds simply 'blew up' and
made an awful scene . . . I, young as I was, had the awkward position of being great friends
with Mrs. Ronalds and Sir Arthur, each one confiding in me. . . ."

CHERCHEZ "L.W."

90e [Ronalds, Mary Frances.] Manuscript copy of a poem, "In Remembrance," by "L.W." [?], 23 August 1896. 1p.

The original "L.W." in Sullivan's life was Louise Scott Russell, as dozens of her "L.W."/ "Little Woman" letters attest, kept by him along with scores of "Fond Dove" love letters from his fiancée, her sister Rachel [see 24a–j]. Why did he save these evidences of his earliest dalliance, and no other love letter from any woman for the rest of his life? What about the "L.W." who persists in his diary entries for twenty years after the original had died? It was not Mrs. Ronalds, for both "Mrs. R." and "L.W." appear independently. The possibility must be considered that "L.W." became Sullivan's security shorthand for "girl friend," with as many identities as there were women in his life (including Mrs. Ronalds herself on occasion). Mrs. Ronalds would have known of this device, in fact there were times when "Mrs. R." made a threesome with A.S. and "L.W." This poem, "In Remembrance," was written in her hand at a time when she knew he was involved in a serious affair ("Miss Violet," see Leslie Baily, pp. 390–392.), and on her very birthday that he had misremembered. It had a double-edged purpose: The words were certainly heartfelt—the "L.W." signature *in her hand* was calculated to turn the knife, showing him that now she too was another of Sullivan's nameless "L.W."'s.

Four months later she wrote on the flyleaf of a New Year's gift book: "To Sir Arthur Sullivan with every good wish for 1897 from M F R" [and in the corner in the same hand] "L.W."

THE JUBILEE HYMN—BISHOPGARTH

A success story in three letters: On Easter Sunday (18 April) 1897, William Walsham, the Bishop of Wakefield, wrote Sullivan.

91a Walsham, William (Bishop of) Wakefield. Als, Bishopgarth, Wakefield, Easter Day 1897, to Sir Arthur Sullivan. 2pp.

"The Prince of Wales (alas!) asked me to write a hymn to be sung in all churches on June 20, the only scrap of consolation being that you have promised to write a tune for it. That may possibly redeem it, tho' I feel awfully dry & dusty. . . ."

A week later, Sir Arthur Bigge, Private Secretary to Queen Victoria, wrote Arthur Sullivan.

91b Bigge, Sir Arthur. Als, Excelsior Hotel Regina, Cimiez, 24 April 1897, to Sir Arthur Sullivan. 4pp.

"Here is the Bishop of Wakefield's hymn—which the Prince of Wales forwarded for Her Majesty to see—I gather that it meets with general approval and is considered worthy of the occasion. As the Bishop says 'Sir Arthur Sullivan's genius will light it up a little!' . . ."

Little more than a month later, Sullivan sent his collaborator-Bishop a letter with a copy of an enclosure from Sir Arthur Bigge.

91c Sullivan. Als, 1 Queen's Mansions, 27 May 1897, to "My dear Lord Bishop." 4pp.

"A succession of worries about the hymn" started this letter of which the entire first half was unnecessary. Sullivan had obviously been working on his royal family connections— "And now, just as I am writing this, a telegram comes from Sir Arthur Bigge, which is . . . more than satisfactory. (I enclose a copy of it) This will be announced in the papers tomorrow or Saturday." The enclosure was a copy of the official notice that the hymn was "ordered to be used in all Churches and Chapels in England and Wales and in the town of Berwick-upon-Tweed upon Sunday the twentieth Day of June 1897." Sullivan, in closing, matched the protest gesture of his Bishop: "My only regret is that I do not think the music is quite up to the level of the words; but I did my best, and it is not easy to be devotional, effective, original *and* simple at the same time."

91d Sullivan, and The Bishop of Wakefield. "Hymn," written by the Bishop of Wakefield and set to music by Arthur Sullivan (by Request). Printed by Eyre and Spottiswoode, Printers to the Queen's most Excellent Majesty, copyright 1897. 4pp.

The inside two pages of this four-page folder give the music and four verses of words to "O King of Kings," the Jubilee Hymn.

92a Sullivan (scenario by Carlo Coppi). *Victoria and Merrie England*, the Grand National Ballet, Suites I, II, and III. Piano Duet, pianoforte arrangement by Wilfred Bendall, London: Metzler & Co., Limited, copyright 1897. Maroon morocco gilt on limp boards. Suite I: 30pp., plate no. M.7987; Suite II: 51pp., plate no. M.7989; Suite III: 45pp., plate no. M.7997. 35 x 25½ cm.

The presentation on the title page of Suite I: "Auntie wishing her a Happy New Year. Dec: 1897. Arthur Sullivan."

This Ballet, and the Queen's Jubilee Hymn, represented Sullivan's participation in Victoria's Diamond Jubilee. The Ballet had opened at the Alhambra Theatre on the night after the Queen's seventy-eighth birthday, Tuesday, 25 May 1897. The composer conducted on this occasion, although the fact was not mentioned in the program.

92b Program: *Victoria and Merrie England*, Alhambra Theatre, Tuesday, 25 May 1897 (opening night). 4pp.

92c "*Victoria and Merrie England* Lancers," arranged by Charles Godfrey, R.A.M., from The Grand National Ballet composed by Arthur Sullivan, London: Metzler & Co. (Limited), copyright 1897, plate no. M7974.

THE SUN NEVER SETS ON "THE LOST CHORD"

93a Bok, Edward W., 1863–1930. Als, [n.p.], 24 November 1896, to Sir Arthur. 1p.

93b Sullivan, and Adelaide A. Proctor, 1825–1864. "The Lost Chord," song. Published in *The Ladies' Home Journal*, December 1897, pages [24]–25.

The Prince of Wales was said to have remarked that he would travel the length of his future kingdom to hear Mrs. Ronalds sing "The Lost Chord." Even though this popular song was already twenty years old, it was still skillful publicity for publisher Edward Bok to feature the entire work in the December 1897 issue of *The Ladies' Home Journal*. A year earlier Bok had made arrangements with Sullivan to pay him £30 for this use of the song, the only compensation the composer had ever received from an American publisher (according to Bok) even though three million copies had been sold in America.

93c Enrico Caruso, 1873–1921. "The Lost Chord," Sullivan and Proctor. New York: G. Schirmer, 1901, plate no. 2060. Page 3, with Caruso's autograph phonetics.

Caruso's own phonetics for "Seated one day at the organ": "Sit-ed uan dei at dhi or-gan / Ai uas uiri and il at üz. . . ."

In order that the great tenor could sing Adelaide Proctor's words approximating English at his American recitals, Caruso interlineated a copy of the sheet-music with his own phonetics, syllable by syllable. The above is a photograph of the first page of music (page 3), from the complete original in the possession of The Peabody Conservatory of Music Library, Baltimore.

93d Sousa, John Philip, 1854–1932. Manuscript of "The Lost Chord," band parts for Tuba, and for Trombones I and II, not signed nor dated. 2pp. 23 x 27½ cm.

The March King's own autograph arrangement.

LETTERS FROM OPERA STARS

94a Calvé, Emma, 1858–1942. Als, [n.p., n.d.], to "Cher Maestro" [Sullivan]. 2pp.

The famed soprano wrote Sullivan [in French], "I accept with the greatest pleasure, happiness and pride to sing with the first musician of England. . . ."

94b Melba, Dame Nellie, 1859–1931. Als, Savoy Hotel [n.d.], to Sir Arthur. 4pp.

"A thousand congratulations on your enormous success last night; how lovely everything was & what an ovation they (we) made you. I feel as happy as though it was I. I think you are greatly to be envied . . . yrs most sincerely Nellie Melba Bravo! Bravo *BRAVO*." It seems likely that Melba wrote this letter on 1 February 1891, after attending the first night of *Ivanhoe*.

94c Palmer, Emma Nevada, 1859–1940. Als, No. 4 Boundary Road, St. John's Wood, Wednesday [n.d.], to Sir Arthur. 4pp.

"How would you like the duo of Lakmé, "C'est le Dieu de la jeunesse,"? Either in French or Italian! If you prefer the Mireille, or anything else I am quite ready for it, as I wish to sing what *you* like. . . ."

94d Reszke, Edouard de, 1855–1917. Als, Hotel Continental, London, "Lundi" [n.d.], to "Cher Monsieur Sullivan." 2pp.

The distinguished Polish basso wrote of his great regret that he was unable to accept Sullivan's invitation to dinner to meet H.R.H. The Prince of Wales. He had accepted another invitation in the country which he could not refuse.

LETTERS FROM COMPOSERS

Sullivan's position as Musical Director of the Leeds Festival created correspondence with other composers who were scheduled to appear. In the instances of Fauré, Humperdinck, and Elgar, it was the Leeds Festival of 1898.

95a Fauré, Gabriel, 1845–1924. Als, 154 Boulevard Malesherbes [Paris], 6 September [1898], to "Monsieur" [Sullivan]. 2pp.

The composer was scheduled to conduct the first performance in England of one of his own choral works, *The Birth of Venus* (1895), on Saturday, 8 October. He wrote this note of inquiry to Sullivan, asking the numbers of players in each of the various string sections of the Festival orchestra.

95b Humperdinck, Engelbert, 1854–1921. Als, 1, Canterbury Villas, Worthing, 30 September 1898, to "Verherter Meister" [Sullivan]. 3pp.

Humperdinck had been commissioned to compose a new work for the Festival. It was his *Moorish Rhapsody*, conducted by him on Friday, 7 October. He wrote to thank Sullivan "for the kind forbearance with which you supported me yesterday at the rehearsal." And he asked, "could one perhaps seat the Celli together as it is the case everywhere . . . The sound would decidedly gain by this."

95c Elgar, Sir Edward, 1857–1934. Als, 43 & 44 Albermarle Street [London], Thursday [n.d., ca. 1898], to Sir Arthur Sullivan. 3pp.

The success of Elgar's cantata, *Caractacus*, 5 October at Leeds, was an important factor in his surge ahead at the turn of the century. Sullivan, busy though he was, had found time to help the younger composer, particularly at rehearsals. This letter is as rare an example of outspoken gratitude, as is the occasion that inspired it, according to Elgar: "I could not let the last day of the rehearsals go by without sending my thanks to you for making my 'chance' possible & pleasant—this is of course what one knows *you* would do but it contrasts very much with what some people do to a person unconnected with the schools—friendless & alone and I am always yours very gratefully Edward Elgar."

THE BEAUTY STONE

96a Sullivan, Arthur W. Pinero, 1855–1934, and J. Comyns Carr 1849–1916. *The Beauty Stone*, an original romantic musical drama in three acts. Vocal score, arranged from the full score by Wilfred Bendall, London: Chappell & Co, Ltd., copyright 1898. [i]–[iv], 1–211, [212], 2 advt. pp. Blue-grey printed paper wrappers. Plate no. 20528. 27½ x 21½ cm.

Arthur Sullivan's penultimate opening night at the Savoy was *The Beauty Stone*, libretto by Arthur Pinero and Comyns Carr. This was certainly no comic opera, nor—with its overlong passages of dialogue—was it properly a grand opera. Perhaps as its description "Romantic Musical Drama" suggests, it may have fallen between two audience interests. It opened on 28 May 1898, the composer conducting, and played only fifty performances. Sullivan's biographers [Sullivan and Flower] quoted a revealing diary comment on the unsatisfactory collaboration: "Both Pinero and Carr, gifted and brilliant men, with *no* experience in writing for music and yet obstinately declining to accept any suggestions from me, as to form and construction . . . they declined to alter. 'Quod scripsi, scripsi' they both said."

96b Program: *The Beauty Stone*, Savoy Theatre, Saturday evening, 28 May [1898] (first night), "On this occasion the Opera will be conducted by the Composer." One card folded in thirds.

SULLIVAN, THE INVENTOR

In 1896 Lady Alice Lathom, wife of the Lord Chamberlain and friend of Sullivan, was among Mrs. Ronalds' guests at the first night of *The Grand Duke*. In 1897 she was killed in a runaway horse accident, not an infrequent pre-petrol hazard. Brought close to the problem posed by this tragedy, the composer turned his inventive genius to devising "a means for releasing draught animals from road vehicles," as the Provisional Patent Specifications termed his "S.S.S."—Sullivan's Safety Shaft. His partner for leg-and-paperwork in this enterprise was S. M. Barry, personal man-of-business for Mrs. Ronalds. Letters passed between them in late 1898. One of 30 November is amusing for the *stretto* it showed which penetrated the composer's calm:

97a Sullivan. Als, 1 Queen's Mansions [London], 30 November 1898, to Mr. Barry. 2pp.

"As is always the case when the goal is in sight, I am getting feverishly anxious, lest anyone should snatch the prize from me. Things get about in an unaccountable way, & I am terrified lest someone should forestall us with the patents."

97b Sullivan. Als, 1 Queen's Mansions, 14 December 1898, to Mr. Barry. 2pp.

The inventor had the revised Statement ready for the Patent Agent to copy and to enter in the Patent Office. "I have finally settled to buy the model . . . it is beautifully made, quite perfect. If I send it up to you, will you get the invention (the S.S.S.) applied to it at once, so that I can take it to H.R.H. without delay?" Naturally Sullivan was moving toward the Prince of Wales' interest.

97c Leaflet: The Sullivan Safety Shaft. One page of description of the invention, and advice as to where it was on view.

97d Patent Office Specifications; No. 26,624 for The Sullivan Safety Shaft. A three-page stitched folder with two fold-out diagrams of illustration.

97e Wallet: Gold-stamped, dark-green leather, containing Letters Patent for The Sullivan Safety Shaft.

"THE ABSENT-MINDED BEGGAR"

98a Sullivan, and Rudyard Kipling, 1865–1935. "The Absent-minded Beggar," song. Manuscript, signed and dated by Sullivan, 6 November 1899. 4pp. 26½ x 34½ cm.
Loaned by the Berg Collection, The New York Public Library.

Sullivan and Kipling met only once as collaborators, unfortunately not for "The Recessional," but on a fund-raising stint for Boer War relief: "The Absent-minded Beggar." The manuscript, with words in Kipling's autograph, and music and musical directions in Sullivan's hand (signed and dated by him), was bought by Alfred Cooper, board chairman of Pegram & Co. (Tea Merchants) for £500 "handed to the 'Absent-minded Beggar Fund.' " Cooper promptly arranged for a facsimile reproduction of the manuscript to be made in a "Special Edition de Luxe," which was widely sold (with slightly varying front wrapper illustrations) for the relief fund. The song inspired many formats for fund-raising use. For example:

98b Song, "The Absent-minded Beggar," Special Edition de Luxe, a facsimile reproduction of the original manuscript. London: Ridgways, Limited [n.d.], copyright. Front cover with photographs of Arthur Sullivan and Rudyard Kipling; inside cover, sketch by R. Caton Woodville, 1899; 4 pages of the facsimile; inside back cover, four verses of the words; back cover, notes on this edition.

98c Song: "The Absent-minded Beggar," sheet-music, first edition. London: Enoch & Sons, copyright 1899 by "The Daily Mail" Publishing Company, London. 9pp. Plate no. E. & S. 2702. The first edition of 75,000 copies, entire proceeds to the fund.

98d March on the celebrated song, "The Absent-minded Beggar": sheet-music, London: Enoch & Sons, copyright 1899. 7pp. Plate no. E. &. S. 2708. Front cover carries the R. Caton Woodville sketch, 1899, by permission of "The Daily Mail" Publishing Co.

98e Linen handkerchief: words and music of "The Absent-minded Beggar" together with a map of the South African Republic, portraits of Lord Roberts and Queen Victoria, printed in blue ink. 52 x 47 cm.

98f Sullivan.   Agreement: Enoch & Sons and Sir Arthur Sullivan, 10 November 1899. Signed by Arthur Sullivan. 3pp.

The publishers' contract shows, on page 3, the special arrangement for participation of the Boer War Relief Fund, but not "as regards the Colonies and the United States."

98g Sullivan.   Al draft, 1 Queen's Mansions [London], 22 November 1899, to Mr. Kipling. 2pp.

"Your splendid words went, and still go every night, with a swing and an enthusiasm which even my music cannot stifle. It has been a great pleasure to me to be able to set words of yours; and although my academical friends (who form a strong element in our Art) regret, without doubt that I have treated the words in a simple and *ad cap*: spirit, with a catching tune, (a heinous offence in their eyes)"—[the draft is unfinished]. Perhaps Sullivan's crystal ball had already shown him Fuller-Maitland's obituary and article in *The Cornhill Magazine*, only three months after his death: ". . . how can the composer of 'Onward Christian Soldiers' and 'The absent-minded beggar' claim a place in the hierarchy of music among the men who would face death rather than smirch their singing-robes for the sake of a fleeting popularity?"

98h Kipling, Rudyard, 1865–1935. Als, The Elms, Sussex, 27 May 1900, to Sir Arthur. 2pp.

"I entirely agree with you that something should be done to wipe out the disgrace of the A.M.B." These opening words of Kipling make clear that those "academical friends" Sullivan had mentioned in his letter of 22 November (very nearly with bravado) had got to him, and had provoked quite a different point of view. Kipling was willing, perhaps with tongue in cheek, to go along with the "disgrace of the A.M.B.," and was overjoyed that Sullivan would set a new march song he had in mind, but not yet written. "Meantime I send you with this *Recessional*. I do hope the spirit will move you to set it." Alas! Sullivan had but six more months to live, and he never set *The Recessional*.

THE ROSE OF PERSIA

99a Sullivan, and Basil Hood, 1864–1917. *The Rose of Persia; or, The Story-Teller and the Slave.* Comic opera, arranged from the full score by Wilfred Bendall. London: Chappell & Co., Ltd, copyright 1900. [i]–[iv], 1–237, 2 advt. pp. Plate no. 20872.

His "Persian opera," as he called it, was Sullivan's last opening night at the Savoy. His diary read: "November 29th [1899], Wednesday—1st performance of 'Rose of Persia' at Savoy Theatre. I conducted as usual. Hideously nervous as usual—great reception as usual—great house—excellent performance as usual—everything as usual—except the piece is really a great success I think, which is *unusual* lately." Indeed, it played 213 performances.

99b Sullivan. *The Rose of Persia*. Manuscript of a cadenza for " 'Neath my lattice," not signed nor dated. 1p. 27 x 34½ cm.

On the front is written in another hand: "Original Mss. of Sir Arthur Sullivan written about 1907 for a cadenza of the principal song " 'Neath my lattice" in the opera "The Rose of Persia" which he wrote for me. Ellen Beach Yaw."

The principal soprano role, that of the Sultana, "Rose-in-Bloom," was sung by Ellen Beach-Yaw on the opening night. Very early in December she was replaced by Isabel Jay, but not before Sullivan had apparently written an unusually high cadenza for her for the close of her song, " 'Neath my lattice through the light." Obviously for a unique voice, this cadenza requires a G sharp above high C (the legendary "Queen of the Night" aria, "Ah infelice!", in *The Magic Flute* only goes to F!). Sullivan's manuscript of this cadenza includes Miss Beach-Yaw's recollection of its history.

99c "*The Rose of Persia* Lancers," by Warwick Williams, on melodies by Arthur Sullivan, London: Chappell & Co. Ltd., and Hopwood & Crew Ltd., copyright 1900 by Chappell, plate no. 20,918.

99d Poster: *The Rose of Persia*. D'Oyly Carte's Opera Company, by Dudley-Hardy, Waterlow & Sons Ltd, London Wall, copyright regd., ca. 1900. 29⅜ x 19⅜ inches.

A whirling dancing figure.

99e Sullivan. Photograph, semiprofile, signed and dated July 1899, taken by Kilpatrick, Belfast. 14½ x 10½ cm. (without mat). [See page 157.]

THE EMERALD ISLE

100a Sullivan, and Basil Hood, 1864–1917. *The Emerald Isle; or The Caves of Carrig-Cleena*, a new and original comic opera in two acts. Vocal score arranged from the full score by Wilfred Bendall, London: Chappell & Co., Ltd, copyright 1901. Original blue-grey wrappers. [i]–[iv], 1–220, 4 advt. pp. Plate no. 21266. 28 x 22 cm.

Early in 1900, Sullivan lost one of his dearest friends in the death of George Grove. He was depressed and unable to come to grips with his work, a dual commitment—the "*Victory Te Deum*" and the new comic opera that Carte had scheduled for the Savoy in November. A few weeks after finishing the *Te Deum*, on 3 July came another blow, the death of his closest friend in the royal family, Alfred, Duke of Saxe-Coburg (Duke of Edinburgh). Unwell himself, and sensing the approach of his own end, he was in no mood to compose, and comic opera perhaps least of all. Yet he finished setting the songs and choruses of Basil Hood's libretto by the end of August, working in Switzerland. He started orchestrating, but a severe cold with complications frightened him, and he returned to London. He did no further useful work on *The Emerald Isle*. On the verso of the title page of the vocal score, a Publishers' Note summed up the status of this final opus: "The numbers of the Opera composed by Sir Arthur Sullivan, with the exception of Nos. 1 and 2, which were completed by him, have been orchestrated and harmonized by Mr. Edward German."

100b *"The Emerald Isle* Waltz," by Carl Kiefert, on melodies by Arthur Sullivan and Edward German, London: Chappell & Co. Ltd., copyright 1901, plate no. 21,324.

100c Poster: *The Emerald Isle*. Savoy Theatre Opera Coy., Mr. William Greet, manager. By Dudley-Hardy, 1901, David Allen & Sons, Ltd, London. Chromotype. 29½ x 19¾ inches.

A red-haired female figure with her arm around a young man whose eyes are bandaged; shamrocks abound.

"IT WAS THE COMPOSER'S LAST FINISHED WORK"

101a Sullivan. *Te Deum Laudamus (A Thanksgiving for Victory)*, for chorus, strings, brass instruments and organ. Full score, Novello and Company, Limited, printed by F. M. Geidel, Leipzig. Printed paper wrappers. 35pp. Plate no. 11445.

In midsummer 1900, Sullivan was harassed and depressed by the state of his health and spirits. However, he managed to finish the *"Victory Te Deum"* in early August, as the exuberant letter of Sir George Martin, organist of St. Paul's Cathedral, testified [see No. 101b].

101b Martin, Sir George C., 1844–1916. Als, 4 Amen Court, St. Paul's, E.C. [London], 14 August 1900, to Sir Arthur. 4pp.

"This is splendid! I am delighted to hear you have entirely finished the Te Deum, & I am longing to see it. As to printing. I should like it to proceed . . . *providing it can be done entirely secretly*—without anyone knowing for what occasion it is intended. This war drags on & may last some time yet . . . I cannot thank you sufficiently for writing it & I hope the performance when it takes place, will not be disagreeable to you." (Sullivan had been dead a year and a half when it was first performed at St. Paul's on 8 June 1902.) Sir George added a nice *vox humana* at the close: "We go away (amongst the partridges) in September. . . ."

101c Sullivan. *Te Deum Laudamus (A Thanksgiving for Victory)*. "Novello's Original Octavo Edition," London: Novello and Company, Limited, copyright, 1902. Paper wrappers. 41pp. Plate no. 8312. 26 x 17½ cm.

There is the following paragraph on the verso of the title page: "This setting of the Te Deum was written by request, with a view to its performance at the Thanksgiving Service to be held in St. Paul's Cathedral at the close of the War in South Africa. It was the Composer's last finished work. [signed] May 1902 George C. Martin."

ARTHUR SULLIVAN BY MAX BEERBOHM

102 Beerbohm, Max, 1872–1956. Original caricature of Sir Arthur Sullivan, signed but not dated, line and wash over pencil on white paper. 24 x 17 cm.

In a letter written by Beerbohm from Rapallo in 1952, he recalled: "About drawing of Sir Arthur Sullivan, – I think it was the only one I ever did. I don't think it was ever reproduced anywhere; but I fancy it was included by me in my very first exhibition, in 1901. He was at that time of course an old man, and he looked rather tragically ill."

THE FINAL YEAR

103a Sullivan's last birthday party: Menu, Savoy, 13 May 1900. 19 x 14 cm.

The signatures of Sullivan and five of those closest to him are on this colorful Savoy Hotel menu: Richard and Helen D'Oyly Carte, Mrs. Ronalds, Herbert Sullivan, and Wilfred Bendall. Other members of the party were: Walter Pallant, Fred Vincent, Miriam Herring, Alfred Oakley, Ida Newhouse, Sybil Crutchley, (Lady) Katherine Coke, and Lionel Monckton.

103b Sullivan. Als, 1 Queen's Mansions [London], Sunday [n.d., 21 October 1900], to B. W. Findon. 2pp.

In a letter written to his cousin, B. W. Findon, only a month from his death, he asked his help to have a paragraph run in the newspapers to refute: "that I was seriously ill, & had passed through Paris [en route] to Monte Carlo. I have been ill it is true, but I am much better now, and only remaining result is an 'extinction de voix'—I can hardly speak." And a closing P.S. "I am hard at work on my opera." (*The Emerald Isle* he was never to finish.)

103c Sullivan. Carte de visite, with a note, 60 Victoria Street, 1 November 1900 [n.p.], to M. le Directeur du Grand Hotel.

On his visiting card Sullivan wrote in French to the hotel manager asking that he do his best for a member of his family, Herbert Sullivan. This was dated three weeks before he died.

103d Sullivan. Photograph, [n.d., n.p.], a sick, old man. 8½ x 7 cm.

GILBERT'S LAST LETTER TO SULLIVAN

104 Gilbert, W. S. Als, Grim's Dyke, Harrow Weald, 9 November 1900, to Sullivan. 2pp.

Patience had been revived for the first time on 7 November. There had been a plan for Gilbert, Sullivan, and D'Oyly Carte to take a curtain call together, even if in wheelchairs, for all three were ill. Gilbert and Carte did manage to attend (without wheelchairs); Sullivan was too sick. Gilbert wrote him expressing his great disappointment. He had looked forward to the opportunity of "shaking hands over past differences." He wrote again two days later (9 November) when his own enfeebled condition from rheumatic fever precluded a chance to get to London before leaving for Egypt for his health. "I've lost 60 lbs weight & my arms & legs are of the consistency of cotton wool." And of the *Patience* revival, he added: "P.S. The old piece woke up splendidly."

SONGS—PIANOFORTE ACCOMPANIMENT

Words by Tennyson:

105a "Tears, Idle Tears," from *The Princess*, The John Church Co., copyright 1900, plate no. 13500-5.

105b "O Swallow, Swallow," from *The Princess*, The John Church Co., copyright 1900, plate no. 13501-7.

These two songs were sung at St. James's Hall in October 1900 at the Butt-Rumford Concert, by Kennerley Rumford, Clara Butt's husband.

Words by Benjamin Disraeli:

105c "My heart is like a silent lute," from "Henrietta Temple," Novello & Co., Ltd., 1904, plate no. 11786.

Words by Jean Ingelow:

105d "Longing for home," Novello & Co., Ltd., 1904, plate no. 11787.

Words by Edgar Allan Poe:

105e "To one in Paradise," Novello & Co., Ltd., 1904, plate no. 11785.

FINALE

"Directions for my funeral To be opened directly after my death." Shortly after the death of his mother in 1882, Sullivan wrote a short memorandum on the subject of his own death. He directed that: "My funeral is to be conducted in the same manner as that of my dear Mother . . . [and that] My body is to be buried in the same grave with My Father, Mother, & brothers in Brompton Cemetery. . . ."

106a   Sullivan.   Manuscript of his funeral directions, 1 Queen's Mansions [London], 18 August 1882 (on mourning stationery, with cover). 2pp.

Little did the composer realize when he wrote these instructions, that they would be disregarded by Royal Command. Queen Victoria directed that his funeral service be conducted at the Chapel Royal, and that his interment be in St. Paul's Cathedral.

106b   Sullivan.   Will and Testament, signed. Page 1 of the calligraphic original.

106c   Sullivan.   Will and Testament, draft by Sullivan. Page 4. Manuscript on 1 Queen's Mansions stationery, in ink by Sullivan on nine recto pages, all verso pages blank, except verso 3, which contains additions in pencil.

On page 4 is that portion treating the residue and special bequests: "The residue of my money, copyrights, performing rights, and of all my personal estate I leave to my nephew Herbert Thomas Sullivan whom I appoint residuary legatee of everything I may die possessed of, with the exception of the following bequests"—there follow, among others:
   —The Millais portrait, to the National Portrait Gallery;
   —MS of *The Mikado* and of *The Martyr of Antioch*, to The Royal Academy of Music;
   —MS of *The Yeomen of the Guard* and of *The Golden Legend*, to The Royal College of Music;
   —MS of *King Arthur* and of the *Macbeth Music*, to Wilfred Bendall. . . .

106d   Order of Service at the Funeral of the late Sir Arthur Sullivan, Chapel Royal, St. James's Palace, Tuesday, 27 November 1900. 4pp. With printed covers, stitched, Harrison & Sons, printers.

Mrs. Ronalds' copy, the front cover bears her name.

   Page 4 of the Order of Service is concerned with the interment service at St. Paul's Cathedral. On this page appears four stanzas of Sullivan's anthem, "Brother, thou art gone before us," which "will be sung by the Ladies and Gentlemen of the Savoy Theatre." This the Company did, *a cappella*, "with a strange pathos, as a last tribute to the dead composer" (*Westminster Gazette*).

106e Mrs. Ronalds' ticket of admission, No. 7, to the Centre section of the Chapel Royal, St. James's Palace, 27 November 1900.

106f "Brother, thou art gone before us," anthem, from The Sacred Musical Drama, *The Martyr of Antioch*, composed by Arthur Sullivan, London: Chappell & Co., plate no. 17,320. Cover, (2)–7pp.

106g Birch, William A. Als, 41 Albert Gate, Knightsbridge [London], 27 November 1900, to "Dear Madam" [Mrs. Ronalds]. 2pp.

Mrs. Ronalds had approached the head of the funeral directors who was in charge of Sullivan's funeral. She had asked that her floral cross be put in the grave with the casket. But she was outranked. This letter was written on the very day of the funeral: "I have again been to St. Pauls Cathedral with the intentions of putting the Cross into the Grave, but was told that only The Queen's Wreath would be buried with the Coffin. This information was given quite privately, so perhaps it would be as well not to mention it to any one."

106h Gilbert, W. S. Als, Helouan, Egypt, 4 December 1900, to Herbert Sullivan. 2pp.

Gilbert, travelling in Egypt for his health, had not learned of Sullivan's death for more than a week. He wrote Herbert immediately, 4 December, a warm letter of sympathy. "It is a satisfaction to me to feel that I was impelled, shortly before his death, to write to him to propose to shake hands over recent differences & even a greater satisfaction to learn, through you that my offer of reconciliation was cordially accepted."

THE UNVEILING OF THE MEMORIAL BUST OF ARTHUR SULLIVAN ON THE VICTORIA EMBANKMENT, FRIDAY, 10 JULY 1903

107a Photograph of the pedestal and bust.

Photograph by Donald Southern.

The sculptor was Mr. Goscombe John, A.R.A., who was also responsible for the bas-relief for Sullivan in St. Paul's Cathedral.

107b Description of the Unveiling Ceremony, reprinted from *The Daily News*.

107c Program of music to be played on the occasion of the Unveiling.

It was an all-Sullivan program, including such selections as: Cornet Solo, "The Lost Chord," and Euphonium Solo, "Ho, Jolly Jenkin" (Friar Tuck's song from *Ivanhoe*).

107d Program for the Unveiling Ceremony.

This included speeches by Lord James of Hereford and Lord Monkswell, for the County Council, and the unveiling by H.R.H. Princess Louise. W. S. Gilbert moved the vote of thanks to H.R.H., and reply was made by her husband, the Duke of Argyll.

107e Two tickets of admission to the ceremony.

One in the name of composer F. H. Cowen, a member of the Committee; another showing on its reverse side the list of members of the Sir Arthur Sullivan Memorial Fund Committee.

107f Gilbert, W. S. Als, Grim's Dyke, Harrow Weald, 19 March 1903, to Herbert Sullivan. 2pp.

"Marshall [Capt. Robert Marshall, dramatist] tells me that you want a quotation from one of the libretti, to inscribe on your Uncle's bust. What do you say to this (from the Yeomen)

'Is life a boon?
If so, it must befal
That Death, whene're he call
Must call too soon.'

It is difficult to find anything quite suited to so sad an occasion, but I think this might do."

Lovely day – stayed at home – 3 letters from Gilbert. 2 answers – his last a rough & insolent refusal to come to the performance of "Ivanhoe" Busy all day with tickets &c. Went to the theatre (R.E.O.) at 7.40. Tremendous crowd outside – at 8 – Prince & Princess of Wales, with Pss Victoria & Maud & Duke & Duchess of Edinburgh entered their box. "God save the Queen" played by orchestra – Cellier conducting. at 8.5 I entered. Tremendous reception by a brilliant & packed house. The sight was really superb.

Began "Ivanhoe" – but the 1st 60 or 80 bars quite inaudible owing to the noise made by the ship on account of standees in the gangway – then they were removed & the opera went on. Event splendidly, without a hitch from beginning to end – all sang well. Kim Macintyre, Pallier & Grueble – Ben Davies, Oudin, Salmand, Françon Davies, Saxon, Kenningham, Copland, Stephens & R. Green.

Went up after the 1st Act to the Prince's room – he & the Duke came & smoked cigarettes in my room afterwards.

Great enthusiasm at the end – everyone called – I went on with Sturgis. Gave all the stage hands 5/- each afterwards

Supped at the Orleans – large party given by E. Dresden & P. Joä. Then to Portland – home at 4.

Sullivan's diary, *Ivanhoe*, first night. (78a)

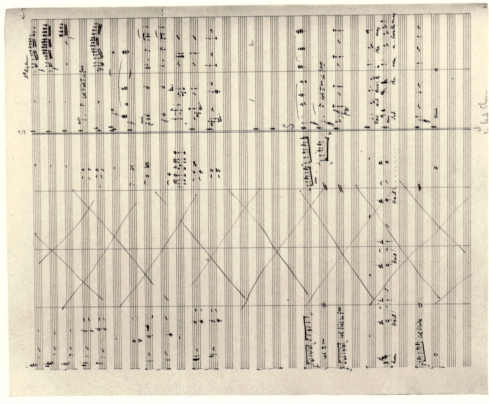

The chorus, "Fair and lovely is the May," *Ivanhoe*, Act 1, scene 3, 1890. (78b)

Sullivan (back row, first right) and Mrs. Ronalds (first lady standing at right), at Blenheim Palace (1891). (80)

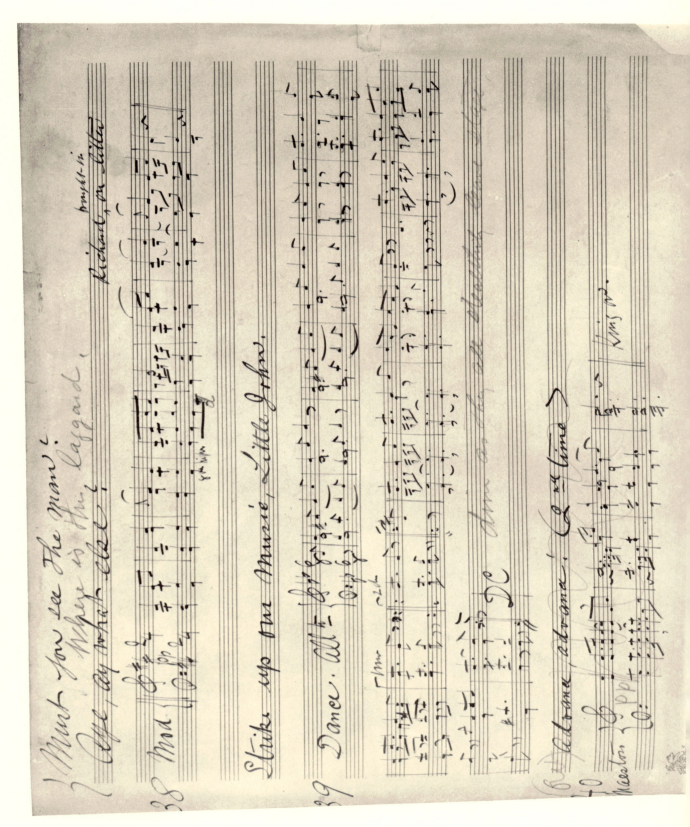

The Foresters, Act 4, scene 1 – MS by Sullivan and copyist (1892). (82a)

Utopia, Limited

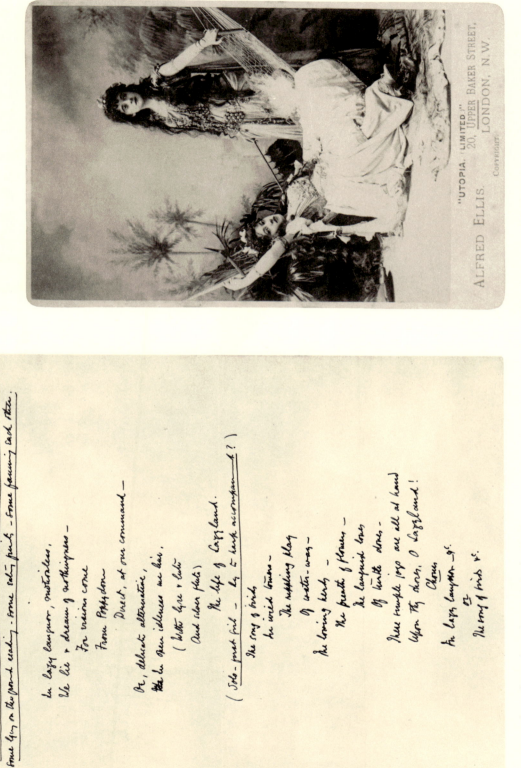

Opening scene, "In lazy languor" (1893). (85d)

Gilbert's manuscript of opening chorus (1893). (85c)

The Chieftain – poster, ca. 1895. (86e)

Haddon Hall – poster, Leeds (1889). (83f)

The Herald's Song, *The Grand Duke*, Act 2. (89b)

The Absent-minded Beggar

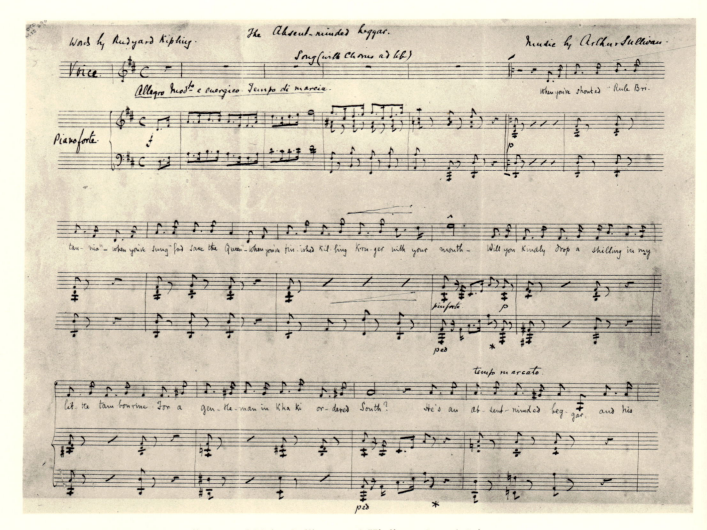

"The Absent-minded Beggar," song – MS by Sullivan and Kipling, 1899. (98a)

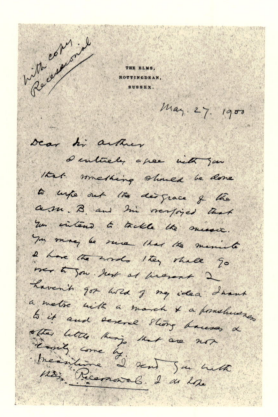

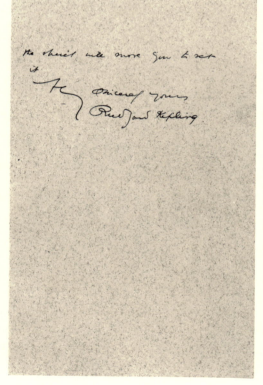

Sullivan to Kipling, draft letter, 22 November 1899. (98g)

Kipling to Sullivan on the "AMB" and "Recessional," 1900. (98h)

From No. 13, Act I, Sullivan's *King Arthur*, 1895. (88a)

The Emerald Isle – poster, 1901. (100C)

The Rose of Persia – poster, ca. 1900. (99d)

Sullivan's MS cadenza written for Ellen Beach Yaw, *The Rose of Persia* (1899). (99b)

Autographed menu of Sullivan's last birthday party. (103a)

Sir Arthur Sullivan by Max Beerbohm, ca. 1899. (102)

All the above legacies are to be paid ~~net~~ that is free of duty.

1877. The residue of my money, copyrights, performing rights, and of all *(state of whatever nature or kind soever)* my personal estate I leave to my nephew Herbert Thomas Sullivan whom I appoint residuary legatee of everything I may die possessed of, with the exception of the following bequests —

17 — I give the following specific bequests

(1) To the National Portrait Gallery, my portrait painted by John Everett Millais R.A.

(2) To the Royal Academy of Music, my original autograph full scores of "The Martyr of Antioch" and "The Mikado" with a signed photograph of myself

(3) To the Royal College of Music, my original autograph full scores of "The Golden Legend" and "The Yeoman of the Guard", with a signed photograph of myself

(4) To H.R.H. The Prince of Wales — some memento

(5) To H.R.H. The Duke of York — some memento

(6) To H.R.H. The Duke of Saxe Coburg and Gotha, my original autograph full score of "The Light of the World", in remembrance of the many happy hours I spent with His Royal Highness when I was writing it — also the music stand belonging formerly to my friend Joseph Barnby.

(7) To my friend Wilfred Bendall the original autograph full scores of the "King Arthur" and "Macbeth" music — also the Russian silver cigarette case, I brought back from Peterhof with me, and my Tiffany spirit flask, ~~and~~ also twelve full orchestral scores ~~which proved at or belong to me at my death~~ of any works (not by me) which he may select himself.

4

Page 4 of Sullivan's draft Will, listing special bequests, 1 March 1899. (106c)

& my arms & legs are
of the consistency of cotton
wool.

I sincerely hope to
find you all right again
on my return. & the new opera
running merrily

[signature]

P.S. the old piece looks up
splendidly.

My dear Sullivan,

I would gladly come up
to town & see you before I
go, but unfortunately, in my
present enfeebled condition, a
carriage journey to London
involves my lying down for
a couple of hours before I am
fit for anything — besides slightly
all night in town. A railway
journey is still more fatiguing

Gilbert's last letter to Sullivan, 9 November 1900. (104)

Arthur Sullivan, ca. 1899. (103d)

206

Bibliography

SULLIVAN

Dunhill, Thomas F.: *Sullivan's Comic Operas, A Critical Appreciation*. London, Edward Arnold & Co., 1928.

Findon, B. W.: *Sir Arthur Sullivan, His Life and Music*. London, James Nisbet & Co., Limited, 1904.

Hughes, Gervase: *The Music of Arthur Sullivan*. New York, St. Martin's Press Inc., 1960.

Lawrence, Arthur: *Sir Arthur Sullivan: Life-story, Letters and Reminiscences*. London, James Bowden, 1899.

Saxe Wyndham, Henry: *Arthur Seymour Sullivan (1842–1900)*. London, Kegan Paul, Trench, Trubner & Co., Ltd., and J. Curwen & Sons, Ltd., 1926.

Sullivan, Herbert, and Newman Flower: *Sir Arthur Sullivan, His Life, Letters & Diaries*. London, Cassell & Company, Ltd., 1927 and 1950.

Wells, Walter J.: *Souvenir of Sir Arthur Sullivan, Mus. Doc. M.V.O.: A Brief Sketch of his Life & Works*. London, George Newnes, Limited, 1901.

Willeby, Charles: *Masters of English Music*. London, James R. Osgood, McIlvaine & Co., 1893.

Young, Percy M.: *Sir Arthur Sullivan*. London, J. M. Dent & Sons Ltd., 1971.

GILBERT

Allen, Reginald: *W. S. Gilbert, An Anniversary Survey and Exhibition Checklist*. Charlottesville, The Bibliographical Society of the University of Virginia, 1963.

Pearson, Hesketh: *Gilbert, His Life and Strife*. London, Methuen & Co. Ltd., 1957.

G. & S.

Allen, Reginald: *The First Night Gilbert and Sullivan*. New York, The Heritage Press, 1958.

Baily, Leslie: *The Gilbert & Sullivan Book*. London, Cassell & Company Ltd., 1952.

Goldberg, Isaac: *The Story of Gilbert and Sullivan or The 'Compleat' Savoyard*. New York, Simon and Schuster, 1928.

Bibliography

Mander, Raymond, and Joe Mitchenson: *A Picture History of Gilbert and Sullivan*. London: Vista Books, 1962.

Rollins, Cyril, and R. John Witts (Compiled by): *The D'Oyly Carte Opera Company in Gilbert and Sullivan Operas*. London, Michael Joseph, 1962.

GENERAL

Dictionary of National Biography, London.

Fuld, James J.: *The Book of World-Famous Music*. New York, Crown Publishers, Inc., 1966.

Gilbert and Sullivan Journal: The official Publication of the Gilbert & Sullivan Society, London.

Grove's Dictionary of Music and Musicians, Fifth Edition. New York, St. Martin's Press Inc., 1955.

MacPhail, Ralph, Jr. (Introduction by): *Additional Adventures of Messrs. Box and Cox*. Bridgewater (Virginia), The Parenthesis Press, 1974.

The Times (newspaper), London.

"THE KIND INDULGENCE OF THE AUDIENCE IS REQUESTED . . ."

Whether for the sudden indisposition of a principal contralto, or for the severe cold of the leading tenor, or for the considerable delay between the first and second acts in consequence of the complicated scenery, the kind indulgence of Opera Comique or Savoy Theatre audiences was traditionally requested by Richard D'Oyly Carte in program inserts known popularly as Indulgence Slips. This is such an indulgence slip.

The following errata have already been noted. For these and others yet undetected, indulgence, please.

ERRATA

ix Herr *not* herr

2d *The Tempest not* the *Tempest*

6g *No part of this inscription is in Sullivan's hand. It is entirely his mother's.*

Page 11, l. 6; 19a; 19b; Index: Jephtha *not* Jeptha

43a Two leaves. *not* Four leaves.

47e Zugrundelegung *not* Zugtundelegung

57b, 59a, Index: *Delete* Sir *from* Gladstone, William E.

62b 3–335 *not* 3–333

62d Arturo *not* Artura

62d, Index: Gargano *not* Goirgono

62f Gab man *not* Gab Man

Page 127, l. 8 of the introduction to *The Yeomen of the Guard:* Der Königsgardist *not* Die Königsgardist

67b "Lied des Wilson" *not* "Lied Des Wilson" Wem Leben Glück *not* Wenn Leben Gluck

67c Lied der Mary *not* Lied Der Mary Wien *not* Wein dis-guised *not* dis-guished

67d *Yeoman not Yeomen*

74c *The letter of Franz Liszt was written to Sullivan.* regretted *not* regreted

78b *Ivanhoe* opened *not* Ivanhoe opened

81i 2pp. *not* 22p.

84 Diner *not* Dinet

95b Verehrter *not* Verherter

Index, "Last night of the year, The": 25i *not* 25

Index

Index

C

Calvé, Emma, 94a
Calvert, Charles, 37a
Capitän Wilson, 67a–c
Carmine, Mlle., 4b
"Carol for Christmas Day,"
  51c, k
Carr, J. Comyns, 88a, 96a
Carte, Helen D'Oyly, 81f, l,
  103a
Carte, Richard D'Oyly, 47d,
  53a, 54c–d, 58, 60a–b,
  61a–b, 62n, 69f, 71a, 78a–b,
  d–e, 79a, 81a–d, f–i, 83f,
  85a, 86c, 89c, 99d, 100a,
  103a, 104
Caruso, Enrico, 93c
Cellier, Alfred, 47b, 57
Cellier, François, 60a–b,
  78a, c, 82a
Chapel Royal, The (St.
  James's Palace), 1e–h, j,
  l–m, 106d–e
Chappell, Arthur, 35a
Chieftain, The, 15b, 86a–e,
  89e; poster, 86e
Chorley, Henry F., 1v, 2g, 3a,
  5a, 6e, 16c, 25i, 26i
"Christmas bells at sea," 42a
Church Hymns with Tunes,
  51m–p
Clarke, Sir and Lady Camp-
  bell, 2b, 67g
Clarke, Hamilton, 47a–b
Clay, Frederic, 2g, 35b
Cliffe, Frederic, 42a
Coke, Lady Katherine, 103a
Cole, Alan, 34a, 35c, 44a, 46d
Cole, Sir Henry, 34a, 46d
Cole, Nita, 83f
Comedy Opera Company,
  The, 47a
Commission Britannique, 12e
*Concerto in D Major for
  Violoncello*, 9a–b
Conneau, Madame, 37b
Conservatorium der Musik zu
  Leipzig, 1u, ix

Contrabandista, The, 14a,
  15a–b, 86a, c
Cooper, Alfred, 98a
Coppi, Carlo, 92a
Costa, Sir Michael, 4a, 6c
"Courage, brother! do not
  stumble!", 51d
Covent Garden, 4a–b, 47a,
  64e, 78b
Cowan, Samuel K., 50m
Cowen, F. H., 107e
Cowper, Mr., 44a
Cox and Box, 13b, 14a–h,
  15a–b
Crampton, Louisa, 26b
"Crépuscule (Twilight),"
  17, 24c
Crutchley, Sybil, 103a
Crystal Palace, The, 1i, 2f,
  7b–c, 9a, 13a–c, 21e–f, 23a,
  37b, 39b, 74b
Cummings, William H., 6a, e,
  11, 26a, 40d–f
Cunliffe-Owen, Sir Philip, 63b
Currier & Ives, 62l
Curtis Publishing Company,
  87c

D

D'Albert, Charles, 43e, 46f–h,
  50j–k, 53h–i, 56f–h, 74b
D'Albert, Eugene, 55f, 74b
Daly, Augustine, 82a, c
Daly's Theatre, New York,
  82a, c; London, 82d–e
Dalziel, George, 51q
Dalziel, Thomas, 51k
Dannreuther, Edward
  George, 1u
David, Ferdinand, 1u, 22b
David, Paul, 1u
Davison, James William, 16b,
  24c, 37b, 40g
Day Dreams, 18
Denny, W. H., 69a, 83f
De Vere, Aubrey, 25e
Dickens, Charles, 5b–c, 16c

Disraeli, Benjamin, 105c
"Distant Shore, The," 50h;
  "Waltz," 50j
Dodgson, C. L., "Lewis
  Carroll," 49e
Dohm, Ernest, 47e
"Dominion Hymn, The," 77a
Don Giovanni, 31
Döppler, V., 16a
"Dove Song (Polka), The," 20
Drew, John, 82d
Dreyschock, Concertmeister,
  22a
H.R.H. Duchess of Edinburgh
  (H.I.H. Grand Duchess
  Marie Alexandrowna of
  Russia), 40a–c
*Duo Concertante for Violon-
  cello & Pianoforte, Op. 2*, 10
Duprêt, Paul, 85f

E

"Echoes," 25f
"Edward Grey," 76a
Elgar, Edward, 2e, 95c
Eliot, George, 50c
Emerald Isle, The, 100a–c,
  103b; "Waltz," 100b;
  poster, 100c
Enoch & Sons, 98f
"Evening," 25c
Exhibition Ode," 63a–c, 66c

F

"Fair Daffodils," 25h
Fan (Henschel), 75
"Father, by Thy love &
  power," 51p
Fauré, Gabriel, 95a
Festival Te Deum, 39a
Fifth Avenue Theatre,
  53a, 62p
Findon, B. W., 103b
Forbes-Robertson, J., 88b
Ford, Ernest, 82a

PRINTED BY THE STINEHOUR PRESS

WITH ILLUSTRATIONS BY THE MERIDEN GRAVURE COMPANY